# PROFESSIONAL
# SOCIAL WORK
## IN AUSTRALIA

# PROFESSIONAL
# SOCIAL WORK
## IN AUSTRALIA

R.J. LAWRENCE

Australian
National
University

eVIEW

Published by ANU eView
The Australian National University
Acton ACT 2601, Australia
Email: anupress@anu.edu.au
This title is also available online at eview.anu.edu.au

National Library of Australia Cataloguing-in-Publication entry

| | |
|---|---|
| Creator: | Lawrence, R. J. (Robert John), 1931- author. |
| Title: | Professional social work in Australia / R. J. Lawrence. |
| ISBN: | 9781921934278 (paperback) 9781921934285 (ebook) |
| Subjects: | Social service--Australia--History. |
| | Social work education--Australia--History. |
| | Social workers--Training of--Australia--History. |
| Dewey Number: | 361.320994 |

Cover design and layout by ANU Press. Cover photograph adapted from www.flickr.com/photos/jariceiii/6300339393/ by jar [o].

First published 1965 by The Australian National University

# Contents

# Foreword to the New Edition

This book was only possible because The Australian National University was willing to grant me a PhD scholarship, and its History Department was willing to accept my application, despite the novelty of my topic, and the absence of supervisors without any direct knowledge of it. When I commenced my work on it in 1958, ANU was still relatively new and its only students were doctoral students. It was a stimulating academic environment and we had considerable free rein.

My pioneering work was not assisted by well-kept archives – either by people or institutions. The keeping of systematic records over any period of time was a rarity. Inevitably, I had to develop an archival system of my own, within which I could place whatever relevant records I could find. The work was often slow and tedious: chasing up missing minutes and annual reports (if they ever existed); sometimes copying by hand what I did locate because it was the only copy (photocopying was not yet available); persuading people to hold on to material; and so on.

The whole project obviously was a considerable challenge, only made possible by the amount of goodwill and cooperation I received at the time. The only disappointment was how little serious comment the book elicited subsequently, and its manifest failure to stimulate further historical research into the profession. Only twice since have others asked for access to my extensive data collection for this early period. In 1979, Laurie O'Brien and Cynthia Turner did produce *Establishing Medical Social Work in Victoria* (Department of Social Studies, University of Melbourne), but without any help from my collected data. At least partly assisted by my 'invaluable archive', Elspeth Browne produced *Tradition and Change: Hospital Social Work in NSW*. (This was commissioned after a 1995 celebration in Sydney of the centenary anniversary of the establishment by the

Charity Organisation Society of hospital social work, at the Royal Free Hospital in London.) In 2011, Jane Miller, president of the alumni association of social work graduates of the University of Melbourne, spent a few days staying with us to study files in my archives in preparation for her PhD on American influences on social work education in Melbourne 1920–60. This was successfully completed in 2015, and I have appreciated the opportunity to give her considerable assistance along the way. Her historical interest had been aroused by realising how little had been written about Jocelyn Hyslop, the first director of social work training in Melbourne. I am aware that the University of South Australia has had a project to collect material on social work history in that state, and recently I have been told about a joint AASW and university historical social work project for which ARC funds were being sought.

In 1976, I wrote an introduction to the published proceedings of the 14th National Conference of the AASW, which brought up to date the historical story of the profession in Australia, but no one has attempted anything of a general kind since. According to the editors, I was, without question, 'the foremost authority on the history of Australian social work today'. It was cold comfort, for I considered Australian society and the profession itself needed a considerable amount of continuing serious historical work by a substantial number of scholars for enlightenment and this was not yet forthcoming.

What is needed is for this to be an ongoing group enterprise for social work historians in the schools of social work, working in close collaboration with other historians, and with archivists to develop a national system of social work archives and historical research. Without such a system in place, assumptions and generalisation about professional social work in Australia cannot be confidently grounded.

On the initiative of the AASW, this lonely pioneer study is being republished by ANU Press, as part of the celebrations of the 70th anniversary of the national professional association. If this is a clear sign of an emerging awareness of the need for historical study, I would suggest the following steps to build on the initiative:

1. Appointment of a Steering Committee by the heads of schools of social work in Australia and the AASW to establish a National Standing Committee on Australian Social Work History.

2. The National Standing Committee would have a national convenor, and have coordinators in each of the States and Territories, who may or may not be members of the national Committee.

3. The National Standing Committee would report to interested parties (these to be determined) at least annually on:

   • The development of a national system of social work archives:
     - where the archives are held, in what form, and conditions of access
     - steps to improve these as part of a national and international system
     - steps to make social workers and their employing agencies more archive-conscious, as an essential professional responsibility.

   • The development of social work history
     - in social work schools, schools of history and other schools
     - publications
     - current research.

The problem needs to be tackled by appropriate national organisation, not to restrict genuine historical research, but to stimulate it as effectively and efficiently as possible within its national and international contexts. Resources should not be a difficulty. Currently, with accredited social work courses in about 30 Australian universities, and an AASW of more than 9,000 members, resources could be found to study the historical processes which have shaped the size and nature of the profession in this country. When this book was written, there were only four schools of social work and an AASW of less than 1,000 members. (It reached 1,158 in 1968.) Surely the time has come to tackle this societal task. I believe we owe it to our profession and the people we profess to serve.

No attempt has been made to update this historical publication. It stands as it was written.

John Lawrence AM
Emeritus Professor of Social Work
University of New South Wales
Honorary Life Member AASW, 1975
Sydney, 2016

# Introduction

The well-established professions rank high in the social structure of modern Western societies. Entry is restricted by the cost of the basic training and the intellectual capacity required, their practice tends to be surrounded by a certain mystique, they are used extensively by the ruling and propertied classes, and their members are generally in the higher-income groups.

In a recognised profession such as medicine, law, architecture, or engineering, there are seven notable characteristics. First, members of the profession and the rest of the community understand that it is a distinct occupational group with certain rights and duties. Second, a general common purpose, for example healing the sick, guides the members' work, and this is in accord with the goals of the wider community. Third, there are shared intellectual techniques which are acquired only after prolonged training at a tertiary educational level, and which require originality and judgement, not routine application. The development of technique is the responsibility of the group. Fourth, the fundamental knowledge, or theory, at the basis of the group's practice is capable of being set forth systematically, is scientifically based, and is at a level of difficulty requiring tertiary education. The group recognises a responsibility to define, develop, and systematise its theory, and is free to do so. This is a direct responsibility with regard to the members' own clinical or practitioner experience. For the part of their theory borrowed and adapted from other groups, it is an indirect responsibility to support the work of those groups.

The fifth, sixth and seventh characteristics relate to the group's general ethical position. Fifth, the group conforms to certain standards of behaviour, because its practice involves them in private affairs and they are experts advising non-experts. Sixth, in their dealings with clients, service to the client and the community rather than gain to the practitioner or the group is stressed in their ethical code. And seventh, the group accept collective responsibility to use their knowledge for the benefit of the community, over and above services to individual clients.

Two kinds of institutions are necessary to the professions: training bodies and professional associations. The training body usually transmits intellectual techniques, theory, and ethical position, and formally tests the competence of a person for professional practice. The professional association watches over the rights and duties of the profession and is concerned generally with the professional competence of its members. It plays an important educational role, for the intellectual basis of professional practice calls for a continued mutual interchange of ideas and information.

Training bodies and professional associations had an especially important unifying role if the Australian social work group were to acquire the features of a profession – the training bodies, because there could be different ideas as to what constituted adequate training for social work, and the professional associations, because the group's members, scattered among many different agencies, needed a sense of unity.

This study concentrates on three main things: the development of social work training bodies and their courses; the spread of qualified social workers into various employment fields; and the growth of professional associations and their programmes. It is roughly divided into pre-war, war, and post-war, since each of these periods had its own set of influences.

Social work's goals may be achieved in a number of ways: by helping individuals and their families; by helping groups of people with personal and social problems; by helping social agencies to work together; by influencing the community's social policies; by administering social welfare programmes; by undertaking social welfare research; and by teaching people who will perform these tasks. Of these, the first, social casework, retained its importance throughout the period (although, as will be seen, the other methods did gain some ground) because of a natural early concentration upon the units of social breakdown, the greater theoretical formulation of social casework, and the continued identification of social work with women who, primarily for culturally determined reasons, tended to leave the broader aspects of community organisation to men.

From its inception, the group had two characteristics that had widespread effects on the nature of its development: the majority of its members were women, and it depended upon social agencies for its employment. The first characteristic, in what was still very much a man's country, had important status repercussions for the group and its work.[1] The second, to some extent, limited the group's freedom of practice and kept remuneration comparatively low. Yet there was no apparent desire for private practice, mainly because it was more effective to work through agencies, and because the group's clientele were not accustomed to paying a professional fee for this kind of help.

Among social work fields, medical social work took the lead. For a time it had its own training bodies and its own specialised professional association, but these were additional to, not substitutes for, the general training bodies and the general social workers' association. In Australia, as in the United Kingdom and the United States, a concentration of the community's social problems was found in the large public hospitals. The connection, in many instances obvious, between the patients' health and social conditions led to an early recognition of the need for medical social work. It was not surprising, therefore, that the medical social work group advanced first along the road of professionalism, encouraged by their close association with the well-established medical profession.

Why, in general terms, did professional social work begin to develop in Australia during the late 1920s? Briefly, the answers are urbanism, industrialisation, social and economic change, a large social service expansion, particularly in the government sector, overseas example, and the stimulation provided by qualified social workers themselves.

In Australia, as in the United States and Britain, professionalism in social service work began in the larger cities, and by the later 1920s Sydney and Melbourne, each with at least a million inhabitants, were large by any standards. There were always people with problems in

---

1    For a serious study of the place of women in Australia society, see Norman MacKenzie, *Women in Australia*.

big industrial urban communities, and the inadequacy of ill-informed, usually part-time or spare-time, attempts at helping them was obvious earlier than in smaller communities. The resources of a large city could maintain social agencies employing trained social workers, and also support a training body. In addition, the need for the co-ordination and rationalisation of social services in a large city was evident, and trained social workers were seen, among other things, as instruments of coordination.

As part of each community's social service system, or series of systems, professional social workers, with trained observation and working full-time, were in the best possible position to know the actual needs of individuals and groups, and the extent to which the community's social services were adequate. This generally meant that the professional social workers were keen to coordinate and rationalise the social services, to extend them to all needy sections of the community, and to remove the stigma of charity, to broaden the concept of need to include other than material want, and to emphasise preventive rather than palliative measures. They were not, of course, alone in furthering these things. The depression years, war, the post-war reconstruction, unprecedented industrial growth with concomitant inflation, a large-scale immigration programme creating a more culturally diverse society, a population growth of over three million during the 30-odd years and its even greater concentration in the capital cities, and a beginning to scientific inquiry into the precise nature of Australian society – all these played a part in stimulating interest in social conditions and the adequacy of social provisions. During the period there was an enormous expansion of social services. The professional social work group, despite its small numbers, played its part in stimulating this expansion.

The earlier growth of professionalism in social service work in the larger and more industrialised communities in the United States and the United Kingdom provided the Australian group with useful experience, and they used it freely. In the early stages, this was a source of strength, for already overseas the basic training issues had been defined, a modern framework for social work had been developed, and teaching material, with at least a rough relevance for any Western industrial society, was in existence. The great part of the published experience was American, which meant that the Australian group was very strongly influenced by both American and British ideas.

Towards the end of the period, reliance on overseas experience began to be an impediment, for a local literature was very slow to appear, questions as to the degree of cultural relevance of much of the overseas material were still left unanswered, and, in addition, the constantly unfavourable comparison of Australian professional conditions with those in America was causing, in some quarters, despair rather than stimulus.

As its numbers grew, the group became status conscious, and this was closely linked with the question of salaries. The members did not look for high professional remuneration, for the voluntary service past of their work was not far distant and lived on in many parts of the community. The idea of becoming rich in such work repelled them. They began to realise, however, that salaries had to be competitive with other professional salaries to attract sufficient people with the requisite talent, particularly men, and they found, especially in government service, that low salaries and low status for themselves and their work were closely linked. Further, they could see no reason why, in the practice of such stressful work of direct social usefulness, which required a difficult and expensive preparation, they should not enjoy at least a comfortable standard of living.

Because the general conditions were favourable for the development of professions in Australia, it is possible that this period will become notable for the number of aspiring professional groups it produced and the extent to which existing groups were strengthened. It is hoped that this account will not remain isolated as a study of a profession in Australia.[2]

---

2    At present its only companion is R.D. Goodman, Teachers' Status in Australia. PhD thesis, The Australian National University.

# Acknowledgements

To explain the origin of this book, I need to indulge in some personal history. A social work course was included in my university education, but it was not the major part, nor at the time did I regard it specifically in vocational terms. Eventually, however, I found myself working as a social worker. The work convinced me that here was a worthwhile career, but I wanted to know more about its development and scope in Australia, and it was apparent that I was not alone in this. Nothing but widespread ignorance on the subject could exist for no one had yet written about it. I am doubly thankful to The Australian National University. One of its PhD research scholarships gave me the opportunity to become better informed and to become better qualified academically, and now its Publications Committee has made it possible for the fruits of my labour to be shared with others who are interested.

Many people have given freely of their time, ideas, knowledge, and support. I would like to acknowledge individually their diverse contributions, but this is impossible because the list would be so long, and I would not be satisfied that it was complete. Yet special mention must be made of my thesis supervisors, particularly Dr Robin Gollan and Dr George Zubrzycki; my thesis examiners, Professor W.D. Borrie and Professor Richard Titmuss; my present colleagues in the University of Sydney Department of Social Work, especially Tom Brennan and Norma Parker; and the scores of social workers who have so willingly contributed.

Without the free access to relevant records granted by the Universities of Sydney, Melbourne, and Adelaide, by the Australian Association of Social Workers, and by various other organisations, the work could not have been undertaken.

Finally I would like to record my gratitude to my wife and children, who have been a considerable source of inspiration and support.

University of Sydney, June 1964
R.J. Lawrence

# THE EARLY YEARS

# CHAPTER 1

# Meeting the Social Challenge of Industrial Society

In the half-century or so before 1930, a feature of industrial societies such as Britain and the United States was the extension of social provision, both government and non-government. By 1930, through a combination of economic, political, and social factors, these societies contained a great number of specialised social agencies helping selected categories of people who were seen to need outside assistance. Their particular concern was with the destitute, deprived children, legal offenders, the physically and mentally handicapped, the physically and mentally ill, unmarried mothers, migrants, the poorly housed, the aged, the idle, the ignorant, the lonely. Often the provision was, by later standards, inadequate or misguided, but it was in this period that the foundations of the modern welfare society were laid, for corporate responsibility for the personal well-being of all individuals within national boundaries was increasingly recognised. This was modern mass urbanised society, subject to continuous economic and social change, establishing the specialised, institutional equipment to meet its social responsibilities.

The emergence of political democracy, closely linked with the rise of labour movements and the elimination of illiteracy, brought in its train an emphasis on democracy as a social philosophy. Equality of consideration and a sense of interdependence were stressed in the face of intolerable differences between the conditions of life of citizens and in the face of the new extreme social separation between citizens, both aspects of the huge urban agglomerations of industrial society. The social and cultural poverty, as well as the harsh economic poverty, demanded agencies to combat it, for individuals could not fight it alone. A great many organised groups, humanitarian in purpose and mixed in motive, arose.

Many problems demanded broader, stronger, and more continuous action, and the state was the only agency with the authority and the potential resources to combat them. The Church had lost its medieval dominance. It had neither the internal strength, the material resources, nor the mass allegiance to respond to the challenges of the new industrial age, although helping people in distress was still strong in the Christian ethic. Much of its welfare work with sectarian strings attached was suspect to an essentially secular society, just as much of the welfare work of the upper classes which helped to maintain the established social order was suspected by those who wished for a basic reform of society.

The organisational demands of a changing mass society, as well as political developments, caused the downfall of the supremely optimistic *laissez-faire* doctrine; depressions and war hastened the process. The increasing national income achieved by technological change, greater division of labour, and specialisation, made its more even distribution both necessary and possible. Increased taxation, especially of personal income, strengthened the sinews of state action through an effective public service.

But without insight into the true nature and extent of the problems of the new society, neither private nor state action was likely to be effective. The Royal Commissions, and towards the end of the nineteenth century, the charity organisation societies, the social settlements, the social surveys, the growth of statistical analysis – all contributed to the diagnosis of the ills of society and the prescription of treatment for them. The application of scientific method to human affairs was seen as the key to social progress. A significant factor in the growth of social provision was the interchange of ideas between countries. The spread from Britain of the charity organisation society, the social settlements, the social survey, and certain kinds of social legislation, and from Germany of social insurance schemes, are examples of a widespread willingness to use the experience of other countries in the meeting of similar problems. It is difficult to tell, however, whether these attitudes and institutions would have emerged spontaneously. The twentieth century terms – 'social service', 'social welfare', 'social administration', and 'social work' – began to supplant the older terms – 'charity', 'philanthropy', 'benevolence', 'alms-giving', and 'poor relief'. This change in terminology was closely connected with changed attitudes to the recipients and the altered nature of the service given them. It was now the community's duty to ensure for all its citizens certain minimum standards of welfare, and each citizen had a right to expect this. The condescension, pity, and implied superiority of the giver to the receiver with which the older terms had become encrusted were not to be condoned in the new democratic society.

## The Training Movement

With the growth of social provision came increasing numbers of men and women engaged in its administration, and its complexity in the mass industrial society forced them to realise that full-time, trained work was needed. It was wasteful not to use the accumulated experience of previous workers, and the new insights about men and society gained from scientific study. The training movement, therefore, developed with the growth of social provision, and at what point the need was felt was partly determined by the chance of personalities and the existence of overseas models, but more by the society's degree of complexity, the size of the cities, and the extent of social provision.

What has been described as the first real school of social work in the world began in Amsterdam in 1899. By the mid-1920s there were schools in Belgium, Canada, Chile, Czechoslovakia, Finland, France, Germany, Italy, the Netherlands, South Africa, Sweden, Switzerland, the United Kingdom, and the United States. The experience of the training movements in the last two countries had a strong influence on the Australian training movement. As it was overwhelmingly British in heritage, Australia tended to look to British experience. On the other hand, in the United States the training movement gained root more firmly than anywhere else in the world, and this, together with the connected factors of size, wealth, and vigour, produced an increasing quantity of useful American social work literature. Moreover, though its population dwarfed Australia's population much more than did Britain's, its geographical size, the comparative newness of the society, and its federal system of government, gave Australians and Americans attitudes in common as well as their broad European heritage and language.

In Britain, Octavia Hill began in the 1870s a scheme for training housing managers, who were responsible for helping tenants in addition to acting as landlords, but she recognised the need for a more systematic training and pointed to an analogy with the nursing and teaching professions. Such a training was started at the Women's University Settlement at Southwark in the East End of London in the 1890s.[1]

In 1912, the London School of Economics established a Department of Social Science and Administration and this was a direct descendant of the Southwark Settlement training scheme. Meanwhile, outside London, mainly associated with the new universities in the large industrial centres, other training schemes were started: at Liverpool, Birmingham, Bristol, Leeds, Manchester, Edinburgh, and Glasgow.

Until World War I, progress was slow. Many new social welfare measures, both government and non-government, were brought in during the early years of the century, but the qualifications required of those administering them remained unsettled. For the most part, student numbers were small, and were mainly women who wished to do voluntary social work, or those willing and able to risk possibly unsuitable positions.

The war strengthened the training movement. Social study departments gained government recognition, the demand for trained workers for the first time exceeded the supply, and a variety of new training schemes was established. In April 1918, a Joint University Council for Social Studies was formed to coordinate and develop the work of social study departments in the universities of Britain and Ireland. All existing university schemes were represented on the council, and it did much to publicise and increase understanding of the training movement.

---

1    Elizabeth Macadam, *The Equipment of the Social Worker*, pp. 28–9.

In the mid-1920s, a Joint Honorary Secretary of the Council, Elizabeth Macadam, described the British training movement in these terms:

Students, generally older than the average undergraduates, fell into three classes: graduates, experienced workers with little or no previous academic training, and students who desired to train for some career for which a university degree was not necessary. Some schools granted diplomas to graduates only.

In each school, the length of the course, except for graduates, was two years. It consisted partly of attendance at lectures or tutorial classes and partly of actual participation under supervision in various activities which gave the candidate some first-hand acquaintance with working-class life, the operations of public departments and of voluntary organisations for social work.

There was variation in the names and arrangements of subjects, but such subjects as economics, economic history, social and political philosophy, psychology, and public administration were included. Generally lectures from regular university degree courses were used for at least some of the academic requirements of social study courses, but several schools were large enough to have their own staff of lecturers. The Joint University Council had stressed the importance of securing teachers who had more than mere academic knowledge of social questions. The term 'school of social study' had come to refer to a department of a university, in which different subjects, which could be grouped together under the comprehensive heading 'social science', were taught not only in close relation to each other but to actual social and economic conditions.

From the beginning, practical work had been considered an essential part of the course. It now included, where possible, training in public administration in connection with health, housing, employment and unemployment, administration of justice, adult and continuation education, juvenile organisations of all kinds, relief work, voluntary organisations for social welfare, as well as investigation into social conditions. Before a diploma or certificate was awarded, a student had to satisfy examiners in both academic and practical work.

Visits of observation were arranged to introduce students to relevant social organisations.

Research into social problems was recognised as an indispensable function of a school, but largely owing to lack of funds, little had been accomplished.

Most of the schools tried to meet the needs of officials in new forms of social service or of social workers already in the field. Glasgow and Dundee had provided systematic evening courses leading to a certificate. Other schools insisted that social training required full-time work, but provided periodically lectures for those who had received no professional training and 'refresher' courses for trained workers.

The courses were under the direction of a Committee or Board on which were representatives of those university departments which offered subjects included in the course, and persons of experience in practical social administration.

In a few cases, schools provided teaching for those engaged in other occupations, such as the clergy, district nurses, health visitors, domestic science and continuation school teachers. During the war, intensive courses for welfare workers in factories and relief workers were instituted as emergency measures. In addition, the leading schools opened selected classes to the general public.[2]

Many of these features were later to appear in the Australian training movement.

As well as the schools of social study, and linked with particular areas of social work, a number of specialist training schemes were established which provided an apprenticeship training rather than a course in general social work principles. For Australia, the most significant of these was the course in medical social work run by the Institute of Hospital Almoners.

Beginning at the Royal Free Hospital in London in the mid-1890s, social work in hospitals, or almoning as it was called, spread first to other voluntary hospitals and later to municipal hospitals. With it grew an almoner training scheme which was, until 1907, under the control of a special Charity Organisation Society committee and then under the Hospital Almoners' Council, consisting of almoners, Charity Organisation Society members, and other interested people. This council was incorporated as the Institute of Hospital Almoners in 1924.

---

2    Ibid., pp. 44–8.

Another of the specialised courses had some influence in Australia. The child guidance movement penetrated Britain from the United States in 1927, and a mental health course, taken after a general social studies course, was later developed at the Social Science Department of the London School of Economics.

In many respects, the first 30 years of the training movement in the United States resembled the British development – the growth in the large cities, the connection with the rise of social science, the majority of women students, the early reliance on voluntary agencies, the growth of full-time social work, and the leading position of medical social work – and the early Australian training movement demonstrated the same features. But there were important differences, arising mainly from the size and strength of the social agencies in the much larger American society, and from its more democratic temper.

In 1898, the first school of social work in the United States had its rudimentary beginnings in a six-week course for practitioners held by the New York Charity Organisation Society. By 1904, this had become a one-year course provided by the New York School of Philanthropy, primarily for students inexperienced in social work. From 1910, the curriculum covered two years; in 1919, the school's name was changed to the New York School of Social Work.

In the meantime, other schools had been founded, at first in the east and then unevenly throughout the country. That at Chicago, like the New York school, became especially prominent. Arising from training experiments in Chicago settlements, the Chicago Institute of Social Science was opened in 1903 by the Extension Division of the University of Chicago. Five years later, it became the Chicago School of Civics and Philanthropy, and in 1920 it gave up its independent status to become the Graduate School of Social Service Administration in the University of Chicago.

By 1910, the American training movement was still largely confined to the five largest cities in the United States: New York, Chicago, Boston, Philadelphia, and St Louis. As in Britain, however, World War I stimulated social work training and encouraged formal cooperation between training bodies. Many universities combined with the American Red Cross to provide emergency home-service training schemes. These demonstrated the need for full social work courses in new parts of the country and helped to arouse university interest. In 1919, the 17 known schools of social work met to discuss formal cooperation. From this arose the American Association of Professional Schools of Social Work, which became highly influential in setting standards of social work education in North America, and in other countries.

The older schools in the east of the United States at first remained largely independent of the universities for they wished to be free of academic regulations. At the 1915 National Conference on Charities and Correction, however, both Abraham Flexner and Felix Frankfurter asserted that training for a profession should be university based. Frankfurter urged a preparation for social work equivalent to the training for the professions of law and medicine.[3] Soon after the Association of Schools was formed, no new non-university schools were admitted to membership. By the mid-1920s, only three of the 23 member schools were independent of universities, and other schools were moving towards membership.

Yet even among the association's members there was wide variation, one of the main reasons being, according to Edith Abbott in 1927, the extreme specialisation that agencies had demanded of schools of social work. They had been asked to provide special training courses for family welfare workers, for child welfare workers, for psychiatric social workers, for travellers' aid work, community chest executives, and so on, instead of being allowed to develop 'a solid and scientific curriculum in social welfare'.[4] Earlier in the 1920s, the executive committee of the Association of Schools had, however, managed to agree that the most satisfactory preparation was a broad professional education.[5]

Comparing the American and British training scenes in the mid-1920s, Elizabeth Macadam noted that both continued to have a large majority of women students and both had medical social work in a well-established position, but the American schools were much more strictly professional and much more concerned with social work

---

3   Felix Frankfurter, 'Social Work and Professional Training', *Proceedings of the 42nd National Conference on Charities and Correction*, p. 595.
4   Edith Abbott, *Social Welfare and Professional Education*, pp. 24–32.
5   Macadam, *The Equipment of the Social Worker*, pp. 174–6.

techniques.[6] The demand by powerful voluntary social agencies in the United States for trained 'executives' had stimulated student numbers, and had given courses a professional orientation which included concern for social work technique. This latter concern remained in the courses after they were fully adopted by the American universities. The course at Chicago University, for instance, had important subjects called 'case analysis and diagnosis' and 'principles of casework'.

In Britain there was resistance to this type of study and attention had become increasingly focused on wide social and economic issues. The teaching in the universities had become remote from the actual practice of social agencies. On the other hand, the non-university courses were too close to agency practice and were weak in theory. The objective of university social training in Britain was to equip socially educated workers of all grades 'with the right outlook on life and its problems'. The social studies departments were offering a university education rather more relevant to effective participation in the modern industrial society than the traditional classical or general Arts education, but the degree of its relevance could be debated.

The emphasis in the United States on 'the profession' and its technique was not evenly distributed among the various methods of achieving social work goals. There was a concentration on directly helping individuals, groups, and communities, and an especial concentration on the techniques of working with individuals (social casework) both in terms of the numbers engaged and as a systematic field of practice and study.

## Social Work Methods

Collective action to help people in distress reappeared in nineteenth-century Britain after a period of neglect; but the new, organised humanitarianism had to find a method appropriate to changing social and economic conditions.

The origins of social casework may be traced back at least as far as Thomas Chalmer's work and writing in a Glasgow parish in the early part of the century. His views were later developed by Octavia

---

6    Ibid., pp. 121, 180–1, 188–9, 191.

Hill, Denison, and Loch, and the whole Charity Organisation Society movement. Formed in London in 1869, the Charity Organisation Society had a profound influence on social service work throughout the world, including the United States. It insisted upon cooperation and organisation in charitable work, strict adherence to cases covered by the resources and aims of the agency, help to deserving cases only, and help adequate to re-establish the individual and his family and to promote independence.[7]

Despite the attitude of the Charity Organisation Society leaders who accepted the need for government provision only as a last resort, by the 1890s Britain was turning increasingly to broad government action. In both Britain and the United States, caseworkers began to realise that it was social conditions rather than individuals' weakness of character that were causing widespread distress. At the turn of the century, the findings of the so-called 'school of environmental determinism' seemed to confirm this.

Though both countries then passed through a social reform phase, the United States also paid attention to the development of social casework and assumed leadership in individual case study and treatment (a leadership which it still retains).

Social reform measures raised basic living conditions, but many individuals still needed outside help to understand their personal problems and to make best use of the available community services. Until World War I, social casework was mainly concerned with rehabilitating impoverished clients through the charity organisation societies, or family welfare societies as they had come to be called. Now, however, there were also agencies, dealing with delinquency, mental or physical illness, and troubled childhood, who used social casework as their method but who concentrated not on material relief but rather on education, guidance, or psychological support.

In the various agencies, casework was passing through a 'sociological' phase. Emphasis was on the effects of environment on the individual, and social caseworkers specialised in their knowledge of the environment and how to change it.

---

7    A.F. Young and E.T. Ashton, *British Social Work in the Nineteenth Century*, pp. 81–105.

In 1915, Abraham Flexner decided that social work had not become a profession mainly because it lacked a transmissible professional technique.[8] American social work then began to define its methods, at least with respect to work with individuals. The first major definitive book on social casework, Mary Richmond's *Social Diagnosis*, appeared in 1917, and almost immediately social casework came to be seen as *the* social work method, and, moreover, the recommended casework procedures were not used with discrimination. There was an almost ritualistic, excessive history-taking which often actually interfered with the understanding of the client and his problems. The sociological dimension was present, but not the psychological. The caseworker still tended to consider he knew what was best for the client even though in theory he was working with, not for, him. The client was persuaded, albeit tactfully, to accept the plans made for his good.

World War I ushered in a new phase. The Home Service Divisions of the American Red Cross brought a new clientele for casework help. This, together with a more democratic viewpoint which did not look upon the poor, and those in need of help, as outside the general community, encouraged a shift away from paternalism. The growing knowledge of psychology, and particularly psychiatry, was given considerable impetus by the war. In the following decade, the psychoanalytic theory of human behaviour was incorporated in casework theory and practice to the partial exclusion of the social sciences.

Analytic psychology offered new insight into people and their problems and emphasised the importance of the relationship between social worker and client. The client's own ideas and feelings became the core of the diagnosis and treatment, and 'process' became one of the most used words in the social workers' vocabulary.

The long-term implications of these developments were revolutionary. In Britain, social work had been largely a class activity, the upper orders helping the lower orders to maintain their stations in life in a fairly rigidly stratified society. In the United States, social work had

---

8    Abraham Flexner, 'Is Social Work a Profession?', *Proceedings of the 42nd National Conference on Charities and Correction*, pp. 576–90.

become more the successful helping the unsuccessful to copy their solutions in adapting to 'the great American way of life'. The genuinely client-centred approach brought a change in all this.

One other important development in social casework in the United States was the Milford Conference Report in 1929: 'Social CaseWork, Generic and Specific'. This asserted that, despite the tendency to create specialised forms of social casework under different agency auspices, the problems of social casework and the equipment of the social caseworker were fundamentally the same for all fields.

Unlike modern casework agencies, social group work agencies had no direct historical antecedents. The university settlements, boys' clubs, Boy Scouts, Girl Guides, the YMCA, the YWCA, and many other organisations were established to offer opportunities for social gathering and recreation in the new urban industrial society. This was a society characterised in the early stages by unstable social relations, weakened social controls, greatly reduced opportunities for outdoor recreation, and new temptations for antisocial behaviour. At the beginning, casework agencies tackled problems of material impoverishment, but these group work agencies tackled problems of social impoverishment. Leading group work agencies in the United States in the late 1920s claimed that satisfying group activities developed richer and better adjusted personalities, and that group life was a means of passing on society's social patterns, customs and conventions.[9]

The techniques used by the group worker, as in casework, passed through an early paternalistic stage when programmes were arranged by the group worker for the members of the group. Gradually, however, direction of this kind gave way to the indirect stimulation of the initiative, the group consciousness, and the self-direction of the group.

Social group work crystallised as a professional social work field much later than social casework. Not until the 1920s did group workers discover common professional interests. Many of the organisations employing them did not consider themselves social agencies and were

9    Philip Klein, 'The Social Theory of Professional Social Work', in H.E. Barnes et al. (eds), *Contemporary Social Theory*, p. 774.

outside the influence of social work education. Much of such theory as was slowly constructed came from the writing of John Dewey and the progressive education movement, and was adapted for use in informal educational settings. When group work began to be taught in the American schools of social work in the second half of the 1920s, there existed only rudimentary theory about group processes, in contrast to the well-developed psychoanalytic theory of individual behaviour taught in the casework courses.

Community organisation for social welfare may be traced back, as a social work method, to the work of the charity organisation societies in the nineteenth century. From their attempts to promote cooperation between agencies, to avoid duplication, and to use funds as productively as possible, grew a new social work method. Later this method came to be defined as 'establishing a progressively more effective adjustment between the social welfare needs and the community welfare resources within a geographic area'.[10]

Councils of social agencies in the United States were separate from the charity organisation societies. In this way, responsibility for setting standards was placed upon the whole group and not upon a single agency. These councils helped agencies to work together, to coordinate and rationalise their services, and to publicise their work. Closely linked with the councils' development was the community chest movement, strongly stimulated by World War I. Social agencies combined to appeal for funds, using expert solicitation methods and tapping new industrial sources, and the funds were carefully allocated with due regard to raising agency standards. In addition to the general coordinating councils, there emerged coordinating 'functional' organisations, often at a national level, which concentrated on the needs of particular sections of the community.

In Britain, various communities formed general coordinating councils of social service, but the community chest idea was not strongly supported. A National Council of Social Service was inaugurated in 1919, on which were represented central and local government bodies, national voluntary social agencies, and various local cooperative organisations, including the councils of social service.

---

10    Walter A. Friedlander, *Introduction to Social Welfare*, pp. 186–7.

By 1930, however, community organisation, even in the United States where techniques were being studied, was less advanced in its systematic theory than social group work. Yet five years later, the United States National Conference of Social Work, in reorganising its programme, indicated that the four major functions of social work were social casework, social group work, community organisation, and social action. This conference, in providing a national forum for the discussion of all social welfare matters, was itself an important enduring community organisation tool.[11]

Formal and informal conferring between the different welfare agencies became an important aspect of the welfare work of Western countries, and was not confined to national boundaries. International conferences of representatives of private and public charities began in the mid-nineteenth century. These conferences, meeting in Europe and later in the United States, were concerned with particular areas of social service work. The meeting of the International Conference of Social Work in Paris in 1928 provided for the first time a general international social welfare forum. Because of the growth of the social work training movement in more than 12 countries, it was not surprising that one of the conference's main sections was devoted to such training, and that an outcome was the formation of an International Committee of Schools of Social Work.

## Professional Association

So far, particular attention has been paid to the various ways in which, by the end of the 1920s, the social welfare field in Britain and the United States was becoming organised. Training bodies had arisen and were to some extent cooperating on a national and international level. Various methods of achieving social welfare were being examined and defined; and social agencies were sometimes cooperating both formally and informally on a local, national and international level. One other important institutional development remains to be noted: the growth of professional association between paid, trained employees of social agencies. Again, American developments need to be considered.

---

11   See Frank J. Bruno, *Trends in Social Work, 1874–1956*. Until 1917, the conference was called the National Conference of Charities and Correction; from 1956, the National Conference of Social Welfare.

Professional associations of social workers arose in the United States as training courses, social workers' clubs, and the National Conference of Social Work encouraged a group consciousness among paid workers. In 1921, the American Association of Social Workers was formed with the *Compass* as its journal. Its purpose was to develop professional standards and organisation, and its membership was restricted to paid social workers. By 1930 it had 5,030 members. Three years later, however, it restricted entry to those with a qualification from an accredited school of social work, which meant mainly a casework qualification.[12]

Before the conception of a general association was widely held, associations arose according to the social work setting. The first of these was, not unexpectedly, the American Association of Hospital Social Workers (later the American Association of Medical Social Workers) formed in 1918. At first it covered psychiatric social workers, but in 1926, the American Association of Psychiatric Social Workers became a separate association. By 1930, this body's membership was 364; that of the American Association of Medical Social Workers approximately 1,700. The National Association of School Social Workers at the same time had approximately 275 members.[13]

In Britain, some specialist associations, notably the almoners', were in existence by 1930, but the British Federation of Social Workers, the general professional association in the United Kingdom, was not formed until 1935.

Characteristic institutions, methods, and attitudes were thus being evolved which smaller societies, such as Australia, could adopt or adapt when they too moved into a more complex phase of social provision.

---

12   Ibid., pp. 145–51.
13   Nathan E. Cohen, *Social Work in the American Tradition*, pp. 137–50.

# CHAPTER 2
# Social Provision in Australia

In the late 1920s, some 140 years after the first European settlement, the Australian population was approaching 6,500,000. During the previous 40 years it had doubled, and had become even more concentrated in the six capital cities which now contained close to half the total. Melbourne with a million persons, and Sydney with just over a million, had reached a size and a complexity in their social provision which made them ready for the growth of a social work training movement and full-time trained social work.

Most of the history of Australia's health and welfare services is still to be written, but there are signs of an interest in the subject.[1] An adequate history of a nation's social welfare policies and services requires delving into many aspects of the society. These include the nature, pace, and evenness of its economic growth; the distribution of wealth; taxation levels; the use and effectiveness of economic controls; the social effects of industrialisation; the nature and stability of its political constitution; the strength of its labour movement industrially and politically; the roles of the state and of voluntary associations; the prevailing notions of social justice; the educational system and educational opportunities; the extent and quality of urban and rural living; demographic features of the society, its age, sex, and family composition; its migration patterns and its rate of growth; the effects in a complex society of wars and depressions; the place of religion, both in the work of its institutions and in the ideas and morality of the society; the extent of humanitarianism; the notion of basic social

---

1    For example, Professors R.M. Crawford and Ruth Hoban have begun a long-term study of the history of the social conscience in Australia.

standards; the changing balance between *laissez-faire* and controlled development; the extent of knowledge of the society and its social problems; the individual stories of welfare organisations; the nature of the people directly involved in social welfare matters; biographies of leading social workers and reformers.

## Early Patterns

Is the lack of Australian writing on non-government social provision and on social reformers because voluntary social effort in the Australian colonies was weak compared with nineteenth-century Britain? Australian society was not yet heavily industrialised, its poverty was not so widespread nor as chronic, and the climate made it less harsh. In addition, there existed no leisured class with time and money to help the less fortunate, nor well-established churches to undertake social service work.

Colonial governments did, however, subsidise private charity, and in so far as social needs were met, they were met by voluntary organisations. Migrants' memories of the harsh 1834 English Poor Law together with general nineteenth-century distrust of positive government activity limited direct government provision.

The Melbourne relief scene was complex enough in 1887 to warrant the formation of a charity organisation society. Three years later, it sponsored the first Australasian Conference on Charity, followed by a second in 1891. Many voluntary agencies were represented at these conferences, and a significant proportion of the delegates were women and clergymen. The scope of the conferences was broad. For instance, topics proposed for discussion at the first conference included 'principles of charity organisation', 'hospitals and treatment of the sick', 'indoor relief', 'outdoor relief', 'treatment of the dependent', and 'reformation of the criminal'. It was hoped that by establishing communication between charitably minded colonists, the conference would begin an important era in the history of Australian philanthropic effort.

The idea that each man could be master of his personal destiny was strong in the colonies. If he became destitute this was largely because of moral weakness. One of Australia's most notable early social workers stated that generally it was vice and extravagance and improvidence that brought people to destitution.[2]

The first two Conferences on Charity met in the shadow of a deepening economic depression, and papers on 'The Unemployed' were presented. One of these was ahead of its time in claiming that the unemployed were victims of the economic system, that the 'deserving' and 'undeserving' distinction was unsound, and that all people in need should be helped.[3]

## 'The Social Laboratory of the World'

The 1890s did usher in a new era for Australian philanthropy and charity, but scarcely in the way the sponsors of the First Conference on Charity had expected. During the period 1880–1900, there were two related general developments which had a lasting effect upon provisions for those in, or likely to be in, material distress. The Australian people, or, rather, a vigorous vocal section of them, became conscious of their nationhood and at the turn of the century a federal system of government was inaugurated. In addition, there emerged a working class industrial and political movement – the Australian labour movement.

One of the driving forces in Australian nationalism was an egalitarian social philosophy which claimed a fair deal and a good life for all, and ridiculed those who just accepted their stations in life. This outlook was not kindly disposed to private charity, however much distress needed alleviating. For it, the only self-respecting course was self-help through political and industrial action.

---

2    C.H. Spence, *The Laws We Live Under*, p. 105.
3    The Rev. Alexander Macully, M.A., 'The Unemployed', *Proceedings of the First Australian Conference on Charity, Melbourne, 1890*, pp. 114–9.

The depression of the 1890s shook the young country's faith in its unlimited progress and prosperity. It demonstrated the inadequacy of private charitable provision for those in material distress, and witnessed the failure of direct industrial action. The arguments of those who advocated political action therefore won increasing support.

At Federation, 'residual powers' over all matters not specified for the Commonwealth were left with the states, including services of such social significance as education, health, housing, child welfare, and care of the destitute. These were handled in a highly centralised way with little devolution to local government bodies. The only powers directly given to the Commonwealth in the social service field were over quarantine, and invalid and old-age pensions. Yet, up to World War I, it was the socioeconomic legislation brought in by the Commonwealth parliament, as well as that of the state parliaments, that earned Australia the reputation of being 'the social laboratory of the world'. The actions of the Commonwealth parliament have been summed up in this way:

> Humanitarian liberalism, whether of the Deakin or Fisher variety, was in the ascendant until the war of 1914. Liberal and Labour governments testified in action to their belief in the efficacy of State enterprise. Their social and economic principles were worked out in the field of public policy, and by experimentation they endeavoured to forge new instruments of social and economic justice, of which arbitration, the basic wage, and 'new protection' were perhaps the most striking. Social aims, however, touched almost all legislation, as may be seen in the fields of immigration, taxation, social services and defence.[4]

Although it has recently been challenged,[5] the usual interpretation of this comparatively early extension of the functions of the state is that it was the product not of theory but of circumstances. Either because of changed circumstances, or because the labour movement was split and weakened by the conscription issue, or both, the first period of government social experimentation ended with World War I, and in the 1920s there was much greater emphasis on economic development.

---

4    Gordon Greenwood, 'National Development and Social Experimentation, 1901–14', in Gordon Greenwood (ed.), *Australia – A Social and Political History*, pp. 210–1.
5    J.F. Cairns, The Welfare State in Australia, PhD thesis, University of Melbourne.

Up to the end of the 1920s, government social policy, in the effort to achieve minimum material standards of well-being, had been concentrated on wages and working conditions rather than on social services. With the threefold purpose of preventing sweated labour, holding industrial disputes in check, and providing a living wage for the average Australian family, a complex system of wage regulation had come into existence. Acting under federal and state Arbitration Acts, industrial tribunals decided on the basic wage and what margins for skill should be paid, taking into account the cost of living, the size of the family unit, and the capacity of industry to pay. One effect of the wage-fixing system had been to encourage unionism amongst a people already inclined to collectivist industrial action; about one Australian in seven was now a trade unionist, a proportion unequalled in any other country.

In the previous few years the idea of supplementing wages by payments for dependent children had received attention from both Commonwealth and state governments. Since 1920 the Commonwealth government, for its own officials, and since 1927 the New South Wales government, for everyone, had had limited child endowment schemes. Two Commonwealth Royal Commissions – on the Basic Wage in 1920, and on Child Endowment in 1927 – and premiers' conferences had considered a national child endowment scheme, but no action had been taken because of difficulties over finance and because the Commonwealth had been unable to secure full control over wage-fixing machinery.

By the end of the 1920s, Australia's population policies had already had a long history. Colonial governments, since the 1830s, and the Commonwealth government, since 1920, had offered assisted passages to capture their share of British emigration. From 1861 to 1929, the average rate of growth of Australia's population had been among the highest in the world. A quarter of this growth had come from immigration in three main periods – up to 1891, 1907–13, and 1920–29 – and much of this had been assisted immigration from the United Kingdom. No vigorous government action had been taken, however, against the rapidly declining birth rate, which had become general throughout Western industrial societies. Since 1912 there had been a universal Commonwealth maternity allowance but this was not envisaged as a baby bonus. Also the very limited child endowment schemes in existence made only a small contribution to the economic costs of child-rearing.

Early in the life of the colonies, the political and social concept of 'White Australia' had begun to appear. At Federation the exclusion of non-European or coloured people had been accepted as a national policy to protect the Australian way of life, in particular its material standard of living. For more than a generation, by the late 1920s, Australian society had been sheltering behind this policy and also behind a tariff wall. The Australian standard of living had become sacred, at least as far as the wage earners were concerned. But what government provision existed when earnings were interrupted or ceased?

Some measure of security in old age and disablement had been provided by the Commonwealth government since its 1908 Act.[6] Ten million pounds annually was now being paid to 145,000 age pensioners and almost 60,000 invalid pensioners.[7] The limited non-contributory principle was still being used – that is, pensions were paid from general revenue subject to a means test. Contributory schemes had been considered periodically since 1910. In particular, a full-scale inquiry by a Royal Commission on national insurance covering not only old age and invalidity, but also casual sickness, maternity, and unemployment, had recently been held.

The Commission had found existing systems of mutual and other assistance very inadequate.[8] Their recommended compulsory national insurance scheme, which covered sickness, invalidity, maternity, and old age, their national health scheme, and their proposed unemployment insurance scheme and national system of employment bureaux, had not, however, been implemented. The main obstacles had been Commonwealth–state relationships, political change, and difficulties over finance as the Depression began. The only government-sponsored social insurance scheme, one for unemployment insurance, had been in operation in Queensland since 1923. In 1925,

---

6    This had superseded the old-age pensions introduced by New South Wales and Victoria (1901) and Queensland (1908), and the invalid pensions introduced in New South Wales (1908).
7    *Commonwealth Year Book*, No. 23, 1930, p. 268.
8    *First, Second, Third and Fourth* and *Final Report of the Royal Commission on National Insurance*, 1925 and 1927.

the New South Wales government had introduced a widows' pension, but like the Commonwealth age and invalid pensions it was on a means test, non-contributory basis. Only in relation to a special section of the community, ex-servicemen and their dependants, had the Commonwealth government's social provision been extended since the war. War pensions, medical treatment, assistance with surgical appliances, living allowances, vocational training, help with children's education, with settlement on the land, and with home building, had all come to be included in the Commonwealth repatriation scheme.

By the late 1920s, there had already come into existence an extensive array of health services, many of them government-run or government-subsidised. Yet the Royal Commission on National Insurance had found them deficient in a number of respects – hospital accommodation in the capital cities was generally insufficient, the middle income groups were not covered adequately for hospital care, local government authorities were responsible for much of the detailed administration of public health measures but were ill-equipped for it, in some states maternal welfare was not connected with the State Health Department, the medical examination of school children was an underdeveloped service, and Australia was far behind in preventive medicine (despite its low mortality rate), and so on. Increasingly, however, a national viewpoint on health matters had developed. In 1921, the Commonwealth Department of Health had been formed. Five years later, after a Royal Commission on Health, a Federal Health Council had been established to secure closer cooperation between the Commonwealth and state health authorities.

From a long-term point of view, one of the most important of the trends was a general shift of governmental power, particularly financial power, from a state to a federal level. Already in the fields of loan policy and credit policy, federal authorities had virtual control over the states. Many important social policies, for example, in connection with education and child welfare which were still theoretically entirely in the hands of the states, were now likely to be influenced by the Commonwealth's economic policy.

While government social policy and provision were being built up over the past couple of generations, there had been a parallel growth in non-government provision. In fact, 'the welfare society' of which 'the welfare state' was just a part, had been emerging, encouraged by urban and industrial expansion, a recognition of new categories of need (some of them not confined to material things), a community response to a nation at war, and an increase in the numbers of middle-class citizens, women in particular, with time and money to devote to 'charity', or 'welfare work', or 'church work', or whatever else they called it.

The 1925–27 Royal Commission on Social Insurance had found that numerous charitable organisations were then operating throughout the Commonwealth. Some had existed for many years. Many had been founded by the principal religious denominations 'to relieve the poor, the distressed, and afflicted and also to assist in the suppression of begging and the encouragement of self-help'. Special investigation officers visited applicants regularly to ascertain their 'character and general circumstances'.

The outdoor relief provided was usually in the form of food, fuel, clothing, bedding, financial aid, finding employment, purchasing tools for employment, starting small businesses, and arranging for a rest and change in the country – cash was seldom given. Single men were provided with food and shelter, but there was an unwillingness to assist able-bodied men. Some temporary assistance was given, however, to 'the deserving unemployed'.

The Commission had found that indoor relief consisted of benevolent asylums, even-tide homes for the aged, homes for patients awaiting hospital treatment, hospices providing free shelter and food for destitute men, refuges for women in distress, industrial homes for adults, homes for the care of girls and boys, and homes for infants and young children. If any charge was made for accommodation it was small.

Many organisations were providing relief for the same class of person – sometimes in the same area of a city. Several attempts had been made to establish a central coordinating organisation in each state, but many factors had prevented cooperation between the various societies.

The funds of charitable societies were privately donated or collected from charitably disposed people, and generally were subsidised by the state governments, although some societies had remained independent of government aid. Appeals were constantly being made through the daily press for assistance in special cases of extreme distress. Most of those dispensing outdoor relief for charitable organisations were unpaid.

As well as this voluntary social welfare activity concerned with basic material needs, there was a growing number of voluntary groups concerned with other aspects of the community's social welfare: health, recreation, education, the reformation of legal offenders, and so on.[9]

It is probable that many of the Australian social agencies had been moulded by overseas example, particularly that of the British. Few of the Australian agencies were large and well-endowed, however, and they would therefore have been but pale reflections of overseas models. Two distinctly Australian agencies, Legacy Clubs and the Flying Doctor Service, were innovations in social welfare work. The members of Legacy Clubs were ex-servicemen whose principal aim was to assist the dependants, particularly the children, of fallen comrades. The Flying Doctor Service began modestly on a denominational basis in 1928. Thirty years later it covered two-thirds of Australia, and its radio network afforded a means of social and business intercourse as well as calls for medical help. This service, and the Country Women's Association, made family life much easier in the Australian hinterland.

## A Stirring of the Social Conscience

This was the state of social provision when, in 1929, Australian society began to find itself engulfed in a major economic depression, whose misery, fear, and despair were to leave their mark on a generation of Australians, and which eventually helped to shape new social policy. At no stage during the next decade were less than 10 per cent of the workforce unemployed; at the worst period, in the early 1930s, there were more than 30 per cent.

People left the higher rental sections of cities and towns to live in shanties on the urban fringes or to overcrowd the already crowded slums. When the Brotherhood of St Laurence was established in

---

9    Compare J. Carlile Fox, *The Social Workers' Guide for Sydney and New South Wales, 1911*, with New South Wales Board of Social Study and Training, *Directory of Social Agencies*, Sydney, 1933.

Fitzroy in Melbourne during the darkest days of the Depression, it was appalled by the living conditions around it, and despaired of being able to assist even some of 'those thousands of decent Australians sleeping in parks and under bridges and walking the slum streets during the day in order to seek help from overworked and understaffed charitable organisations'.[10]

Australian welfare authorities were ill-equipped to cope with widespread and continuing poverty. Moreover, despite the emphasis in the early years of the century on minimum standards of individual welfare, this had not become a strongly established guide to policy. Relief during the Depression was badly handled. There was reliance on short-term emergency measures with little regard to the conservation of skills, or the maintenance of self-respect, or the preservation of families at a reasonable level of subsistence. The 'dole' was given not as a right but as a charitable gift; the view lingered that many of the unemployed could find employment if they tried.

The relief of the unemployed was still seen as a state not a Commonwealth government responsibility. Although non-government relief-giving expanded greatly, the state governments found they had to assume a far greater proportion. Yet their resources were limited, and they in turn had to look to the Commonwealth for financial assistance.

In contrast with the makeshift arrangements for relief, the economic measures adopted by the Australian governments were carefully planned and executed. They were designed, misguidedly according to modern theory, to bring about deflation and economy. Under these conditions money was not likely to be spent on new government social services, and, in fact, some of the existing provision was reduced in its scope.

In the second half of the 1930s, however, there was a little expansion in infant and child welfare services, and an awakening interest in slum-clearance and low-cost housing. In 1936, the Commonwealth government expanded its Federal Health Council into the influential National Health and Medical Research Council, which was to have a wide advisory role in public health matters, and, in 1937, the Victorian state government introduced limited non-contributory pensions for

---

10   Gerard Kennedy Tucker, 'Thanks Be', Melbourne, 1954, pp. 70–1.

widows. The movement towards social insurance schemes, which had been interrupted by the Depression, gathered strength during the mid-1930s but again it was without result. Reports on unemployment insurance and a health and pensions insurance by two British experts were acted upon. The first scheme, however, foundered on the question of the respective responsibilities of the Commonwealth and state governments, and a 1938 National Health and Pensions Insurance Act was abortive because many disagreed with its form; the Labor Party opposed contributory schemes, and the medical profession was hostile.

The social provision primarily concerned with mental health remained markedly underdeveloped. By the end of the 1930s, the child guidance movement had made little headway. Mental illness and mental defectiveness were frequently confused. Most of the mentally ill were still segregated from society in huge state government, prison-like custodial institutions called asylums. Psychiatry, not yet a respectable field of medical practice, was largely confined within their walls and was mainly practised by doctors with little or no psychological training. Yet the development of mental health associations in the larger states during the 1930s was a sign of an increasing awareness of the size and importance of the modern mental health problem. Unfortunately, these pre-war mental health associations lapsed and were only revived after the war.

Another noticeable trend during the 1930s was a movement towards coordinating social service effort. Many who supported the social work training movement saw this as a coordinating activity, and some saw the cooperation of the numerous agencies on the training bodies as a forerunner of wider cooperation. The Central Council of Victorian Benevolent Societies, formed in Melbourne in 1929, and the Council of Charitable Relief Organisations, formed in Adelaide in 1936, both attempted to use a central index of cases, and there was a move in 1937 to expand the Victorian Council into what was in effect to be a council of social service. Only in Sydney, however, was such a council actually established.

When compiling a directory of social agencies, the only one published in the 1930s, the Sydney general social work training body considered the time ripe for a renewed attempt to coordinate the city's 'philanthropic efforts'. In August 1935, a large gathering agreed to launch a general coordinating body, and early in 1936, after accounts of British and American experience had been studied, the Council of Social Service of New South Wales was formed. Its aims were those of a fully developed, general coordinating council, but its resources were very small, and actually its main function at first was to keep a central index.

## The Cleavage in Social Administration

By the time the social work training movement appeared on the Australian scene, a general pattern of administration of social provision had become set, and in fact it remained little changed during the 1930s. Paid Commonwealth and state male public servants, drawn from the general public service pools, were administering social legislation. There was little recognition that persons working in this or any other part of the public service needed special ability or training. Most non-government social agencies relied upon unpaid, voluntary work, which usually meant women attending to the execution of policy, and men, employed elsewhere, sitting on boards and committees in their spare time, helping with financial and general policy matters.

Attitudes to women in early twentieth-century Australian society channelled them into this work. Despite their early political recognition, women were still not expected to be active in the business world or in the affairs of the nation. The woman's place was in the home, but it was acceptable for her to undertake welfare work – indeed in some circles, membership of certain welfare organisations became a badge of social respectability. This was one of the few areas outside the home in which women could use their talents. A woman supported by her husband, or by a private income, was, from a financial viewpoint, the ideal worker for agencies short of funds. Moreover, some felt that women had greater sympathy for, and understanding of, people in trouble, particularly women and children. The general public were not excited by social problems without obvious political overtones. Their view was, as in other matters, 'there will be a government department dealing with that'. Those few problems which were not covered by government departments could well be left to the gentle ministrations of womenfolk and, to a lesser extent, clergy.

Whatever the reasons, and cause and effect are difficult to untangle in this question, the performance of non-government social work had become strongly identified with women.

There was, then, a cleavage in Australian social administration. On the one hand, there was an approach through broad legislative measures, sponsored by political parties and administered by government, largely male, officials; on the other was an approach through numerous small voluntary organisations, catering for individual needs, sponsored by a wide variety of citizen groups or churches, with detailed work largely in the hands of unpaid women in the higher income groups.

# CHAPTER 3
# Taking up the Training Challenge

Before examining the immediate origins and early years of the Australian social work training movement, how was the case for training presented in Australia during these early years – in talks given on various occasions, in newspaper articles, and in other printed material?[1]

## The Case for Training Social Workers

Three main arguments were used: community trends favourable to social work training, the defects of untrained social workers, and the advantages of trained ones.

It was pointed out that social problems were becoming more complex because of industrial and urban growth, and the tensions and anxieties of industrial society were emphasised in a depression. Social service, to be service, needed a new understanding backed by continuous study. As yet, social welfare measures had not kept pace with the improvement of industrial technique. Even seemingly simple social problems were more complex than had been realised.

Matching this complexity, so it was argued, was a growing fund of knowledge, which could be used to revise older methods and experiment with new ones. The beneficial pooling of knowledge by professional people – doctors, psychologists, psychiatrists – would come about only if social work was also a profession. The realisation

---

1    For detailed references, see R.J. Lawrence, The Development of Professional Social Work in Australia, PhD thesis, The Australian National University, Chapter 2.

that social service work could be studied systematically was recent, but not to use available knowledge was wasteful in human and monetary terms. Voluntary social workers, because they usually had other claims on their time, could not be expected to study the subject in detail or learn of modern methods and experiments overseas.

It was further asserted that the increased sense of community responsibility, which was demonstrated by the striking growth in social services over the previous 50 years, was less satisfied with 'haphazard and comparatively uninformed tinkering with problems'. This did not apply only to voluntary work. Unless public servants were trained, 'routine administration of social legislation affecting masses of lives' was likely to be detrimental to individual welfare. The growth in social provision emphasised the need for coordination and cooperation if it was to be effective. Money available for welfare purposes was limited, especially during a depression.

Arguments relating to the voluntary, untrained worker had to be handled with care, because the training movement needed the support of all people in social service work. It was stated that the untrained worker still had a part to play but it should be more restricted. Well-motivated amateurs were liable to rush in where professional people would tread with some circumspection. Untrained social workers had to learn through a system of apprenticeship and experience, which, it was claimed, was slow, haphazard, and a strain on the worker, and costly in terms of mistakes and general inefficiency; and at least a few of them were aware of this. Mistakes in social work were often paid for by human suffering – a high price for humanitarians. Put bluntly, inadequate social work was worse than none.

It was claimed that mistakes in relief-giving arose mainly from a lack of thorough investigation of the circumstances of applicants. Investigation, or study as some preferred to call it, was a necessary prerequisite for assisting people, whether with material or other help. Indiscriminate giving was likely to be harmful to applicants as well as a waste of funds. The untrained worker tended to become immersed in 'doing' and 'giving' instead of finding out the facts of the case, particularly how the client saw his own problem. Helping people to help themselves was too little the aim and still less the achievement of untrained workers. If agencies now needed to pay their social workers, to be worthy of their hire they should be trained.

The protagonists of training further argued that general community arrangements for social welfare were not critically evaluated. A common assumption was that because social agencies were in existence, social welfare was being promoted. A closer examination of welfare programmes would lead to a greater consideration and respect for other people, and was also likely to reveal that one section of the community was inextricably involved in the social services but the rest were aloof from them. Australians needed to think more about social progress, it was asserted.

The advantages claimed for trained social workers over their untrained predecessors or colleagues were many. It was said that they had learned ways of being reasonably efficient in a complex society. They had knowledge of the community's resources for aid and relief, and were aware of the need among the multiplying remedial organisations for cooperation to prevent overlapping. This avoided imposture, but more important, it meant that handling of cases from a social casework point of view, did not have to be divided. In addition, widespread employment of trained social workers by social agencies would help to make apparent a shared general purpose for all social services and make cooperation more of a reality.

Trained social workers had had an opportunity to broaden their knowledge of social conditions, not only through academic study but through actual observation and experience. This, together with their knowledge of the social services, equipped them to be constructively critical of the community's arrangements for social welfare, and about the social welfare of the community in general.

It was stated that, instead of being content with palliative measures, trained social workers tried to find the root causes of social breakdown, and did something about them, both in individual cases and in community action. It was in this sense that their work was 'scientific'. They recognised that they had an important preventive role to play.

For their responsibilities, trained social workers were equipped with relevant knowledge about individuals and the community, and had skill in tested social work techniques. They were keenly aware of individual differences and were alive to the multiple causes of maladjustment. They helped individuals to adjust on a psychological and social level as well as on the economic; they recognised that their work affected 'the moral and mental welfare as well as the physical well-being of people'.

It was declared that trained workers respected the personality of the client. They were not condescending, neither were they 'Nosey Parkers' nor 'Lady Bountifuls', and they did not make themselves indispensable. Apart from other considerations, their aim of helping the client to help himself precluded these things. Not only were they aware of the personality needs of their clients, but they had a heightened self-awareness which helped them to guard against fulfilling their own personality needs at the expense of their clients.

Those who supported training agreed that it was no substitute for natural aptitude for social work, but insisted that the aptitude needed to be developed fully. All trained social workers had been screened at least to some extent on the grounds of their personal suitability to do the work. They could be a powerful force for helping people with social problems, and thus reduce the cost of social provision by making it more effective.

Taken together, these various arguments constituted a strong case for social work training, provided they could be proved. Depending upon the occasion, the speaker, and the audience, only a selection of the arguments, however, were used at any one time, and in the absence of appropriate research, many of the arguments appear to have been rooted as much in opinion and hope as in fact. In general, the case was nurtured by the size of the cities, the increased difficulty of effective social provision despite ever-growing funds for the purpose, some advance in knowledge of psychology and the social sciences in Australia, and by observation of developments overseas.

In the troubled decade during which these arguments were voiced, five social work training bodies were formed in Australia. Three of them – in Sydney, Melbourne and Adelaide – were general; the other two – in Melbourne and Sydney – were concerned with training for medical social work. This was a period of struggle for the Australian training movement – to find appropriate standards, to gain community acceptance, and to remain solvent – and its tensions, especially in

Sydney, carried over into more secure times. By 1940, the product of the movement was still only 54 social workers in Sydney, 53 in Melbourne, and 12 in Adelaide; moreover, only some of these were in social work employment. But a start to an important venture had been made.

In the founding of each of the training bodies, overseas example played a significant part, and in the rather later developments so too did interstate example.

## The Creation of Training Bodies

The suggestion for a general training scheme for social work in New South Wales came from the National Council of Women, a non-sectarian federation of a large number of women's organisations. The council's interest originated in October 1927 from Isabel Fidler, first tutor to women students at Sydney University and the convenor of the council's Standing Committee on Education, and later several senior members of the university's academic staff combined with representatives of the council to draw up a scheme of studies. In July 1928, 17 people representing 14 organisations interested in social work enthusiastically agreed to form a board 'to establish and control a specialised educational course for social workers'. Early in 1929 a constitution was adopted and the New South Wales Board of Social Study and Training, the first Australian general training body for social work, came into existence.

Meanwhile, in Melbourne, a series of events was leading to the establishment of a training body for medical social work. In 1927, after an overseas tour, R.J. Love, the Inspector of Charities and Secretary of the Victorian Hospitals and Charities Board, reported to the Victorian Parliament.[2] He had been impressed in other countries by the way a hospital was seen as part of the whole social welfare structure. Hospital almoner departments were instrumental in achieving this and he recommended their adoption in Australia; but they must be run by full-time, qualified staff. Further, each non-medical society or group of societies was urged to appoint a full-time, qualified officer.

---

2    *Victorian Parliamentary Paper 1927*, Vol. II, No. 45.

R.J. Love envisaged one grand scheme of social welfare in which overlapping and duplication were eliminated by a comprehensive system of referrals.

Shortly after this report appeared, the president of the Queen Victoria Hospital for Women and Children, Mrs Norman Brookes, visited several large hospitals in England. Her scepticism about 'the almoner system' changed to enthusiasm. On her return to Melbourne, she convened a meeting of representatives of charitable organisations to hear R.J. Love speak on the need to establish an almoner system in Victoria. At this meeting support was given to the idea, but there were doubts about whether the hospitals could bear the cost, and whether the state government would assist financially; also the value of hospital auxiliary workers was emphasised.

At a follow-up meeting held in the office of the Hospitals and Charities Board and presided over by an eminent doctor, Sir George Syme, a decision was made to inaugurate a scheme for training almoners. Early in May 1929 it was resolved that a Central Almoners' Council should be formed; that in organisation and development it follow the London Institute of Almoners (with modifications to meet local conditions); that it consist of representatives of interested organisations; that it confine its activities primarily to 'the education and training of almoners and to essential propaganda work'; that it try to secure the services of Anne Cummins of the British Institute; that, for efficiency, it be closely linked with the Charity Organisation Society; and, finally, that philanthropic trusts and benevolent citizens be asked for financial support (there was to be no public appeal). At the end of May, on a motion of R.J. Love, 'The Victorian Institute of Almoners' was formed.

Early in 1930, these developments joined fully with another development which had centred on the Melbourne Hospital. In 1922, an auxiliary unit run by volunteers had been formed at the hospital and this included a relief section. In 1927, Mrs Kent Hughes, a member of the unit and formerly a nursing sister at the hospital, spent a period with Anne Cummins at St Thomas's in London. On her return she urged the employment of a qualified almoner at the Melbourne Hospital. The outcome was the appointment, in June 1929, of Agnes Macintyre from St Thomas's, her boat fares and salary having been guaranteed by the hospital's auxiliary.

Soon after her arrival in Melbourne, she began training three prospective almoners within the Melbourne Hospital. Early in 1930, after the Institute of Almoners had been unsuccessful in gaining Anne Cummins's services, it invited Agnes Macintyre to become its Directress of Training, and clerical help was offered to the hospital to compensate for the time she would spend on institute affairs. She and the hospital accepted, and so training for medical social work in Melbourne became established at the Melbourne Hospital.

In 1933, 'Hospital' was inserted before 'Almoners' in the Institute's name to signify a narrower scope than that envisaged by its founders. Until then, certainly, it had trained hospital almoners only, but its two-year course had included much general social work training. Now that a general social work training of two years under another body was being developed, the institute decided to provide a one-year specialist training in medical social work following the general training.

As early as April 1930, Dr Ethel Osborne considered that the almoner training might be developed into a university School of Social Science. Shortly afterwards, the recently founded Victorian Council for Mental Hygiene approached the Melbourne University to establish a School of Social Training, but the University Council decided that it was not equipped for the purpose. The Institute of Almoners immediately wrote urging the university to develop the course as soon as possible.

In June 1931, the presidents of the Council for Mental Hygiene, the Institute of Almoners, the Charity Organisation Society, the Central Council of Benevolent Societies, and the National Young Women's Christian Association of Australia, and the Director of Education, convened a meeting at the Melbourne Town Hall. Sir Richard Stawell, president of the Council for Mental Hygiene, presided. Beforehand it was decided to use this meeting to stimulate interest and to make a fresh approach to the university through a selected committee, rather than to form a large, unwieldy body to promote training.

This Committee on Social Training was to investigate developing a general social work course, preferably in association with the university. For a year and a half it did much public relations work, at the same time consulting the university about a course and its management. The university remained firm. It was willing only to be officially represented on an independent controlling body, for it considered it could have neither adequate nor expert control over the practical work, nor could it provide teaching in psychology.

To make a start in the 1933 academic year, the Committee on Social Training appointed a Board of Studies to supervise a course. It also decided to have a direct link with many more organisations than those originally responsible for its own formation. So at a meeting in the Melbourne Town Hall in June 1933, a widely representative Victorian Council for Social Training was formed, and Australia's second general social work training body came into existence.

Meanwhile, events in Sydney were moving towards the founding of Australia's second specialist training body for medical social work. In October 1931, the Directress of Training and the secretary of the Victorian Institute of Almoners joined representatives of the Rachel Forster Hospital,[3] and the Board of Social Study and Training to discuss the establishment of medical social work training in Sydney. The discussion ended with a meeting attended by 'many prominent citizens' who were addressed by the board's president, Professor Tasman Lovell, and Dr R.B. Wade.[4]

Soon after this the Royal Alexandra Hospital for Children sent Stella Davies, one of the first people trained by the board, to do the British Institute of Hospital Almoners' course. In 1932, the Rachel Forster Hospital also sent its former secretary, Katharine Ogilvie. In 1934, both these women, now qualified almoners, assisted in the training of three students who were taking a specialist course in medical social work established by the board. This followed the board's general course and was organised by a sub-committee. Its management was severely criticised by the two qualified almoners, Katharine Ogilvie in particular, and an impressive case was made for setting up a separate Institute of Hospital Almoners, as in Melbourne and in London. The board's director expressed disapproval of the English-type apprenticeship almoner courses run by independent specialist bodies, but the move for a separate institute gathered strength.

---

3    This hospital, situated in the Sydney suburb of Redfern, provided 'medical care by medical women for necessitous women and children'.
4    In 1932, Dr R.B. Wade became president, Royal Alexandra Hospital for Children; 1935–37, president, Royal Australasian College of Surgeons; 1937–44, president, New South Wales Institute of Hospital Almoners.

3. TAKING UP THE TRAINING CHALLENGE

In October 1935, the Hospitals Commission appointed a committee to explore the possibilities of forming an institute, to make preliminary arrangements, and to appoint an experienced almoner in charge of training who was to work in a general hospital.

The Medical Superintendent of the Sydney Hospital, Dr C.A. Telfer, had recently returned from abroad and was keen to have an almoner department in his hospital. Mainly through him, the Sydney Hospital and the Hospitals Commission appointed Helen Rees, an experienced English almoner who had been the Directress of Training at the Victorian Institute of Hospital Almoners, to open an almoner department at the Sydney Hospital and to establish a training scheme. She took up her post in June 1936.

In November of that year, the Minister for Health presided over a meeting of 60 people – representatives of the Sydney University, the Board of Social Study and Training, the hospitals and public health services, prominent members of the medical profession, and people interested in social work. Dr R.B. Wade, after tracing the growth of the almoner movement in Britain, successfully moved that the New South Wales Institute of Hospital Almoners be formed, to act as a training body, and, like the Victorian Institute, to keep a register of trained almoners and to develop their work and opportunities for employment. In April 1937, a constitution was adopted.

The Board of Social Study and Training was not happy about this development, but it gave the institute grudging cooperation when it saw there was no real alternative. Relations between certain members of the two training bodies remained very strained however.

The immediate reason for the appearance of a training body in Adelaide, a city much smaller than Sydney or Melbourne, was the energetic promoting by Stella Pines.[5] In April 1935, she began to enlist

---

5    A nursing sister of World War I, Stella Pines spent some years in North America, including a period in Ida Cannon's social service department at the Massachusetts General Hospital. In the early 1930s she was in Sydney, then was connected with the beginning of the Victorian Centenary College of Nursing in Melbourne. In 1934 she was not accepted as a trained almoner by the Victorian Institute. She was unsuccessful in her application to become the Director of the South Australian training body she did so much to create. Her next move was to Brisbane where again she attempted to promote social work training, but this time without success. In 1943 she was connected with the forming of an Institute of Occupational Therapists in Melbourne.

the interest of people connected with philanthropic and educational organisations. In September, on her prompting, the Lord Mayor presided over a meeting at the Adelaide Town Hall, and the 25 people present formed themselves into a committee, to be called a Board of Social Service Training, to draw up a constitution (which was adopted in November) and a curriculum. A sub-committee later successfully approached the University of Adelaide for its cooperation; although Sir William Mitchell, its influential Vice-Chancellor, was particularly interested in the idea he declined to become the president of the board because of his university position. In April 1937, the name of the training body was changed to 'Board of Social Study and Training'.

During the early period of these training bodies, occasional correspondence passed between them, and their officers met unofficially, but they had no formal machinery for cooperation. In 1937, a suggestion came from Sydney that an 'Australian Council of Social Studies', similar to the British Joint University Council for Social Studies, be formed, and also that an Australian Conference of Social Work might be sponsored by the general social work schools the following year as part of the 150th anniversary celebrations of Australia's founding. The Sydney Board eventually dropped the latter suggestion, but organised a conference of the three schools in May 1938 to discuss common problems and consider a federal organisation. By the end of 1938, after considerable debate on the most appropriate name, a constitution had been decided upon, and the 'Australian Council of Schools of Social Work', formally came into existence. It was to promote the education and training of social workers, to provide for cooperation between members, to encourage them to attain standards which would ensure reciprocity with recognised schools abroad, and to act on an interstate, Commonwealth and international level with these objects in mind. Before the Australian council had had time to become more than just a name, the war came.

# Financial Insecurity

A strong factor in the formation of the council was hope of financial assistance from the federal government. The general training bodies experienced extreme financial insecurity in their early years. A comment of the director of the Melbourne school in 1935, that the work was being crippled by poverty, and that the constant anxiety about money sapped the energies of the staff,[6] could well have been made on all three general training bodies in the 1930s.

The Melbourne director quickly saw that another professional staff member was needed. Not until 1939, however, was a second appointment made, and even then it was financed not by the training body but, through the almoners' institute, by the Anti-Cancer Council which wanted to increase the number of trained almoners. A second staff member was appointed in Sydney in 1939, although there was no money available, because of the insistence of the local almoners' institute. In Adelaide, additional staff was completely out of the question because of the cost.

For most of the 1930s, the general training bodies employed only a director with some secretarial assistance. Yet even so, salaries were still the largest item of expenditure. For a brief period, the Sydney and Melbourne training bodies did rely upon voluntary directors, but in 1932 and 1934 respectively, each paid its director a full salary. The Adelaide Board offered only £100 for its director's starting salary, and eventually did little more than double it, which meant that the Adelaide director gave the greater part of her time voluntarily. All three training bodies depended on voluntary assistance in the overall planning and supervision of the course, in some of the general office work, and in the supervision of students doing fieldwork inside social agencies. In Sydney and Melbourne much of the office accommodation was free of rent.

Although costs were kept to a minimum, students' fees usually covered only between a third and a half of the total expenses. This meant that outside financial assistance was vital. In Adelaide, the state government provided a small subsidy, but state government financial assistance was not forthcoming in either Melbourne or Sydney, despite deputations seeking it.

Each of the training bodies had thus to rely on private contributions, and this was made the more difficult because already abnormal claims were being made upon such sources. As a rule they did not make

---

6    Victorian Council for Social Training, *Annual Report 1935*.

appeals to the general public. A recurrent theme in written approaches to possible donors was that the work had little emotional or general appeal, but that 'it must touch the imagination of thoughtful citizens'.

Only one really substantial gift came the way of any of the training bodies, and this was to the Sydney board from outside the country. In 1932, the Carnegie Corporation of New York provided $10,500 and $2,000 for an overseas tour by its director. Three years later, it gave an additional but final $15,000. Shortly after this, the Melbourne council applied to the corporation for help but was told the policy now was to make grants only to university training bodies. From 1936 to 1940, the Sydney board's accumulated funds dwindled rapidly. Not even a Finance Committee sponsored by the General Manager of the Bank of New South Wales could find support, and by 1940, the board was faced with imminent insolvency.

The Melbourne council had a more constant struggle for funds. The salary of the director for the first three years was guaranteed by a few people prominent in the business and industrial world. The Council's officers had to continue to approach trusts, estates, industrial concerns, and individuals, to keep the body in existence, yet by 1940 its donor list was still small and, though individual contributions were usually much larger than in Sydney, it was still only just remaining solvent.

The Adelaide board, in a much smaller city, faced an even more difficult situation and almost certainly, without the state government grant, and the honorary services given to it, especially by the director, it would have collapsed. Its donors were mainly people connected directly with it.

Compared with the general training bodies, the two almoner institutes were more financially secure. The director of training was employed in and paid mainly by a hospital. The Melbourne institute made a small contribution to the Melbourne Hospital for her services; a similar though larger contribution was made direct to the Sydney Hospital by the Hospitals' Commission. Students' fees again did not cover total costs, but usually the deficit was covered fairly comfortably – mainly by gifts from charitable trusts and similar bodies in Melbourne, and by private individuals and one trust in Sydney.

The character of these early training bodies – their structure, the way they functioned, and the people with influence in them – was as important as any financial limitations they experienced.

## The Nature of the Training Bodies

Each of the general training bodies consisted mainly of representatives of a large number of organisations. For example, the Sydney board had 21 organisations represented on it in 1929, and 53 in 1935; the Melbourne council 61 in 1937, 81 in 1940; and the Adelaide board 24 in 1936, and 32 in 1941. The organisations varied greatly in aim, scope, and resources. Together they covered a wide range of educational, health, and welfare services. For the most part, the representatives held senior positions in their organisations, and they came from various walks of life: the church, teaching, medicine, psychiatry, psychology, law, the army, nursing, the public service, social work, home duties.

With such large and diverse membership, general membership meetings were unsuited for effective policy making, and in fact they were not held frequently. The Sydney board held, roughly, quarterly meetings, the Adelaide board and the Melbourne council rarely met other than annually. Why, then, have the unwieldy membership? For survival, the training needed to gain widespread acceptance and support, particularly in social service circles. Membership of a training body at least implied support of the idea of training, and a large membership had a public relations value. Further, it was thought that existing agencies should have at least some say in the training.

The main work of each body, and the actual control over its affairs, was in the hands of an executive group. No executive group exceeded 20 in number, and was more often about 12. In Sydney and Melbourne, meetings were normally monthly, supplemented occasionally by meetings of sub-committees. In Adelaide, the executive group really consisted of two groups with overlapping membership, the Executive proper which met rather less than monthly, and a Committee for Studies which met about seven times a year.

People in the executive groups of the training bodies were often as much the interested parties as any organisations they happened to be connected with. They fell into four categories: university staff members who usually taught in the course, members of other professions, office-bearers of welfare organisations, and people actually practising social work.

Particular emphasis was placed upon the first category. This was primarily an educational venture, and connection with the highest educational authority had a prestige value. Moreover, the more that university people of good standing were closely associated with the course, the greater the chance of it being taken over by the university. Arguments to support training for social work had a strong intellectual appeal, and this activity gave university people an appropriate opportunity for fairly direct community service.

Some members of the established professions had become aware of the importance of social conditions in the health and welfare of their patients or clients, and had recognised that neither they nor other existing professional people were equipped to cope with this aspect. Apart from bringing knowledge from contingent fields, members of the accepted professions, especially doctors, were high in community standing. In the early years, it was essential that social work training be connected with people respected for their integrity and ability in an established discipline.

The main purpose of the training bodies was of course to produce qualified social workers. At first the executive groups contained no qualified social workers, but later in Adelaide and Melbourne, though not in Sydney, there were a few, mainly almoners.

Within the executive group, the chairman, a person of community standing, and the training body's director, the person with the greatest knowledge of social work education, played the most influential parts. Because there were so few others with specialised knowledge of social work education, a particular responsibility rested with the director.

Inside the executive groups of the two almoner institutes, again special influence lay with the director of training and the chairman, and again the real work and control of the bodies was in the hands of the executive group. Naturally the character of these specialist training bodies differed from that of the general bodies, but also, reflecting the times and nature of their origin, they were different from each other.

Few on the Victorian institute's executive of about 12 members had medical qualifications; many, including a number of married women, were lay members of hospital and other boards. In contrast, the New South Wales institute's executive group, its council, had a high proportion of medical practitioners in its 17 members. It was, however, the training sub-committee of this council which controlled the training in detail, and this was dominated by qualified almoners.

In general, the New South Wales institute placed a much greater emphasis on the participation of qualified almoners than did the older Victorian institute. The almoners' professional association was entitled to a third of the New South Wales institute's total membership, and the other members were representatives of the Hospitals' Commission, the Board of Social Study and Training, the BMA, and Sydney University, and interested persons elected by the executive council. At first the Victorian institute's council had 21 separate organisations represented on it – eight hospitals, a further four organisations medical in character, four sectarian welfare bodies, two central relief-giving agencies, two educational institutions, and a professional association. In 1933, a few general welfare organisations, now represented on the new general training body, relinquished membership of the council. In almost every instance, the institute found organisations willing to be represented, but there was one important early exception, the Alfred Hospital. Largely because of its long-standing rivalry with the Melbourne Hospital, this large general teaching hospital did not agree to cooperate fully until 1936.

Except for a short period at the beginning of the Victorian institute, both institutes had at their head a medical man prominent in his profession and in the community. The identification of these and several other influential members of the medical profession with the institutes helped to give the movement for training medical social workers respectability in the eyes of other members of the medical profession, and of related professions, hospital administrators, and the general public.

Perhaps one of the greatest assets in the Australian training movement's early struggle for recognition was the association of men of community standing with all the training bodies. Significantly, at the head of the training bodies were men; equally significantly, the directors were women. This was a serious activity for these men, but it was a spare-time one. They could not be expected to be experts in social work education.

## The Pioneers

In any small, new development, especially when it is concerned so much with human relations, individual personalities tend to play a dominant role. A very small number of people carried the main burdens of the Australian training movement in its early years; and some of them had a long association with it.

Individuals who may be singled out for the part they played are Professors H. Tasman Lovell and Harvey Sutton, Aileen Fitzpatrick, and Katharine Ogilvie in Sydney; Helen Rees in Melbourne and Sydney, and Dr John Newman Morris, Professors G.L. Wood and A. Boyce Gibson, S. Greig Smith, Jocelyn Hyslop, Agnes Macintyre, Joan Brett, and Dorothy Bethune in Melbourne; and Amy Wheaton in Adelaide. All these people had at least some overseas experience – in either Britain, North America, or both.

For the first nine years of the Sydney board, Professor Tasman Lovell[7] was its president. Its accommodation and most of its money came from his efforts, and in 1937 when pressure of other work forced him to resign, he was warmly thanked by the board.[8] The child guidance movement in the United States had captured his imagination, and child welfare in general was one of his keenest interests. In 1934, while president of the board, he visited the United States.

---

7    Professor Tasman Lovell was educated at the universities of Sydney and Jena; lectured in philosophy, Associate Professor of Psychology, Sydney University, 1920–29; appointed to Australia's first Chair of Psychology, Sydney University, 1929; President, NSW Council of Social Service, 1943–50.
8    NSW Board of Social Study and Training, *Annual Report 1937*.

Professor Harvey Sutton[9] was the Sydney board's president in the difficult period 1937–40. His professional experience had made him well aware of the influence of social conditions on public health. Both Professors Sutton and Lovell continued until 1947 as members of the body controlling the general training in Sydney.

Professor G.L. Wood[10] was the first chairman of the Board of Social Studies of the Melbourne general training body, and had taken an active part in the discussions leading to its formation. He spent a period in 1934–35 visiting centres of social work in the United States. Shortly afterwards, pressure of university affairs forced him to resign his position as chairman, but at his death in 1953 tribute was made to 'his interest in training for social work, undimmed by the expanding calls of his other University and governmental duties'.[11] He believed in close ties between the university and the community and saw this exemplified in the social studies course. His own close relationships with the commercial life of Melbourne proved of financial advantage to the early training body.

Professor Boyce Gibson,[12] his successor as the board's chairman, had been associated with the social studies course at Birmingham University. He was chairman for six years, and his skill in negotiation was an important factor in the eventual decision of the university to absorb the Melbourne training. From 1943–47, he was again the training body's chairman, and not until 1958 did he sever connection with it.

In a special position of influence was Dr John Newman Morris. After observing hospital social work in the United States in 1930, he declared himself convinced of its worth, provided the workers were carefully selected and trained.[13] In the following years, he worked to

9     Professor Harvey Sutton was educated at universities of Melbourne and Oxford; Chief School Medical Officer, Victorian Education Department, 1910–15; Principal Medical Officer, NSW Education Department, 1920–29; appointed Director, School of Public Health and Preventive Medicine, Sydney University, 1929, and Professor of Preventive Medicine, 1930.
10    Professor G.L. Wood was educated at the University of Tasmania; school teaching; Commerce Faculty, Melbourne University, 1925; appointed Commonwealth Grants Committee, 1936; Myer Chair of Commerce, 1944.
11    Melbourne University, Board of Social Studies, Minutes, 10 August 1953.
12    Professor Boyce Gibson was educated at the universities of Melbourne and Oxford; lecturing, Glasgow, Oxford, Birmingham, 1923–35; succeeded to his father's Chair of Philosophy at Melbourne University, 1935.
13    J. Newman Morris, *Social Work in Hospitals – Some American Investigations*, p. 23.

support not only medical social work but all qualified social work. In 1931, he became president of the Victorian Institute of Almoners and remained in this position until the end of the institute in 1950. From 1933, he was also president of the Victorian Council for Social Training until its end 10 years later, when it was said:

> He has done so much to put social work on the map, here and in other States, to get its value recognised by State and voluntary bodies, and to bring its usefulness before the Commonwealth Government. He has lost no opportunity of assisting a very young profession, safeguarding its salary scales, interpreting its aims, and giving always that understanding and encouragement which are so needful in the early stages.[14]

He was a member of the university general training body 1941–56, also the first (and only) president of the Australian Council of Schools of Social Work. A man of high community and professional standing, he was deeply involved in community affairs.[15] To have his sustained active interest meant a great deal to the training movement in its early years.

In 1932, on one of his many trips abroad, Dr Newman Morris attended the Second International Conference of Social Work held at Frankfurt in Germany. In 1936, S. Greig Smith, who was also closely connected with both the general and the medical social work training movement in Melbourne, attended the Third International Conference of Social Work held in London. Like Dr Newman Morris, he was in a special position of influence although of a different kind.

Greig Smith was Secretary of the Melbourne Charity Organisation Society (Citizens' Welfare Service from 1947), 1908–57. Throughout the 21 years of the almoners' institute, he was its secretary. He was the first treasurer of the Victorian Council for Social Training, and was on

---

14  Victorian Council for Social Training, *Annual Report 1942* and *Annual Report 1943*.

15  In 1931, Dr Newman Morris was, *inter alia*, Vice-Chairman of Federal Committee of the BMA; former President, BMA (Victorian Branch); Chairman, Queen's Memorial Infectious Diseases Hospital; member of Victorian Committee of Royal Australasian College of Surgeons Charities Board, Executive Committee of Lord Mayor's Fund, Standing Committee on Convocation of Melbourne University. In the following seven years, he became a member of the National Health and Medical Research Council, Medical Board of Victoria, and Council of Australian Red Cross (Victorian Branch); President, Federal Council of Australian Aerial Medical Services, and the Council of St John Ambulance Association; and Vice-President, Victorian Society for Crippled Children. In 1948 he received a knighthood.

the governing body of the general training course until 1958. In 1935, he convened the meeting which led to the formation of the Victorian Association of Social Workers and was its first president.

Early in 1929, Greig Smith considered that the appointment of an experienced English almoner was not necessary,[16] yet he gave unswerving and vital support to the three English-qualified almoners who were in turn appointed as Chief Almoner and Directress of Training of the Victorian Institute. The success of these three appointments – Agnes Macintyre, 1930–31;[17] Joan Brett, 1931–33;[18] and Helen Rees, 1933–35[19] – in the hospital, the institute, and the community, laid solid foundations for medical social work in Melbourne. Their experience and personal qualities were different, but what they shared was an effective public presence. Agnes Macintyre was the first qualified social worker appointed in Australia, and she proved a worthy ambassador of the British training movement. Her two successors, particularly Joan Brett, played important parts in founding the general training course in Melbourne.

The Victorian institute passed a notable milestone when, in 1935, one of its former students succeeded Helen Rees after a year's experience in England arranged through the British Institute of Hospital Almoners. For the next 10 years Dorothy Bethune[20] steered the fortunes of medical social work in Victoria. On her resignation early in 1945, because of ill-health, she was made a vice-president of the Victorian institute. She was highly regarded personally, although a few thought of her early tendency to see medical social work as quite distinct from social work in other settings, and her disinclination to press for higher salaries and status for almoners as retarding a broad professional growth. She did, however, serve on the university training body's board from its inception, and was still taking an active interest in general social work developments in the late 1950s.

---

16   S. Greig Smith, Notes on Hospital Almoner System, submitted to the Charity Organisation Society Executive Committee, 11 February 1929.

17   AIHA. From St Thomas's, London. In her 40s.

18   MA (Cantab.), AIHA. In her 20s. Left to be married; had three children; was a war widow. Later returned to almoner work in England.

19   MA (Cantab.), AIHA. Methodist minister's daughter; in her early 30s; an excellent training course; almoner, City General Hospital, Sheffield.

20   Directed a kindergarten; qualified almoner, 1932; Registrar of Public Assistance, Bendigo; assistant almoner, Melbourne Hospital, 1934.

In 1936, Helen Rees opened the Almoner Department at the Sydney Hospital and became Almoner-in-Charge of Training for the New South Wales Institute of Hospital Almoners. She returned to England in 1941 at the request of the English Association of Hospital Almoners to undertake a survey of their work under wartime conditions. The fact that she later became Director of Training for the British Institute of Almoners gives an indication of her quality. She was influential in the move to establish a university training body in Sydney, and her knowledge of general training schemes was invaluable. Associated with her in this, and in the Institute's affairs, was Katharine Ogilvie who became a close friend.

The dominant part played by Katharine Ogilvie[21] in the foundation of the New South Wales institute has been mentioned. In 1941, she left the Rachel Forster Hospital to succeed Helen Rees as the institute's Almoner-in-Charge of Training and Head Almoner of Sydney Hospital. In 1954, when Sydney University took over medical social work training from the institute, she became a member of the university staff. Just two years before, she became president of the New South Wales Council of Social Service and was still in this position in 1959. She was at the same time also a leader in the New South Wales Old People's Welfare Council.

Before she opened, in 1934, the Almoner Department of the Rachel Forster Hospital after training at the British Institute of Hospital Almoners, she had already established herself as a community leader by her work, while still in her 20s, as the hospital's secretary. For the next quarter of a century her community and professional standing was extremely high. Her personal qualities and education made her a forceful leader, a formidable champion of a cause which had won her favour, and a compassionate understanding of sick people permeated her social casework. In 1950–51, she revisited England and strengthened further her ties with the British almoners.

The directors of the three general training bodies – Aileen Fitzpatrick in Sydney 1931–40; an English woman, Jocelyn Hyslop in Melbourne 1934–44; and Amy Wheaton in Adelaide 1936–58 – held key positions

---

21    From a well-known country family; BA (History), Sydney University; prominent in international hockey circles; Secretary, Rachel Forster Hospital; observation of hospital administration in UK and USA (this aroused her interest in almoners' work); an MBE; member of the Senate of Sydney University, 1943–49 (a Fellow elected by graduates).

in the Australian training movement. The first and last of these were not qualified social workers. This did not matter very much with Amy Wheaton because she was so well-qualified in other directions.

It has been said that Aileen Fitzpatrick coloured the whole of the pre-war period in Sydney. There exists a strange letter written by her early in 1940. In it she speaks of the New York School of Social Work as having been her 'own old school of social work', and later says, 'It has been no light responsibility to have had the background of a good school in beginning training for social work here'.[22] It is difficult to reconcile this with other evidence. Nothing suggests that she had been to the United States before her appointment as director of the Sydney board in 1931.[23] From September 1932, on money provided by the Carnegie Corporation, she did spend nine months observing schools of social work in the United States, Canada, the United Kingdom, and Europe; and in the long vacation of 1934–35, again with Carnegie assistance, she visited, in charge of a group of Australian students, many centres in North America. But she did not hold a social work qualification, and the quality of her professional teaching was one of the main points at issue with the almoners. She managed, however, to make good professional contacts with American social workers, and until the almoner group challenged her training standards she secured a lot of support for the board's work.

If the board had been under different direction, the separate training body for medical social work in Sydney might never have come into existence, and the intrigue and bitterness which characterised the training movement in the late 1930s might never have developed. Her directorship was not without positive accomplishment – she was influential in forming an association of social workers, in founding the New South Wales Council of Social Service, and in establishing the Australian Council of Schools of Social Work – but, on balance, her appointment was a mistake.

---

22    Aileen Fitzpatrick to Dr Wallace, Vice-Chancellor, Sydney University, 16 February 1940. (Fisher Library Archives.)

23    Aileen Fitzpatrick. In her early 30s; BA (Classics), a contemporary of Katharine Ogilvie at Sydney University; teaching classics in a high school; voluntary church work; trip to UK and Europe; member of National Council of Women; General Secretary of Country Women's Association of NSW for three years. The position of Director was not advertised before an appointment was made.

Jocelyn Hyslop was a very distinctive person. Highly intelligent and energetic, she could hold the attention of any audience, but her fluctuations in mood and cutting wit did occasionally cause difficulties with students and agencies. She was a psychiatric social worker, well-qualified academically and professionally.[24] Her experience included work with children and this remained one of her keenest interests.

With Carnegie assistance, she travelled to her Melbourne post in 1934 via the United States, and noted there the accepted professional status of social work, the large proportion of men, particularly in administrative positions in federal agencies, the extension of social work beyond relief-giving and into the middle classes, and the community chests whose funds were distributed by qualified social workers. On her arrival in Australia she was well aware of the different patterns of training in America and Britain, and said:

> Perhaps a better form of training than either may be yet evolved in Australia, but much must depend upon the attitude of the public and whether it demands a professional standard in the field of social administration, whether voluntary or State.[25]

An important factor in the transference of the general training course to Melbourne University in 1941 was the high academic standing of its director. When she resigned in 1944 to enter a religious order, Australian social work lost one of its most colourful and effective figures.

---

24    Jocelyn Hyslop. Educated at St Andrews and London University; BSc (Econ.), Acad. Dipl. of Sociol., Cert. of Soc. Sc.; Cert. of Mental Health; school teaching; lecturer, teachers' training college; organiser, school care committees for London County Council; psychiatric social worker, child guidance clinic, Liverpool, and the Babies Welcome Association, Leeds. Was in Melbourne in 1933, on a world tour.
25    *Argus*, 8 December 1934.

Amy Wheaton returned from London to her home city Adelaide in 1936 to direct the newly established training body, with an up-to-date knowledge of the social sciences.[26] She managed to maintain her broad academic interests, but the excessive teaching and administrative load she carried for so long allowed her no time to publish. For the greater part of the 21 years she was director of the Adelaide training body she did most of the teaching in the course, and it is perhaps little exaggeration to say she was the training movement. Yet she was also active in women's organisations and reared three children. Her academic ability was highly regarded by her former university teachers, Sir William Mitchell in particular, and this was a strong influence towards the full acceptance of training by the Adelaide University in 1943.

After carrying the course almost single-handed and being underpaid for it, in the immediate post-war years as well as earlier, she found herself confronted with an unsympathetic Vice-Chancellor and a few young professors ignorant of social work and the local past. She had no bent for university politics and her health broke. In the last years of her directorship, increased staff and a belated rise in her status made some recompense.

In 1950, she returned to England for a visit. She did not go to the United States until after she finished in Adelaide, but from the beginning was aware of the different training patterns of Britain and the United States.

These, then, were the people who were mainly responsible for breathing life into the training bodies which took up the challenge in the 1930s. Different in experience, age, sex, and temperament, each played a significant part in these formative years. They were in fact the pioneers of a new profession in Australia.

---

26    Amy Wheaton. In her late 30s; MA, Adelaide University; father's death diverted her from medicine; eldest of six children; school teaching; BSc, majoring in sociology and social psychology, London School of Economics; periods in Europe, especially in France and Germany (she was fluent in German); 1931 went to live in Melbourne; 1935, Women's International Conference at Istanbul, observed social services and social conditions in Germany and UK, did part of the Mental Health Course in London. An MBE in 1939. In 1950 she attended the first World Congress of the International Sociological Association at Zurich; elected to the Association's Council; studied at the London School of Economics and the Tavistock Clinic. After visiting North America in 1957–58 she became a Professor of Social Work, a temporary United Nations Advisor, in the Department of Social Work of the University of the Punjab, Lahore.

While Australian communities were founding social work training bodies, so too were other communities. An international survey of social work schools and training schemes in 1936 covered 179 schools and 63 non-academic training schemes in 32 countries.[27] Increasingly, social work training was becoming a world movement.

---

27    Alice Salomon, *Education for Social Work*. Zurich, 1937. This study was sponsored by the International Committee of Schools of Social Work and the Russell Sage Foundation.

# CHAPTER 4

# Training Standards

The training standards attained by any educational institution depend upon its curriculum, its teachers, the teaching materials available, and its students. The early experience of the Australian training bodies in each of these aspects is the subject of this chapter. Though their output was small, they were still confronted with basic issues in social work education and many of the problems experienced and the patterns set in this period continued into the post-war years.

## The Curriculum

How long were the courses to be? At what level? What balance was to be struck between classwork and fieldwork, between psychological and sociological subjects, between generic and specific teaching? In designing its curriculum, each of the training authorities had to provide answers to these questions, but they did have the experience of the British and American training movements to guide them, and in fact they drew from both sources.

In the 1920s, some British schools granted diplomas to graduates only. This became the established pattern in the United States in the 1930s, largely as a result of pressure from the American Association of Schools of Social Work. The case for postgraduate education for social work was strong. It gave some chance to give professional knowledge, skills, and attitudes to people with a measure of maturity and with the social education of a university degree. In other words, the American narrow teaching of techniques, and the British broad social education unrelated to agencies' practice could be combined into what was in effect, one long professional course, similar to a medical course, starting from basic 'background' subjects and progressing to professional training enlightened by clinical practice or fieldwork. Moreover, a long course gave the student time to work through the various emotional and intellectual problems peculiar to social work education.

The Australian general training authorities were, at least to some extent, aware of the force of these arguments. At first, in Melbourne, it was mooted that the course should be postgraduate, and from 1933, the Sydney board stated in its prospectus that the most satisfactory educational preparation for its course was a university degree in Arts or Economics. The three schools discussed the question in 1938, and decided that postgraduate courses were *not yet* practicable.[1]

In fact, however, each of the three general training bodies followed the then typical British pattern of two-year undergraduate courses; but the British example was not slavishly followed, for the Australian courses included both a wide range of background subjects *and* classroom teaching of professional skills. With the considerable fieldwork requirements as well, this made too crowded a curriculum for a real grasp of both the background subjects and the professional skills.

All three general training bodies aimed to provide one basic course for every type of social worker, which, in the words of the Sydney board, was to impart 'a knowledge of fundamental principles ... essential in all branches of social work'. It is doubtful, however, if the early courses were generic in more than a rudimentary sense. More likely they consisted of an accumulation of pieces of experience drawn from social work's many fields, from which only the gifted student could extract the common core.

Yet the development of one course was of the greatest importance in producing a unified occupational group. The training movement in Australia in the 1930s was spared the excessive number of claims for specialised educational provision which had been experienced in Britain and the United States. In general, groups in the various

---

1    *Summary of the Discussions, Conference of the Australian Schools of Social Work, Sydney, 25–27 May 1938.*

social work settings in Australia were too small or without sufficient interest to make substantial claims for specialised courses. Practical considerations alone suggested a pooling of educational resources in one course which pointed up similarities rather than dissimilarities.

Two different kinds of claim for specialised training provision were made upon the general training bodies. The more important was for further professional training for a particular field of social work after a general course; the other was to provide or help with sub-professional specialised courses which were taken apart from the general training.

Early, the Adelaide board received sympathetically a request for specialised training for psychiatric social work, but it did not have the resources to do other than provide a general course, which anyway it saw as encouraging adaptability: 'too early specialisation does not tend to produce breadth of understanding and sympathy', it declared in answering a League of Nations' questionnaire. At the end of 1936, the director said, 'We have to think in terms of a future Almoners' Institute'.[2] Until well into the 1950s, however, Adelaide students had to go to Melbourne or Sydney for specialised training in medical social work.

As has been described, such a training in Melbourne was in fact established first, but with the advent of general training it became a third year taken after the two years of the general course. There do not appear to have been moves towards any other similar specialised professional courses in Melbourne, run either by the general training body or by a separate institute.

The Sydney board presented a more confused picture. Two of its students in 1932 took a special course in nursery school work, and the board awarded them a certificate even though this was not primarily a social work field. Two years later, three students with the board's general qualification took a one-year course in medical social work, and the board awarded them a special certificate, but, as has been noted, the almoners' institute then took over this function. There is

---

2    Amy Wheaton to Secretary, South Australian Board of Social Study and Training, 11 December 1936.

no evidence that the board actually provided any other specialised professional training, although some of its statements give a different impression.

When the three training bodies met in 1938, they found that there was considerable uniformity of content in their curricula. The availability of teachers and of existing lecture courses had, however, made for some local variation, and this was possible because any discipline which gave insight into the composition and behaviour of communities, groups, or individuals, had claims for inclusion.

It was expensive, and difficult, to have courses in the background subjects designed specifically for social work education, but if this were not done the degree of relevance of various subjects within a discipline could vary widely. Some sections of, for example, economics, psychology, biology, political science, history, and sociology, would be very closely related to professional social work practice, others only remotely. If the total training time was short, to spend a proportion of it on remotely relevant material was wasteful. Yet there could be advantages. Each of the training bodies used at least some full university degree subjects in its curriculum. In taking these, social work students mingled with students aiming to become, for instance, lawyers, teachers, psychologists, or philosophers, with benefit to the breadth of their outlook. Moreover, contacts and friendships between students of different faculties often carried over into professional life, with advantage to the discipline trying to become established. Also, it could be argued that systematic teaching in a firmly established course would have a greater educational impact upon the student than unsystematic teaching of a new course often by someone outside the university.

The Sydney board's curriculum included three full university lecture series and part of another, and a number of specially constructed lecture series. The Victorian Council for Social Training started with five university subjects in its curriculum, but by 1937 only two remained. To these had been added lecture series of varying length arranged by the training body itself: Social Philosophy, Australian Social Organisation, Physiology, Nutrition and Family Budgeting, Psychology, Mental Hygiene, Social History, Problems of Society, and Casework. The Adelaide board's curriculum included two existing university subjects and a new one, Social Psychology, given by the board's director. In addition, as with the other training bodies, there were a number of specially designed lecture series.

Of particular importance in each of the courses was the lecture series, usually combined with discussion classes, devoted to teaching professional skills. Not unexpectedly, this teaching was concentrated on social casework. Broader problems of community welfare were often stressed, particularly in Adelaide, but the teaching of techniques concentrated upon work with individuals. The theory of group work did advance during the 1930s, but still casework dominated the professional literature. Apart from the available teaching material, there were fewer agencies in Australia which concentrated on group and community welfare, and since, where possible, in their fieldwork students were placed under the supervision of qualified social workers and these worked mainly as caseworkers, the early concentration on casework was maintained.

From the start, each of the three courses included substantial amounts of practical work and these were later increased. At their 1938 meeting the schools agreed that practical work should be between a third and a half of the total work done by the student. As in Britain and North America, it consisted of supervised work in agencies, and visits of observation to agencies and institutions of social work significance. The agencies chosen for student supervision depended upon their relevance to the course, their willingness to cooperate without payment, the quality of the supervision they could provide, and the time available. Between 1932 and 1940, the Sydney board used over 30 different agencies for supervised student placements. The visits of observation did not have the educational potential of supervised work in agencies, but they did give students some idea of the actual nature of social provision and helped to give reality to classroom teaching.

During the 1930s, the International Committee of Schools of Social Work stressed the importance of social research. Occasionally, the early Australian social work students took part in research, but it had no regular place in the already crowded curriculum. In 1932 and 1938, the Sydney and Adelaide boards became members of the International Committee. The curriculum of each of the three training bodies was patterned on overseas models, and if it could have been extended over three or preferably four years, it would have provided a reasonably adequate framework for the training.

The most obvious feature of the one-year curricula of the two almoner institutes was the emphasis on practical work, although later there was a trend towards more classroom training. Under the supervision of a qualified almoner, students saw the working of a number of hospitals, and they studied social and economic factors connected with ill-health.

Reciprocity with the British Institute of Hospital Almoners and with each other was important to both the Australian institutes. Not only did this provide prestige and interchange of knowledge, but it provided almoners with employment, both interstate and British. As early as 1932, the Victorian institute became affiliated with the British institute, and by mid-1939 the New South Wales institute had followed suit, which in turn established full reciprocity between the Australian institutes.

# The Teachers

To put their training schemes into effect, the training bodies required many teachers from a variety of fields. Each teacher was limited as much by the curriculum, the teaching materials available, and the nature of the students as by his own training, experience, personality, aptitude for teaching, knowledge of social work, and interest.

The teachers were in two main groups, those teaching the background subjects and those the teaching directly concerned with social work. The first group were usually not qualified social workers; they were either full-time university teachers or were people practising another profession such as law, medicine, psychiatry, or psychology. In most instances, they were the best available in each city. Not always, however, were the university teachers interested in teaching social work students. Some did not like teaching only snippets of their discipline, and some thought the students' practical work an unnecessary distraction from their academic work. Moreover, the teachers who were prominent in their professions had little spare time for preparing or revising lectures, and were often inexperienced in teaching.

The knowledge of actual social work possessed by the teachers of the background subjects was generally such that they often needed outside guidance, usually from the director, to make their subject as pertinent as possible for social work students. Further, for the course to be coherent, the work of the various teachers needed to be correlated, and this was difficult, for a number of busy people were involved, the directors had many other responsibilities, independent habits of thought were typical of university and professional people, and there was an assumption anyway that the students would see where it all fitted together. In addition, it was expected that much of the integration would occur in the teaching on the professional side of the course. Where possible, qualified social workers were engaged in this, but in the early stages this was often difficult to achieve. The story of the professional teaching is one of a group trying to pull itself up by its bootstraps.

The teaching of the professional discipline proper took place in the classroom and in the field. The first was largely the responsibility of the director, although social workers from agencies regularly helped with discussion classes, and gave some lectures. The second was done primarily by social workers when they supervised students' fieldwork in the agencies, although members of the staff of the training bodies occasionally supervised students' fieldwork directly. Again, the problems of integrating this side of the course were as considerable as integrating the background and the professional parts. In these early years, theory and practice were often unrelated. At least some of the supervisors in the general course did not know the theory, and even if they had, their practice and the theory would have been very different.

As the number of qualified social workers increased, there was a marked tendency to use as supervisors inexperienced trained people, rather than experienced untrained ones. One can surmise that the quality of teaching of the former would not have been high, but the alternative was worse. In May 1933, Joan Brett wrote to Edith Eckhard: 'Very few of the large number of philanthropic societies here, with the exception of the COS have any idea of constructive casework and are quite incapable of handling training'. Three months later, she confided to the Victorian council's president (Dr Newman Morris) that the training of students even at the Charity Organisation Society was unsatisfactory. In 1935, Jocelyn Hyslop, when speaking to the Melbourne Ladies' Benevolent Society, asked existing workers to look on the students as members of a younger generation preparing to carry on the work of their predecessors, and not as nuisances or as people only to be made use of, which had so often happened to her when she was training in England.[3] When agencies were understaffed there was a strong temptation to use students as extra labour and to spend little time on their supervision. This was even greater when supervisors did not know what the students were being taught in the classroom.

Although the standard of supervision of fieldwork could not have been generally high, it did improve. The Melbourne director in 1936 called two conferences of supervisors, and in later years such conferences became customary. This kind of activity, greater consultation between the training bodies' professional teachers and the supervisors in agencies, some direct supervision of students' fieldwork by the teachers themselves, and especially the growth in the experience and number of qualified social workers who could supervise – all these helped to raise the standard of the practical work side of the course.

A reason for the establishment of the separate Institute of Hospital Almoners in Sydney was the dissatisfaction of the qualified almoners with the quality of professional teaching by the general training body. As soon as the institute was formed it began negotiations with the board to raise the amount and quality of the board's professional teaching. Later it pressed specifically for an immediate appointment by the board of a tutor in casework brought from North America or Britain, but not until 1939 was an appointment made.[4]

In these early years, then, there were many reasons why the teachers in the background subjects and the professional subjects, in the academic work and the practical work, could not provide the students with an adequate and integrated education for social work; but there was improvement, particularly on the professional teaching side. Also, at least some of the teachers brought to their task enthusiasm for what they saw to be a significant new venture.

---

3    *Argus*, 6 February 1935.
4    The person appointed, Elizabeth Govan, was to be in a key position during the war years in Sydney.

# The Teaching Materials

Even if the courses had been longer, and the teachers suitable in all respects, there would still have been a lack of appropriate teaching materials – in the background subjects, in the professional subjects, and in the practical work.

Of particular importance in the education of social workers is the condition of the social sciences in their society. Until well beyond the 1930s, the social sciences, especially sociology (the discipline most concerned with social, as distinct from economic and political, phenomena), were in a very underdeveloped state in Australia.

This lack of knowledge about Australian society is not difficult to explain. In the larger, more industrialised societies, social research had spread from the study of social problems to the study of the society in which they were found. The Australian communities, however, had not been faced with sharp destructive social divisions. Their populations were solidly British in origin. There was only a small Aboriginal group. There were no tremendous extremes in wealth. There had never been a political revolution. The society was relatively late in becoming heavily industrialised. There was the myth that it was a classless society.

No local philanthropic trusts were willing to finance large-scale social research. The universities reflected the general lack of interest in social issues. The appropriate departments, if they existed at all, were small, their members lacked the money, time, and often inclination, to undertake empirical research. They leaned heavily upon British and American teaching materials. Further, their disciplines were often at a stage of development when armchair speculation unsupported by empirical inquiry went unquestioned. The position in Adelaide and Melbourne was less developed than in Sydney.[5]

Although government departments in Australia early became involved in social provision, research within them was slow to develop, and when it did it was often of poor quality, concentrating merely upon the collection of statistics in stereotyped categories. The idea that highly

---

5    In 1940, eight of Sydney University's 45 professorial chairs were in social science subjects; in 1941, three of Melbourne University's 28 chairs; and in 1942, two of Adelaide's 24 chairs.

qualified people were needed to do social research worthy of the name was difficult to accept in the public service, and this was not helped by the weak intellectual tradition of the Australian political parties. In political circles, as in the country in general, social questions were frequently considered to be matters of common sense upon which anyone could pass a judgement.

For many years, then, the teaching of the background subjects in the Australian social work courses was badly hampered by a lack of material. The same was true of the teaching material in the professional side of the course.

As late as 1954, an American, after teaching in one of the Australian courses, could say:

> There is a great need to develop teaching materials based on Australian rather than American or English practice. Much of the vitality is lost if one constantly uses materials from a different cultural context. [6]

The pattern of relying upon overseas, largely American, professional teaching materials was set in the 1930s. At the time there was no alternative, and with some modification they could be made at least roughly relevant.

Few collections of social work and social science literature existed in the Australian community then. Each training body built up its own collection, but general lack of funds kept it small, especially in Adelaide. To teach adequately such an eclectic discipline as social work, library facilities for teachers and students should be excellent.

In the practical work part of the course, social agencies provided students with experience from which to learn, but many of them were small and almost all were unaccustomed to careful self-examination. Students would have seen much, particularly in the early years, which was at variance with what they were taught was good practice. A spectacular, though somewhat educationally misguided attempt to show good practice to students was made when the Sydney board's students, with the help of the Carnegie Corporation, visited American centres in the long vacation of 1934–35.

---

6    Frances Hall, Report to the Board of Studies in Social Science, Adelaide University Board of Studies in Social Science, Minutes, 15 December 1954.

# The Students

Of importance to the early training standards and thus to the nature of the new occupational group was the quality of the students.

Each of the training bodies agreed, for practical, educational, and sometimes moral reasons, that those embarking on the full course should be selected on both educational and personal grounds. The principle of student selection was especially difficult to apply in the early years. Opinions differed on necessary standards, interpretation of these standards varied, and a certain flexibility, particularly about experienced social workers, was politic in this transition period.

At their 1938 discussion, the general training bodies considered the selection of students in terms of age, education, and personal qualifications. Most delegates favoured a starting age of 20 years, allowance being made for exceptional cases. In this, they supported the practice of the Melbourne and Adelaide bodies. The Sydney board's only age requirement was that no diploma was to be awarded earlier than the age of 21.

Maturity for practical work or for professional practice were the usual arguments advanced for the age requirements. Sound though these may have been, they presented a recruiting difficulty. During the waiting period after secondary schooling, many influences either in the university or in employment could channel potential social work trainees into other fields. In addition, a waiting period put social work as a career at a disadvantage with the careers for which training was immediately available.

In 1938, the three training bodies considered students should be capable of undertaking a university course and stipulated the Leaving Certificate or its equivalent as a prerequisite. Again provision was to be made for exceptional cases, particularly in the over-25 age group.

Within each student group there could, then, be a fairly wide range of age, experience, and intellectual ability. Striking appropriate teaching levels was, therefore, difficult, but at least while there were few students individual tuition was possible.

In addition to age and educational requirements, students were screened on grounds of personal suitability. If social workers were temperamentally unsuited to help people with personal and social problems (and this was conceived as their prime function), it was felt that they could harm both clients and themselves. Further, no matter how intellectually capable, it was a waste of time, energy and money, theirs and the training bodies', trying to learn a discipline which their personalities precluded them from practising effectively.

Actual selection techniques usually included personal interviews as well as references, but they were not of the intensive character sometimes found in the North American schools. For a brief period in Sydney, all underwent psychological tests, but later this procedure was reserved for doubtful cases.

The 1938 discussion on student selection ended with agreement that educational background and cultural maturity must be considered, and that references should be obtained from people who knew the student personally and who knew the student's work. A student was to have freedom from other commitments, satisfactory health, emotional maturity and stability, breadth of interest, ability to establish constructive personal relationships, and initiative and capacity in planning and execution.

The two almoner institutes reserved the right to determine which of those acceptable for general training were also acceptable for medical social work training. There were two main reasons for the insistence upon independent judgement. First, and this applied more in Sydney, the original selection was not considered rigorous enough; and second, hospital social work was seen as having pressures not found in other social work settings. It seems, however, that in practice most of the general students who wished to do the almoner course were accepted.

The entrance requirements, as with the courses themselves, reflected a conviction that modern social workers should be talented in a number of ways. Only a minority in any community had the natural and general educational endowment to gain the professional qualification, far from all of these had the financial resources, and at that time there was practically no outside aid available to students. Previously the main requirements for social work connected with non-government organisations were interest and leisure, and the one requirement to work in a government department concerned with social legislation, as with other legislation, was literacy. Not everyone in existing agencies was engaged in potential social casework situations or policy-forming, but a great many would have been. It is probable that only a moderate proportion of these had the basic endowment to undertake the new professional courses. On the other hand, many with the basic endowment were not then engaged in social work, partly because it was not yet recognised that relatively rare talents were needed. Recruiting for the new courses therefore had to tap new sources and tactfully ignore some of the older ones.

None of the training bodies appears to have had a definite recruitment policy, something studied, planned, and executed over a period of time. Recruitment literature was sparse and was mostly of an all-purpose nature – directed to recruits, employers, donors, and the general public, all of whom had to be reached if the training was to become firmly established.

Press advertisements for students were not unusual, nor were special newspaper articles. The general coverage of the training bodies' activities, at least in Melbourne and Adelaide, was reasonably good, much greater than at a later stage when they were better established and newspaper space was more competitive. Occasionally time was given them on the radio.

All the organisations represented on the training bodies were possible sources of recruitment, but there is little evidence as to the extent of their contribution. As workers became trained they themselves sometimes recruited for the profession. Most of the effort, however, emanated from the training bodies. Occasional attempts were made to reach students leaving school, and university students, particularly in the Arts faculties. There were occasions such as women's conferences when information about social work training may well have brought recruits. To know precisely where the publicity penetrated, and how effective it was, is now impossible. Possibly personal contacts led many students into the courses.

The unquestioned assumption, based primarily upon British precedent, that hospital social work was women's work meant that recruiting for the almoner courses was directed towards women, as was much of the recruiting for the general social work courses. Partly as a result of this, but perhaps mainly from many other factors of which the limited recruiting was only symptomatic, almost all the pre-war students, and therefore the qualified social workers, were women – despite frequent repetition that the courses were for men and women. It is important to look at this in some detail.

The broad cleavage which had developed in Australian social provision by the time the training bodies were established has been observed. The government, mainly male, sector was often represented on the training bodies, and occasionally took part in the practical work section of the courses, but public servants or potential public servants had little encouragement to take the courses. There is an inbuilt slowness in government action, but by the end of the 1930s the New South Wales Child Welfare Department, through a proposed cadetship scheme, had shown the only sign of really active interest on the part of any state government. Almost all the government authorities had still to be convinced that the training was necessary for some, and worthwhile for many others, in departments primarily concerned with social welfare. Confidence in the existing standards, general suspicion of formal higher education, particular suspicion that much of the training was not relevant to the departments' work, scepticism about the early standards of the training bodies, worry about the cost of training, anticipation of the difficulty of fitting trained people and their new techniques into an established administrative structure, fear for their own personal security, and lack of identification with social work in general either from ignorance or sex prejudice – these must have been some of the factors operating in the minds of the public servants.

The prime sources of advanced professional knowledge were at first the directors of the training courses and these were all women. There were restrictions to the employment of women in the public service, and public servants were not accustomed to working with women, at least not at policy-making levels. To say that sex prejudice did not enter into their judgement of the need for the courses offering would seem to be implausible.

Most of the organisations represented on the training bodies were in the non-government social services. Practically all these were small with slender financial resources. As has been mentioned, many men participated in these agencies, usually at policy-making and general administrative levels but not usually as a vocation. The actual social *work*, the face-to-face handling of individuals or groups in need, was identified mainly with women.

The general training bodies were keen for policymakers and general administrators in the non-government agencies, and also for those in government departments, to take their courses. But it was difficult for people for whom it was a part-time interest, to undertake a two-year full-time course, particularly during the depression years. The small group of men in non-government agencies then actually practising as social workers could not be induced to take the course for a number of reasons. They were poorly paid and could not afford the necessary time or money, and their employers were in no financial or staff position to help, and there was also little chance of substantial financial recognition of the qualification. This applied too, of course, to those coming fresh to the field.

Many of the men worked in youth recreation. The concentration on social casework, to the neglect of social group work, made the courses appear irrelevant; in addition, a specialised, less rigorous training was already available, for at least some of them, through the Young Men's Christian Association.

Coping with the physically tough, antisocial elements and the chronically destitute element in society was usually the concern of men, and of the churches, because these elements were usually male, and it was considered either dangerous or not 'nice' for women to work with them. With no knowledge of effective remedial techniques, attitudes were inclined at the worst to be harsh, punitive and hopeless, at the best, custodial. Further, religious 'saving' rather than social rehabilitation, was often the focus. It was highly unlikely, at least in the early stages, that this traditional area of social provision would have provided many students for the courses. Attitudes were firmly established and the sophistications of social casework seemed irrelevant.

None of the clergy undertook the courses in the 1930s, yet some of them, particularly those attached to missions or in underprivileged districts, spent the greater part of their time in social casework situations. The training movement in Australia, as elsewhere, was essentially a secular movement, and one of its biggest challenges was to make an impact on all the many social welfare functions the churches had traditionally, and were still, undertaking. Pre-war, little was achieved in this direction.

It may be true that some of the women concerned with the training bodies wished to keep the work for their sex, either because it was one of the very few interesting outlets for women's talents in communities where their roles were limited, or because they thought the work inherently more feminine in character. At points, the training movement was connected with the advancement of higher education for women, an aspect of the feminist movement.

These, then, were the factors working against the recruitment of male students. How did women students view it? Society at large was still at a stage when the idea of a professional career woman met with widespread resistance. A woman's natural role was seen as a domestic one, and it is unlikely that many of those taking the social work courses took a wider view. Granted that questions of students' motivation in undertaking any course are complex, it is apparent that the social work courses had advantages for women with marriage in mind. They qualified her for paid, interesting work which had some relevance to the life she would lead after marriage; and, in addition, compared with many university courses, was not too long or too difficult, yet gave her access to the university student body which raised her marriage chances. Somewhat later, when the training was a fully university one, 'the deb. department' was a label occasionally used in university circles for the department which trained social workers. If many of the students did their course without a sense of long-term commitment to professional practice, this would have had an effect upon the quality of their work and the teaching they received, to say nothing of the serious long-term repercussions for the building of a new profession.

The manifold effects of the identification with women of the new training were long-lasting, and made peculiarly difficult the effort to place all the responsible work in social provision, government and non-government, in the hands of people who were aware of its interrelation, and who shared common knowledge, skills, and values. There seems to have been little concern in the training bodies themselves about the lack of male students. Looking at the situation in the practical and short-term way in which they must have viewed it, women students were far easier to recruit than men; in addition, social casework was the technique most advanced in its theory, and it was much more clearly linked with women than social group work, community organisation, or social welfare administration, where lack of theory made teaching more difficult. In any case, dealing with the broader aspects of the community in detail raised questions which could not be adequately handled in the time available in the courses. Uncertainty about the future, lack of time, money, and staff made it necessary to take the easier way.

At the 1938 conference of the training bodies, however, it was agreed, although apparently without reference to the important sex factor, that they must look to the public services to employ the trained people. 'The lack of money in private agencies and the widening sphere of governmental activities' were the main reasons given.

The length, level, and cost of the courses determined that the students were drawn mainly from the higher socioeconomic groups, from the professional and the more affluent of the white-collar families. At a time when educational opportunities were largely ruled by the socioeconomic status of one's family, these courses confirmed the traditional class base of much of the voluntary social service activity. A description of the early students of the Victorian Council for Social Training mentions that many of them came 'from Melbourne's oldest families'.[7] Although the social stratification of Australian communities was not as marked nor as rigid as in Britain, it was none the less real. It is doubtful whether the courses in the 1930s were of sufficient length or educational strength to shake the students' outlook on society and to remould it to a new professional pattern; but this deficiency did prevent the qualified social workers from dividing off from the rest of the voluntary social service field too sharply too early. As for those administering government social provision, it is possible that, on occasions, the different social and educational backgrounds of the qualified social workers set up barriers – 'Nice girls from nice families' was a stereotype of qualified social workers which became established in at least some public service circles.

---

7   *Herald*, 19 July 1934.

By starting with full professional courses, the Australian training bodies were immediately committed to handling many complex issues. Overseas example helped them to pick their way conceptually through their problems, but time and work were needed to give substance to many aspects of local training. Although the students of the 1930s did not receive a basic training comparable with that available later, their introduction to professional practice was much superior to none at all. The training bodies' early concentration, however, upon casework and women, so natural at the time, remained as an impediment to a broad professional growth.

# CHAPTER 5

# A New Occupational Group

After examining the pre-war fortunes of the new occupational group produced by the development of an Australian training movement, it is necessary to consider its employment, the professional activities of the qualified social workers outside their agencies, and the quality of their work.

## Ready But Uneven Employment

As was to be expected from the location of the training bodies, the nature of their courses, and their students, most pre-war qualified social workers in Australia were women working in non-government agencies in Sydney and Melbourne, usually engaged in social casework, often in a medical setting. Although this was a period of general financial stringency, people qualified by the new courses had no difficulty in finding paid employment. This was because only a small number qualified each year, salaries were comparatively low, and agencies hoped that under trained guidance their resources would be used more efficiently, and the social workers' general training fitted them for a variety of jobs. In addition, the most significant group, the almoners, only slightly increased the total labour costs of the large hospitals.

It was appropriate that the first qualified social worker practising in Australia, Agnes Macintyre, was an almoner, for hospital social work was the only field of professional social work which showed any real development in the 1930s in Australia. Vital to the employment of almoners was acceptance by hospital boards, hospital administrators, the medical profession, existing auxiliary medical services, and community welfare organisations.

The Victorian almoner institute actively promoted the employment of almoners. It sent letters to honorary medical staffs and to the Hospital Secretaries Association. It provided speakers for various groups, and its officers wrote articles for the general and medical press. Moreover, many of its members were already closely connected with some hospitals and could informally support the institute's work. A powerful ally was the Charities Board, who at least twice, in 1931 and 1934, urged Victorian hospitals to appoint almoners.

To secure the cooperation of the medical profession, the doctors already convinced of the worth of almoners had a crucial role. The report written by Dr Newman Morris in 1930 after his American tour was used extensively. So also was the strong testimony of a president of the Royal College of Surgeons that hospital almoners saved life and money and alleviated human misery.[1] Almoners' work received publicity at the Australian Medical Congress in Hobart in 1934, and at the annual meeting of the British Medical Association in Melbourne the following year.

Through these activities, a climate favourable to almoner appointments was created, and towards the end of the 1930s the demand both in Victoria and other states for qualified almoners far outstripped the supply. Sometimes special financial assistance – for example, from hospital auxiliaries at the Melbourne and Melbourne St Vincent's Hospitals, from the Junior Red Cross at the Melbourne Children's Hospital, from a private donor at the Adelaide Children's Hospital – supported almoner work until the hospital was ready to accept full responsibility. At least twice, at Hobart Hospital and at the Alfred in Melbourne, almoners worked for periods without pay to demonstrate their usefulness. Probation periods were common, but appointments almost invariably were renewed and the work snowballed.

By the mid-1930s, practically all the important public hospitals in Melbourne accepted the idea of appointing almoners. Six hospitals had taken the Melbourne Hospital's 1929 lead: the Children's in 1931,

---

1    Lord Moynihan, *The Importance of the Almoner's Department in the Hospital*, May 1927.

St Vincent's in 1932, and the Women's, the Alfred, Prince Henry's, and the After-Care in 1934–35. Only one full-time country appointment had been made, at the Geelong Hospital in 1934. Further hospital appointments consolidated rather than extended this position, although at the end of the 1930s, the Queen Victoria Hospital made its first appointment.

The poliomyelitis epidemics of the 1930s produced agencies to help physically handicapped children. The first non-hospital medical social work appointment in Victoria was made in 1936 by such an agency, the newly formed Victorian Society for Crippled Children. Its services extended to country areas. In the late 1930s, the Anti-Cancer Council of Victoria pressed for an immediate extension of almoner services to selected country areas, but the war intervened.

The Royal Melbourne Hospital led in the size of its almoner department. The clinic-by-clinic growth of the department was typical; as also was its early accommodation. Its office was a converted bathroom, patients had to wait in a passageway exposed to the weather, and, for privacy, interviews were often held on seats beside a tennis court.[2]

Largely because of the later development of almoner training in Sydney, almoner appointments there were of more recent origin, and up to 1940, less extensive than in Melbourne. Before the establishment of the New South Wales Institute in 1937, the Royal Alexandra Hospital for Children, in 1933, the Rachel Forster Hospital for Women and Children, in 1934, and Sydney and St Vincent's Hospitals, in 1936, had already appointed qualified almoners, and the Royal Prince Alfred Hospital and Royal North Shore Hospital each had a social service worker who later received partial recognition by the institute. In 1937, Lewisham, and three years later, the Prince Henry and Crown Street Women's Hospitals appointed almoners. By mid-1940, however, there was still no appointment outside Sydney or outside a hospital.

The development of medical social work in the 1930s in South Australia, Western Australia, and Tasmania, was slight; and in Queensland non-existent. The Victorian almoner institute sent information to key persons in Adelaide, and in 1935 its directress

---

2    Dorothy Bethune, *An Historical Survey of Almoner Work in Victoria*. In 1939, prompted by the New South Wales Institute of Hospital Almoners, the Hospitals Commission asked the Public Works Department to provide proper almoner accommodation in new hospitals.

visited there. By 1937, almoners had been appointed to the South Australian Society for Crippled Children, the Adelaide Children's Hospital and the Adelaide General Hospital. The Perth General Hospital early had a social service department run by qualified nurses. One of these qualified as an almoner with the Victorian institute in 1936, and on her return successfully advocated the replacement of nurses by almoners. Shortly afterwards the Perth Children's Hospital made its first appointment. In Hobart, the only appointments were at the Hobart Hospital, 1931–35, and the Tasmanian Society for Crippled Children, for most of the 1930s.

There were difficulties in establishing an independent role for almoners. Social work authorities insisted that medical social work was distinct from nursing.[3] It required higher academic attainments, knowledge that nursing did not cover, and different attitudes from the authoritarian ones often found among trained nurses. Further, it needed greater self-reliance. Almoners' social casework was a discipline in which the doctors had no special competence, and which in other communities was practised more frequently outside medical settings than in them. For this reason, social workers were not providing an ancillary service as nurses did. For convenience and to gain acceptance in the early stages, however, they frequently allowed themselves to be so classified. Their sex helped doctors and administrators to think of them as auxiliary workers, even as 'doctors' handmaidens' working under medical direction rather than with medical cooperation. This had important status and salary implications.

Some responsibility for employment standards for almoners was taken by the two almoner institutes. In 1935, the Victorian institute expressed regret to the New Zealand hospital authorities that the Wellington Hospital used the title 'almoner' for an untrained person. The next year an English visitor, untrained but with some relevant experience, was not accepted by the institute to act even temporarily as an almoner for it feared 'a dangerous precedent' would be set. In 1938, the Victorian institute suggested to employers conditions of employment which it believed would give the Australian almoner a status equivalent

---

3     E.g. the South Australian Board of Social Study and Training, Reply to Questionnaire of the League of Nations Social Questions Committee.

to the British almoner, and proposed a minimum salary of £250 a year. The New South Wales institute almost immediately adopted the same conditions.

Probably some of the early qualified almoners were timid about the question of payment. They and their employers were very much aware of the voluntary tradition of social service work, and for some time social workers' salaries were not realistically assessed in terms of the length and level of the training, and the responsible nature of the work. As late as 1957, one of the leaders during the 1930s spoke of social workers' privilege in being paid to do good. If by 'doing good' was meant 'performing socially desirable work', this did not distinguish social work from many other occupations; and in fact these often received special financial inducements on this account.

Both almoner institutes advised hospitals upon the scope of almoner work. In their view, the almoners' task was to study and treat social disabilities affecting the patient's health and to ensure as far as possible that he received the full benefit from his medical treatment. Although assessing patients' fees was not entirely absent in Australian almoner work, it never assumed the proportion it did in the early stages in Britain.

During the depression years much of the almoners' time was spent in trying to break, for overwhelming numbers of people, the vicious circle of poverty and disease. No less than 2,849 patients were interviewed by the almoner at the Rachel Forster Hospital from June 1934 to June 1935.[4] Material assistance was normally the immediate need, leaving little time for intensive casework. The extensive use made by the early almoners of community resources to help their clients, quickly brought many hospitals from their comparative community isolation.

The position of the non-medical social workers during the 1930s was different from that of the almoners. They may have had considerable impact as individuals on particular agencies, but they were scattered over widely diverse fields of social provision. No special bodies like the institutes were concerned with extending their employment opportunities, defining their functions, or safeguarding their working

---

4    *Report of the Almoner Department, Rachel Forster Hospital, June 1935.*

conditions. The constitutions of the general training bodies contained no direct reference to employment, but their officers, particularly their directors, had to concern themselves with it to some extent, for the survival of the training schemes if for no other reason.

The field perhaps closest to medical social work, psychiatric social work, was, like Australia's mental health services in general, markedly underdeveloped. Two qualified social workers were appointed in 1932 to full-time positions in psychiatric clinics at the Sydney Royal Prince Alfred and the Melbourne Hospitals, and others, for example the almoner at St Vincent's Hospital in Melbourne, gave some of their time to such clinics, but no mental hospital employed a qualified social worker.

In other fields of social provision, by 1940 appointments of qualified social workers were equally rare, and most dated from the second half of the 1930s, and were single appointments. Although the development was thin and uneven, it was a beginning. The majority of the appointments were devoted to social casework, but in rudimentary form social group work, community organisation, and social research were represented.

The correctional field was still left entirely to voluntary probation officers, despite hopes to the contrary, and, more important still, was the failure of qualified workers to be employed in family welfare. General relief agencies, such as the charity organisation societies, were the traditional centres for family welfare work. Benevolent though the Melbourne Charity Organisation was to the social work training movement, it did not appoint its first qualified social worker until after World War II, and this was well before any such appointments by similar organisations in other states.

In the United States, Roosevelt's New Deal programme owed a considerable amount to qualified social workers, in its formulation and administration. Qualified social workers with long experience in the strong voluntary relief-giving agencies were available in that country to help both government social security planning and to assume leadership in its administration. In Australia this was not the case in the 1930s; nor was it so in the 1940s when a general social security scheme was eventually implemented. Not unexpectedly, in view of the nature of the Australian public service, qualified social workers were not employed in administrative government positions – even when social security measures, relief-giving, child welfare programmes, slum clearance, and similar important fields of social policy were involved.

## Professional Association

As increasing numbers of qualified social workers made a corporate existence possible, associations were formed. Matching the development of the social work training bodies, there was a general association and an association of almoners in both Melbourne and Sydney. In addition, towards the end of the 1930s, the almoners joined in a national association. The associations were products of the training bodies in two ways. From the beginning in the almoner groups, and not long after the start of the general groups, they catered for social workers qualified by the training bodies, and in each of the associations, leaders in the training movement at first took an active part.

The qualified social workers had considerable inducement to associate. They encountered similar problems even in widely different spheres of welfare work. An association provided a means of communication and also the opportunity to combine on educational activities and on social action. A further advantage of association, the possibility of collective action on conditions of employment, appears, however, to have been little considered at this stage.

In 1932, for 'discussion on matters of general interest to the profession', the almoners in Melbourne formed the Victorian Association of Hospital Almoners. Only persons with the certificate of a recognised institute of almoners, or its equivalent, could be members. In 1936, because a growing number of qualified almoners were likely to be lost, by marriage, or working in other fields of social work, full membership was restricted to persons 'professionally engaged in medical social service'; others could now be only associate members.

Of the association's 16 members at the beginning of 1934, two were in New South Wales, and one in Tasmania. This induced the Victorian association to become the Australian Association of Hospital Almoners. It was just a change of name for the Victorian group since the Australian association's officers and meetings were to be in the state with the most members, but provision was made for local groups of not less than three members to be formed in other states.

At the end of 1936, the few qualified almoners in Sydney formed themselves into such a group, but called themselves the New South Wales Branch of the Australian Association. A Victorian sub-committee, in consultation with members in other states, later recast the association's constitution. In May 1938, the Australian Association of Hospital Almoners assumed a federal form which it retained until its absorption by the general professional association some 20 years later. The new national body aimed to foster and develop medical social work in Australia by working for adequate and uniform professional standards, by helping the interchange of information and ideas between almoners both interstate and overseas, and by taking collective action for all Australian almoners when it was required.[5]

Under its 1938 constitution, the almoners' association consisted of members of state branches and individual members in states without a branch. Its general government was placed in the hands of a central council, on which each branch was represented. Council meetings were to be at least yearly, in the state of the office bearers.

The association's membership stood at 29, 17 in Melbourne and five in Sydney, when the new constitution was adopted. By February 1940, total membership was about 40, which included 23 in the Victorian Branch and 13 in the New South Wales branch. Throughout the 1930s there were few qualified almoners who were not members of the association.

Members' attendance at the Victorian group's monthly meetings was high. It was a small, tightly knit group, for its members had much in common. Most of the early meetings were devoted to the problems of nascent almoner departments, and throughout the 1930s the main focus remained on members' own immediate work.

The Sydney almoner group met only occasionally during its brief existence in the later 1930s.

---

5    Australian Association of Hospital Almoners, Constitution, adopted 20 May 1938.

While the almoners were forming their association in Melbourne, the Social Workers' Association of New South Wales was formed in Sydney, on the initiative of the director of the local general training body. The declared purpose of this new general association was to bring recognised social workers together to discuss social work problems and to promote in general the coordination of social work throughout the state. Further, it was to improve the standard of social work, in particular by advocating the training of all social workers.[6]

At first, membership was open to all *bona fide* social workers and to social work students, as one of the main reasons for the association was to link the trained with the untrained. Membership conditions were later changed, however, which both reflected and caused a shift towards an association exclusively for qualified social workers. By 1940, some provision was still made for a membership of non-qualified social workers, but in fact a large majority of members was qualified. As early as the mid-1930s, a majority of the association's executive committee was qualified. A striking, though perhaps, not unexpected, feature of the association's membership was that, although at first entry was virtually unrestricted, scarcely any men became members, and none was on the executive committee.

In 1934, following the example set by the almoners in Victoria, the Social Workers' Association of New South Wales for a time considered calling itself an Australian body since there was no similar group in any other state. The next year the Victorian Association of Social Workers was formed on the initiative of S. Greig Smith. Its stated objectives were almost identical with those of its New South Wales counterpart.

The Victorian general association restricted its membership to qualified social workers and to people who had been professionally engaged as social workers for not less than five years. In the first few years, interpretation of its definition of 'a social worker' as 'any person professionally engaged in the readjustment of individuals or families in their social setting', caused some difficulty. A 1935 definition by the New South Wales association was broader – a person 'engaged in the practice of social casework, in group activities, in social administration and in social research'. As with the Sydney general group, few men

---

6    Social Workers' Association of New South Wales, Constitution (as amended 1939).

were members of the Victorian association, and by 1940 a growing proportion of the association's members were qualified social workers, although this trend was not as marked as in Sydney.

The two general associations each had a governing group, a committee in New South Wales and a council in Victoria, which had general control of the association's activities. They met about as often as the general meetings of the association; that is, about five times a year in Victoria from 1935 to 1940, and in New South Wales from 1933 to 1936, and about eight times a year in New South Wales from 1937 to 1940. Compared with the almoner groups, these general associations were much less tightly knit, for the span of interest, knowledge, and employment in them was far wider.

Each of the four groups discussed existing arrangements for social provision and occasionally took collective action to improve them. Usually they did this quietly and informally and they took care not to become associated in social action with irresponsible allies. How effective they were is now impossible to tell.

The Victorian group of almoners were concerned about the shoddy work of a certain relief organisation, transport difficulties of patients on sustenance payments, the financial bar to holidays for many children, the inadequacy of a particular convalescent home, the neglect of persons suffering from venereal disease, the lack of provision for chronic illness, and the need for an emergency housekeeper service.

The interests of the New South Wales group of almoners were different but again the emphasis was on provision available to their own immediate clients – dental and convalescent care for persons on sustenance payments, the admission procedure of an institution, the need for a city hostel for country patients attending deep X-ray treatment, the policy for a new convalescent home, and the provision of teaching for children in hospital for long periods.

The two general groups were rather less involved in social action, although there was still a noticeable interest in it. The New South Wales group were concerned with sewing depots for unemployed women, the central index of the Council of Social Service, the lot of the deserted wife, child welfare provisions, and the need for general educational reforms. The Victorian group were mainly interested in relief, its level and the quality of its administration, but in addition it considered reforms in the treatment of young offenders, in housing and slum clearance, and the coordination of state social services into one department.

These discussions and actions helped the groups to become known in social welfare circles, and this process was aided by their representation on a few bodies, chosen from among the multitude of organisations because of their influence, their social usefulness, or their relevance to the group's work. There was too the community activity of individual members, and occasionally visitors were invited to the general meetings.

During the 1930s none of the associations was active in determining the nature of the professional training. The almoner groups, especially in New South Wales, were, however, well represented on the governing bodies of their local institutes. In contrast, the Sydney general group was represented only on the local training board, not its executive, and then only until 1937, and in Melbourne, there was no representation of the general association on the Victorian Council for Social Training until 1940.

The social work associations at this time were embryonic full professional associations. Their sole income was the few shillings of each member's subscription, the numbers were small, and their officers had little time to give to association affairs, but they were important. They set a pattern of educational activity and at least some social action, and they assisted the community's acceptance of trained social work. Perhaps most important of all for the recognition and development of a responsible new occupational group, they held together the products of the Australian training movement.

## The Quality of the Work

Various factors influenced the quality of the work of the early qualified social workers, in their employment and in their professional associations. The personal and social characteristics of the qualified social workers clearly affected the scope and quality of their work. As a group, they contained a fairly wide range of intelligence and education, though not nearly as wide a range as their untrained predecessors. They were usually from the higher socioeconomic groups, and almost all were unmarried women. There were a few older women, but frequently young women filled positions of heavy responsibility and carried their burdens alone.

Gradually the number and proportion of older women increased and it was they who provided the group's work with continuity and leadership. Intentionally or otherwise, they were 'career women' and as with the older unmarried female teachers and nurses were sometimes unkindly described as 'frustrated spinsters'. In society's general view, women were cast for marriage. If they did not marry they were 'failures' who had to find compensating outlets. Since social workers were so much concerned with the personal lives of other people, they were particularly vulnerable to such comment. These attitudes were a problem for the developing occupational group. How they affected the quality of the older woman's work depended upon whether she herself had fully come to terms with her professional role, and upon the degree of professional acceptance she received from those with whom she worked, both colleagues and clients.

Possibly because of their personal characteristics, the new group of qualified social workers tended to have blindspots, either imposed from without or determined from within. A detailed analysis of their cases may reveal that sexual and marital problems were bypassed, and that more time was spent in interviewing women and children than men, only partly because they were more available. Because of the marriage factor, the proportion of younger qualified social workers in employment was always considerable. Sordid tough cases were not referred to them if the person making the referral saw the social worker not as a professional person, but as a young woman who had had a sheltered existence. 'Protection' of womenfolk, particularly younger ones, was a widespread male attitude.

As yet, there had not been enough time for any of the qualified social workers to have had a long professional experience. Moreover, the basic professional training, though improving, was still inadequate in many respects. Any professional training, however, could have provided only a start on the road to professional competence. Unless experience was related to training and there was the contact with new developments in the profession, the qualification tended to be emptied of its meaning.

The lack of books on the subject set real limits to the reading of the early qualified social workers. Some special library collections became available to them and the Victorian almoners began a collection of their own. This was important because apart perhaps from those directing the training courses, and some who had been overseas, few had personal collections. Books and periodicals were difficult to obtain locally, and they were expensive. As yet no local professional literature had emerged.

During the 1930s, numbers were too small for adequate staff development programmes. For their professional stimulation, the qualified social workers therefore looked outside their agencies to the training bodies and their associations. One regular educational source within the agencies, however, was the supervision of social work students in their fieldwork. This helped the qualified social workers to examine and be explicit about their own practice, and provided some link with the current professional courses.

Occasionally the general training bodies provided educational opportunities for people in the field, but the best chance of learning more about social work came from the meetings of the social work associations. At first their members learnt merely from each other, but as the groups increased in size and confidence other specialists were invited to speak on and discuss a variety of topics. The breadth of interest of the general groups is illustrated by the topics chosen for the 1937 meetings of the Sydney group: child welfare legislation, a discussion on casework arising from this, the employment of youth in New South Wales, government relief-giving, recreation, United States casework methods compared with those used in New South Wales, the housing problem in New South Wales, and venereal disease and its social implications.[7]

To give time for closer study of problems, conferences began to be held. In 1936, the Victorian group of almoners held a one-day conference, and in 1937 and 1939 held weekend conferences. The general group in Sydney held a weekend conference in 1938, to which representatives of the training bodies were invited. The following year plans for a similar conference were stopped by the war. The general group in Melbourne were to have been invited to this. They themselves had

7    Social Workers' Association of New South Wales, Minutes, 17 March 1937.

seriously considered holding at least one conference for all interested in social welfare, but they had decided they were not well-enough established.

No national conferences of social work or of social welfare were held in the 1930s, in spite of the increased interest in social work aroused by the Depression and the existence of overseas models and historical precedents in Australia. None of the qualified social workers attended the two international conferences of social work held in the 1930s. Together the Social Workers' Association of New South Wales and the Victorian Association of Social Workers sent greetings to the third, held in London in 1936, and attended by the latter's president.

It is apparent that for the early qualified social workers in Sydney and Melbourne, and for the almoners rather more than the general social workers, educational habits were set; but as yet they were not strong and were confined within state, indeed city, boundaries.

# THE WAR YEARS

# CHAPTER 6
# An Expansion of Opportunities

Australia, with its seven million people, immediately followed suit when Britain declared war on Germany in September 1939. By the end of the year, troops had been sent to the Middle East, Australian naval forces had joined the British in the Mediterranean, and it had been decided that many Australian airmen should be trained for service in Europe and the Middle East. As the fighting spread, there was increasing anxiety about Australia's own security. Japan's attack on Pearl Harbor and the rapid southward advance of Japanese forces through Malaya and the Netherlands East Indies brought a concentration of Australia's military forces near her shores to withstand threatened invasion. By mid-1943, the danger had passed, but Australia was still fully involved with the organisation needed to act as the base for the American forces in the western Pacific, and at the same time to prepare for the transition to peace.

## New Social Policy

World War II made unprecedented demands upon Australia's economic, political, and social capacity. The pace of industrialism was greatly hastened. During the emergency of 1942, the labour force and non-essential production became strongly controlled. Only the Commonwealth government could handle the large national and international issues raised by the war, which meant that the pre-war trend towards central government authority was greatly strengthened. Of particular importance was the Commonwealth's assumption of full financial supremacy over the states by its exclusion of the states from the income tax field in 1942.

Apart from the increased importance of federal authority, the most notable feature politically was the emergence of a united federal Labor Party under strong leadership. The party had remained in the political wilderness for almost a decade after its destructive Depression experience. In October 1940, however, it almost won the federal election, but it would not enter a national government with the United Australia and Country Parties. An obvious way to gain Labor's support in its handling of the wartime issues was for the government to make social service concessions, and this was the immediate reason for the introduction of a national child endowment scheme in March 1941. The scheme provided flat weekly payments with no means test for each child after the first in every family, and broke the drought of federal social security legislation which had lasted, except in connection with ex-servicemen, since 1912. In October 1941, the Labor Party came into office where it remained for the next eight years, and during this time enacted a wide range of social security measures. From spending less than £17 million on social services in the year 1938–39, the Commonwealth came to spend almost £68 million in 1946–47.

Between the wars, unlike Australia, many countries developed their social security measures, especially on social insurance lines, but the growth was usually piecemeal and haphazard. The war gave great impetus to the development of comprehensive integrated social security systems. The most celebrated plan was Beveridge's, presented in 1942 in Britain,[1] which laid the foundation for the establishment in 1948 of a full British social security scheme, a combination of social insurance and assistance.

In the United States, in 1943, the National Resources Planning Board presented a report which urged the government to ensure sufficient and appropriate employment opportunities, to extend the coverage of social insurance to as large a proportion of the population as possible, to develop a comprehensive general public assistance system, and to study and expand social services which were preventive and constructive in character.[2] During the war years, when such questions of broad policy in the development of social services were raised, the American social work profession made only a small contribution; but there was

1    Sir William Beveridge, *Social Insurance and Allied Services*.
2    Nathan E. Cohen, *Social Work in the American Tradition*, pp. 246–7.

an unprecedented demand for competent professional workers for specific social services. All the American professional social work groups operated through a joint committee: the Wartime Committee on Social Work Personnel. This gave professional classification to social workers in the military and government services; it also helped to unify the social work professional groups who, in the post-war years, formed a single professional association.

In Britain, as in the United States, the demand for specific competent social work services was unprecedented, particularly, for the first time, by government departments.[3]

Of special importance in Australia's great extension of government social services in the 1940s was an all-party Commonwealth Joint Parliamentary Committee on Social Security. For five years, from July 1941, this committee inquired into and reported upon 'ways and means of improving social and living conditions in Australia, and of rectifying anomalies in existing legislation'. Its nine almost unanimous reports covered most of the nation's social welfare services, and strongly influenced much of the Commonwealth's subsequent legislation. Many of its health recommendations were not, however, acted upon, mainly because of difficulties raised by the medical profession.

In its first report the committee stated that there was evidence that a considerable proportion of Australia's citizens were poorly housed, ill-clothed, or ill-nourished. No longer could they sustain the claim that Australia was the social laboratory of the world. If the campaign against poverty was to be successful, it was essential that a national policy be developed – and this was done.

The Commonwealth government introduced non-contributory widows' pensions in 1942, and funeral benefits and a new form of maternity allowance followed the next year. In March 1944, the Unemployment and Sickness Benefits Bill, again on a non-contributory basis, and the Pharmaceutical Benefits Bill were both enacted. In addition, legislation for hospital benefits was introduced, and there was a liberalisation of the invalid and old-age pensions schemes. The confirmation of the non-contributory principle in these new schemes was perhaps a reflection of the political party in power,

---

3     Richard M. Titmuss, *Problems of Social Policy*, p. 289.

but in effect they were only non-contributory in the sense that no close relationship existed between the payment of graduated taxes out of which the social services were financed and the receipt of benefits. To keep costs within bounds, and to distribute money where it was assumed to be most needed, a means test was applied in the administration of most of the benefits, although there was growing opinion that it should be abolished for age pensions.

When the constitutional validity of the Pharmaceutical Benefits Act was successfully challenged in 1945, the validity of many of the other recently instituted social benefits was thrown into doubt. A successful referendum the following year, however, gave the Commonwealth the specific social service powers that it had in fact already assumed.

Closely linked with the establishment of the income security services was the acceptance by the Commonwealth government of a full employment policy. Few more important social policies emerged from the war. From having about 10 per cent of the workforce unemployed immediately before the war, Australia quickly moved into conditions of full employment, and as a result of government action, these conditions were to remain almost unbroken throughout the post-war period. In May 1945, the Labor government defined its employment policy in a white paper. No political party, least of all the Labor Party, could afford to neglect the demand for full employment in the post-war years. The great extension of central government economic power and a new understanding of the causes of depressions made such a policy practical, even though it brought another set of problems in its wake.

Another social policy which was of major importance in the post-war years, Australia's population policy, was greatly affected by the experience of the war. Pre-war, the Depression had halted immigration, and estimates of Australia's capacity to absorb a rapidly growing population had been drastically reduced. In addition, doubts on Britain's ability to continue as the main emigrant nation had been expressed. The threat of invasion by an Asian power made Australians acutely aware of their small numbers. Since natural increase, though the most desirable, was slow, the solution was immigration, and an immigration which included a considerable proportion of non-British, but still European people. Moreover the war greatly increased national confidence to handle a bold post-war immigration programme within a full employment policy.

The small group of qualified social workers in Australia was among the many witnesses from whom the Commonwealth Parliamentary Committee on Social Security gained its evidence, but, in general, on questions of broad social service policy their influence was slight. To specific policies, they did, however, make a much greater contribution, and there was a greatly expanded demand for their professional services.

## Social Workers in Demand

The disruption of family life, the increased rate of juvenile delinquency, the entrance of large numbers of women into industry, the unmarried mothers, the emotional stresses of a wartime society, the need to rehabilitate servicemen – these all created conditions conducive to social work appointments. An attitude that social workers were only concerned with 'the poor' quickly lost ground; but expansion was delayed by the numbers, sex, and inexperience of the qualified social workers available. As will be observed in the next chapter, the output of the training bodies did not increase until the immediate post-war years, women students were still the great majority, and the numbers of social workers were still apt to be reduced by marriage.

In July 1941, only 95 qualified social workers were in employment throughout Australia. Apart from four engaged in social work education, 39 of the remainder were in Victoria, 31 in New South Wales, 11 in South Australia, five in Western Australia, three in Tasmania, and one each in Queensland and the Australian Capital Territory. Altogether only nine worked for Commonwealth government agencies, 10 for state government agencies, and one for local government.[4]

In its first report, the Committee on Social Security mentioned an increasing reliance on trained social workers and research officers as a marked advance in the administration of social services overseas, and recommended their appointment by the Commonwealth Social Services Department. Eventually, towards the end of the war, there was an isolated appointment of an experienced and well-qualified

---

4    Memorandum attached to *Proceedings of the Conference of Representatives of Departments of Social Studies in Sydney, Melbourne and Adelaide, July 4–6, 1941.*

social worker, Lyra Taylor,[5] as the department's chief research officer. As a great many of the Commonwealth's expanded social welfare functions were administered through this newly formed department, it was a crucial appointment for professional social work in Australia. The only other significant social work appointment in Commonwealth agencies during the war was that of Jean Robertson[6] in September 1940, as Assistant Director of the Industrial Welfare Division of the Department of Labour and National Service. This appointment did not extend beyond the war period and few qualified social workers actually worked in industrial settings.

This record of social work employment in the wartime Commonwealth public service is poor, but to be expected. In 1941, acting as spokesman for the training bodies, the Vice-Chancellor of Melbourne University wrote to Commonwealth government officials expressing concern that when nursing, teaching, medical, or scientific skill was required only those qualified were appointed, but for social welfare no training was demanded.[7]

At the end of the war there was a surge of interest by Commonwealth authorities in the employment of qualified social workers. The Director-General of the Department of Post-War Reconstruction, Dr H.C. Coombs, convened a conference of representatives from four Commonwealth government departments, the Universities Commission, the Australian Red Cross Society, and from both the general and medical social work training bodies and associations. His purpose was to examine the extent to which ex-members of the forces could look to social service careers, and the extent of the demand for social workers created by the re-establishment and rehabilitation programmes of various government and non-government agencies.

5    Lyra Taylor, MA, LLB (University of New Zealand); Dip. Soc. Sci. (Johns Hopkins University, Baltimore). A lawyer in New Zealand; went to the USA, interested in Children's Courts; qualified as a social worker; Family Welfare Agency, Baltimore; Family Service Association and teaching for the School of Social Work, Montreal; YWCA Montreal for five years; 1940 General Secretary, YWCA, Sydney, lectured on group work for Sydney University Board of Social Studies; returned to North America in November 1942; came to Australia for the appointment in the Commonwealth Social Services Department. Member, Sydney University Board of Social Studies, 1941–42; NSW Council of Social Service Committee, 1940–42; Melbourne University Board of Social Studies, 1947–52.
6    Jean Robertson, MA, Dip. Soc. Sci. (Glasgow); came to Australia in 1939 to work as fieldwork tutor for the Victorian Council for Social Training.
7    J.D.G. Medley to Dr Roland Wilson, Department of Labour and National Service, 8 July 1941.

Many of the authorities recognised the need for qualified services but wanted them almost immediately.[8] Numerous opportunities were lost on this and other occasions in the post-war years because the qualified people were not immediately available.

Qualified social work made a few piecemeal gains in state government agencies during the war, and there was considerable hope of future development. For example, by 1943 in New South Wales where social work training was now directly financed by the state government, the departments of child welfare, education (in its child guidance clinics and in the play centres of the National Fitness Council), and health (in mental and public hospitals)[9] were employing at least some qualified social workers. In addition, the National Fitness Council was sponsoring plans for community centres and wanted qualified leaders, the Health Department wished to have social workers for its proposed care for children of working mothers, and the Housing Commission expected a demand for social workers in its post-war programme. Moreover, it was being pointed out that, overseas, social workers had proved their value in school social work, assistance with relief cases of chronic dependency, industrial welfare work, probation, work in family relations bureaux, and the rehabilitation of the disabled and people discharged from sanatoria – all of which came, or could come, under the state government.[10]

Towards the end of the war the Adelaide City Council, following the Melbourne City Council, appointed a social worker, and the South Melbourne City Council, after a survey by Melbourne's general social work training body, established a scholarship for one of its residents to qualify to work with its social welfare services. Otherwise, local government was an untouched field for qualified social work.

One or two public hospitals opened almoner departments, for example the Newcastle in 1943, and some added to their almoner strength, but others were unable to obtain any staff and towards the end of the war the established almoner departments in civilian hospitals were very badly understaffed. In mid-1945, nine Sydney hospitals

---

8    Department of Post-War Reconstruction, *Training of Social Workers and Other Officers, Conference with Training Authorities, Melbourne, August 9th, 1945.*
9    Most New South Wales public hospitals were only state agencies in that they received government subsidies and came under the surveillance of the Hospitals Commission.
10    Memorandum (from Elizabeth Govan?) for Professor Stout re State aid to students.

employed 18 almoners, and eight Melbourne hospitals employed 19. No almoners worked in Queensland or Tasmanian hospitals, scarcely any worked in Western Australian hospitals, and Adelaide had only five in its two main hospitals. There were at this stage, however, 19 almoners employed by the Australian Red Cross Society throughout the Commonwealth and eleven more employed in various non-medical settings, five of these with UNRRA in Europe.[11]

After urging from the almoners' association, the Commonwealth government, with the approval of the three services, authorised the Red Cross to undertake a scheme for the rehabilitation of servicemen in military hospital units. In July 1941, the society appointed a qualified social worker, Marion Urquhart,[12] as its Director of Rehabilitation to organise the scheme throughout Australia. Two years later, it was estimated that 31 almoners were then needed. Some qualified social workers without medical social work training were employed, and even then there were too few. The Society's programme, with its offer of a more obvious war service, a uniform, and a higher starting salary, inevitably drew qualified people away from medical and other social work in the civilian population.

The Committee on Social Security recommended that the work of almoners should be developed as part of any national health service. An estimate, in 1943, of New South Wales medical social work needs gives a figure of about 200 almoners.[13] Clearly there had to be an enormous increase in the number of qualified people available before there could be a truly national medical social work coverage.

In Britain, the extreme shortage of almoners together with a greater emphasis on preventive medicine brought a reappraisal of their functions. Casework skills, research, and cooperation with doctors were stressed to the exclusion of routine administrative work. Australian almoners also tried, but with varying success, to avoid becoming immersed in administrative work. The statement of an almoner's

11   New South Wales Institute of Hospital Almoners, *Annual Report 1945*.
12   Marion Urquhart, Certificate of the Victorian Institute of Hospital Almoners, 1934; first almoner at the Woman's Hospital, Melbourne; 1936–41, Almoner and Chief Executive Officer, Victorian Society for Crippled Children, which gave her experience in rehabilitation of the physically handicapped.
13   New South Wales Institute of Hospital Almoners, *Annual Report 1943*.

functions used by the New South Wales Institute was changed in 1943 in the direction of stressing casework skills and working in cooperation with the medical staff, not under their direction.

The Red Cross medical social workers in the military hospitals worked in close cooperation with the Army Medical Service, the Army Education Service, the Repatriation Department, and the various social agencies concerned with the welfare of sick or wounded servicemen. A development closely connected with their work was the establishment of Red Cross social welfare departments to help ex-servicemen discharged medically unfit, or those who later became unfit as a result of war service. These were, in effect, family casework agencies.

Qualified social workers began doing family casework during the war through agencies designed to help servicemen or ex-servicemen and their dependants, and to a very much lesser extent, through church agencies. In Melbourne, the AIF Women's Association was established in 1940, and two years later the Returned Soldiers' League set up a Fighting Forces Family Welfare Bureau which grew out of its Servicemen's Child Welfare Committee. In November 1940, in Adelaide, the Returned Soldiers' League instituted a Family Welfare Bureau financed by the Fighting Forces Comforts Fund. Each of these agencies employed qualified social workers. The most substantial development of this kind was, however, in Sydney. Early in 1940 the Lord Mayor's Patriotic and War Fund set up a Family Welfare Bureau, and by 1944 it employed seven qualified workers.

The Catholic Social Service Bureau was founded in Melbourne in 1936, primarily to screen and help applicants to Roman Catholic institutions for children, but much of its work had developed along family welfare lines. Similar bureaux opened in Sydney and Adelaide in the early 1940s, and, in 1944, the Church of England established in Sydney another general family casework agency – its Family Service Centre. Apart from extending family welfare work undertaken by qualified people, these agencies provided qualified social workers with an opportunity to influence the social provision of the churches.

One other field, psychiatric social work, showed some signs of movement, although it was still greatly underdeveloped. The Committee on Social Security asserted that the general public lacked sympathy with and understanding of mental illness. War neuroses began to create in some quarters, however, a new interest in psychiatry and also the social rehabilitation of psychiatric patients. A completely new development was the Red Cross Society's desire to employ many psychiatric social workers in its rehabilitation scheme, if they had been available. In 1944, it actually sent four social workers to the Mental Health Course in London because no local training in psychiatric social work existed.

A Sydney psychiatrist said in 1943 that the psychiatric social worker was now recognised as a valuable ally of the psychiatrist in child guidance and adult psychiatric clinics, and in mental hospitals.[14] In that year, at Callan Park in Sydney and Royal Park in Melbourne, social workers were first appointed to Australian mental hospitals. The child guidance movement was still to be found only in Sydney, and psychiatric clinics in general hospitals remained without necessary social work services. The psychiatric revolution for the civilian population had to await the 1950s.

Despite their new employment frontiers during the war, the qualified social workers continued to be primarily engaged in helping individuals, although some did work with groups. A great many, in whatever agency they worked, found themselves shaping policy, either singly, or collectively through their associations.

## Collective Activity

Before considering the part played in those war years by the social work associations, changes in the nature of the associations should be mentioned. The most important of these were the establishment of general and almoner groups in South Australia, the coming to life of the federal body of the almoners' association, and the further definite move in 1945 by the New South Wales general association towards an organisation exclusively for qualified people.

In 1941, the six qualified almoners then in Adelaide formed the South Australian Branch of the Australian Association of Hospital Almoners. Naturally, the Australian membership requirements applied which

---

14   Irene Sebire, *The Psychiatrist and the Social Worker*.

meant that only qualified almoners were eligible to join. The immediate reason for the establishment in 1942 of the South Australian Social Workers' Association was to make more effective an approach by the qualified social workers to the Red Cross, Civil Defence and government authorities about the newly created civilian relief depots. The association's objects and membership qualifications were almost identical with those of the New South Wales general association.

The latter, however, three years later, made important changes in its membership rules. Provision for associate members was first restricted, then eliminated. Two main reasons were given: there was now a growing membership of qualified social workers, and the need to discriminate in the choice of associate members had proved difficult. People who had undertaken only the emergency industrial welfare courses, described in the next chapter, were not considered qualified social workers by the association.[15] This trend towards a closed association was to be expected because, generally, provided there were enough members, it allowed the organisation to be more effective in carrying out its own aims. The function of linking the trained and the untrained could be taken over by broad coordinating bodies such as councils of social service.

Towards the end of the war the general associations in Sydney and Melbourne each had roughly 90 members, and in Adelaide there were about 60. The Sydney branch of the almoners' association more than doubled in size in the war years and was drawing level with the Melbourne branch, which in 1945 had 36 members; and the Adelaide Branch about nine to 12. Following the pre-war pattern, the great majority of members of the associations were unmarried women, and all members of the almoners' association were women.

The members and the executive of the Sydney general association met about 12 times a year, which was more frequently than their counterparts in Melbourne and Adelaide. Of the three almoner groups, however, Melbourne was by far the most active, although despite increasing membership, all three continued without executive committees. In the early war years, and still in 1945 in Adelaide,

---

15   In 1941, a group of practising personnel and industrial welfare officers established the Personnel Officers' Association of Australia, with the two foundation divisions in New South Wales and Victoria.

the yearly average of members' attendance at their meetings was over half the total membership. In the general groups the percentage of attendance was rather lower.

The Central Council of the Australian Association of Hospital Almoners began operating during the war years, first in Melbourne and then from mid-1942 in Sydney. In July 1945, it was decided that meetings should be at least quarterly. The council concerned itself with such matters as standardisation of records, reports on Australian developments to members and to British almoners, discussion of salaries, and recruitment of students, but it was hampered by problems encountered by many national organisations in Australia. The state in which the central body was located tended to be over-represented, the travelling of representatives from other states was costly and took time, and executive action was inclined to be slow. By the device of sometimes using local people to represent other states in which they had once worked, the almoners' association increased attendance at its council meetings and reduced costs. Only occasionally could representatives from other states attend and then it was sometimes when they were on other business. No branch challenged the view of the Australian president in 1943 that for the national development of the association, branch representatives should have a degree of voting freedom, without having to refer everything back to the branch.[16]

What did the social work associations do during the war? In 1943, the retiring president of the New South Wales Social Workers' Association urged that a well-balanced programme for such an association should include self-protective activities to prevent exploitation of functions and services, the improvement of the community's social services, and the professional development of social workers.[17] In speaking of the first, self-protective activities, she said that the association had so far almost completely neglected these because there had always seemed to be more important things to do. During the war years, however, more attention was given to standards of employment, in the almoner groups more quickly than in the others. The shortage of almoner students impelled the almoner groups to try to improve their salaries and working conditions, but in both Melbourne and Sydney they became enmeshed in complex negotiations. Many interested

16    Australian Association of Hospital Almoners, Central Council Minutes, 13 March 1943.
17    President's Report, Social Workers' Association of New South Wales, 1943.

but not necessarily informed parties were involved, and there was uncertainty on how salaries should be based – whether on the number of beds, assistants, or responsibility. In New South Wales, wage pegging regulations drew the almoner group into court action which they found slow, expensive, and unproductive. The almoners found themselves being grouped with medical auxiliaries who had lower training standards and less responsibility. General social workers, with only a two-year training, were sometimes commanding salaries higher than the almoners; and, as mentioned, Red Cross offered a higher starting salary.

In the view of the general training bodies, action on social workers' salaries should be the function of the social workers' associations.[18] As yet, however, the general associations had very little interest in such matters. At the end of 1942 the Victorian Association asked the general training body for its cooperation to establish a minimum salary of £225, and in 1944, on request from an agency, it drew up a scale of salaries which it distributed to all agencies employing social workers. On this, the starting salary was £250 and a social worker in charge of an agency was to receive at least £300. The New South Wales Association by the end of 1945 had still taken no action, but it had, since late 1943, collected information on members' salaries and working conditions and had just appointed a committee which promised to act. The newly formed South Australian general group was only slightly involved in such questions.

Another matter in which some of the social work associations began to take an interest was acting as an employment exchange. Only the Victorian general association developed this interest at this stage, and even in the post-war years, this possible function remained underdeveloped in each state.

The question of a professional code of ethics appears to have been first raised in 1945 in the Victorian almoner group, when it was argued that a code was necessary because almoners' work was growing, and because almoners were so often the deputies of the medical profession. In 1944, prompted by action taken by physiotherapists, the question of registration of social workers was raised in the New South Wales

---

18    *Report of the Conference of the Boards of Social Studies of the Universities of Adelaide, Melbourne, and Sydney, held in Sydney on August 16th and 17th, 1944.*

general association. A social work code of ethics was not, however, finally decided even by the early 1960s, nor by then had the question of registration even been carefully considered.

There was, then, what may be described as a beginning interest in self-protective activities on the part of the associations. Their interest in improving the community's social services, already apparent in the 1930s, was developed much more strongly and was given great stimulus by the war. By 1943, the president of the New South Wales general association could assert that the association was likely to be consulted on every important social service move. In urging the full participation of members, she stated that times were abnormal, the association was building for the future, and that social workers should take part in community activities leading to social action and reform, rather than remain working extremely long hours in their agencies doing work which was mainly remedial not preventive.[19]

The wartime activities of the qualified social workers outside their agencies, usually through their associations, were in fact fairly extensive and on some projects intensive. There was very little expert advisory opinion that could be used by those responsible for making rapid and far-reaching changes in social policy and provision. In particular, there existed one underdeveloped council of social service throughout the country, and no general advisory social welfare body existed on a national level. (Yet the movement towards coordinating and rationalising social services did receive some stimulation by the war, for towards the end a council of social service was getting under way in Victoria, in mid-1945 a Queensland Council of Social Agencies was formally established, and a Youth Welfare Coordinating Council, which later developed into a council of social service in July 1946, was established in Adelaide in October 1943.)

In their joint action, the qualified social workers approached premiers, ministers, senior public servants in Commonwealth and state government departments, municipal authorities, governors' wives, officials of voluntary bodies – in fact whoever was likely to have most influence in bringing about a desired change. Repeatedly they advocated that individual differences should be borne in mind by planning authorities; that for economic, humanitarian, and social

---

19   President's Report, Social Workers' Association of New South Wales, 1943.

reasons, preventive and rehabilitative work should be promoted; that individuals' total needs, psychological and social as well as economic, should be recognised; that all sections of the community, not just servicemen and their dependants, should be adequately provided for; and that trained people were needed to make social provision effective.

On a national level the social work associations submitted evidence to the Committee on Social Security. In addition, in 1942, they were among the organisations invited by the Commonwealth Attorney-General to express a view on the proposed change in the federal constitution to give wider social service powers to the Commonwealth government. Moreover, it was action by the almoners' association which led to the Australian Red Cross Society's national rehabilitation scheme. The general association in Sydney was responsible for a quite different development which reached beyond the borders of their state. This was the publication by the local Council of Social Service of a bulletin which, it was hoped, would attract intelligent interest to social questions and services. Neither its content nor its circulation was confined to New South Wales.

On a local level, each of the social work groups helped to prepare their cities for bombing. At the beginning of 1942, the Civilian Aid Service accepted the offer of the New South Wales Social Workers' Association to organise and staff Citizens' Information Bureaux, similar to the British Citizens' Advice Bureaux. The public did not make extensive use of the bureaux which were established and interest in them faded as the possibility of air attack waned. Through this project the qualified social workers did become much better known in the Sydney community, but it sorely taxed their time and powers of organisation.

The immediate reason for forming the general social work association in Adelaide was concern that Civilian Relief Depots should be established. By March 1942, there were 12 of these, staffed by untrained Red Cross volunteers. The Premier later appointed a Civilian Welfare Advisory Committee, which included the whole executive of the newly formed Social Workers' Association, to advise on the organisation of a Civilian Welfare Bureau, an agency to coordinate the work of the existing depots. The association ran lecture courses for the staffs, and eventually gained the appointment of a qualified social worker, on loan from the Children's Welfare Department, to run the bureau.

In addition to this activity to combat enemy attack, the general social work associations in both Sydney and Melbourne assisted government authorities with evacuation plans. Furthermore, in Sydney, the almoner group prepared a classification of patients and receiving houses; almoners were to play a vital role there if it was necessary to evacuate hospital patients.

The qualified social workers showed particular concern for British children evacuated to Australia. In the discussion in Sydney and Melbourne in 1940 between voluntary groups and government authorities about arrangements to receive and place these children, the qualified social workers stressed the need for careful selection of children and foster homes and adequate supervision. In the event, the state child welfare departments took full responsibility for the scheme. Only in Melbourne was outside assistance accepted. There, all the qualified workers combined to assess over 1,200 homes which had offered to take the newcomers. The results were used by the Children's Welfare Department, which appointed a qualified social worker to supervise arrangements.

Perhaps the most spectacular social action in which the qualified social workers played an important part was in connection with government child welfare provision in New South Wales. Towards the end of the 1930s, it seemed that the New South Wales Child Welfare Department was going to be the first state child welfare department in Australia to adopt progressive policies, giving individual consideration to children and parents by qualified staff, and linking government and non-government child welfare programmes. The department already had a history of ineffectual inquiries and Royal Commissions when, in 1938, its secretary initiated a comprehensive permanent Child Welfare Conference which brought together people engaged in, or knowledgeable about child welfare work. The conference ran into official opposition. The department's secretary was removed to another part of the public service and the conference was superseded by a nominated Child Welfare Advisory Council, introduced by the primarily consolidating Child Welfare Act passed in October 1939. Leading qualified social workers and members of the social work training bodies were in the thick of these developments, and were appointed members of the new Advisory Council. Already by 1939, statements which sounded progressive were emanating from the department's minister. For instance, he stated, with reference to staff training, that social work in its present-day form called for high qualities of personality and specific skills and techniques which could best be imparted by fieldwork and formal instruction.[20]

Then came the war, and with it a series of studies which recommended far-reaching changes. In 1942, the Pre-School Child Committee of the Child Welfare Advisory Council made many recommendations to the appropriate minister, Clive Evatt, and in 1944 reiterated the urgent need for change. The Standing Committee for Child Welfare of the New South Wales National Council of Women made recommendations to the Child Welfare Department in 1943 about foster home placement, and, in 1944, on adoption procedure. In each of the reports the need for adequately trained staff was stressed, but none of the reports had any immediate impact. It was over provision for delinquent children that the department was eventually impelled to act.

In December 1941, the Delinquency Committee of the Child Welfare Advisory Council submitted a report to the minister on the prevention and treatment of the mounting delinquency in the community, but it was ignored. The following year it reported on the mass abscondings and riots in the Child Welfare Department's institutions, and also put forward the case for establishing more child guidance clinics. Adverse publicity eventually forced the minister to seek assistance from the Advisory Council. Throughout 1943, members of the Delinquency Committee intensively studied cases of girls at the Girls' Industrial School at Parramatta.

A foreword to the resulting report claimed that the general conditions found at Parramatta could be matched at institutions throughout the Commonwealth.[21] They reflected the community's scale of values which still emphasised punishment and detention rather than re-education. According to the report, the Child Welfare Department needed a large increase in the numbers of inspectors, insistence upon training for all new inspectors, an extensive 'in-service' training programme, the appointment of a trained experienced caseworker to a senior position to organise the in-service training and to act as consultant to inspectors, and, finally, an increase in the staff of the child guidance

---

20    Quoted in *Child Welfare in New South Wales* (departmental booklet), pp. 17–8
21    The Delinquency Committee of the Child Welfare Advisory Council, New South Wales, *A Report on the Girls' Industrial School, Parramatta, NSW, 1945.*

clinics, particularly in the social work field. To obtain the necessary funds, the department was urged to assume community leadership in the care of the children of the state, to be open and frank about its problems, and to seek public support. If this was out of keeping with public service traditions, public opinion should be organised to change those traditions.

The report went to the minister and nothing further was heard. Exasperated, the Advisory Council took action. The Chairman of the Delinquency Committee wrote two trenchant articles for the press slating child welfare practice in New South Wales. An avalanche of public criticism of the Child Welfare Department followed. There was genuine sympathy with departmental officers doing difficult work under bad conditions, but not with official attitudes which refused to admit any shortcomings in the department's administration and which dubbed the critics 'academic theorists'.

The Advisory Council eventually went direct to the Premier, W. McKell. With an election in the offing, the Premier agreed that the minister should be changed, the position going to the best available man, and at the same time ordered a public service judicial inquiry into the running of the Child Welfare Department. The outcome was that by 1945 there was a new minister and a new departmental head, and a strong reform mandate which included an emphasis on training of the department's officers. One of the bitter disappointments of the post-war period was the failure of the department to employ a substantial number of fully qualified social workers.

The qualified social workers' wartime social activities were by no means confined to those mentioned so far. The New South Wales general group trained some voluntary workers for the Women's Auxiliary National Service; it took part in a Women's Forum discussing post-war reconstruction; it prepared a memorandum on housing for the Reconstruction authorities; it sent money to an appeal by the British Mental Health Emergency Committee; it took part in the Legacy Club's deputation on widows' pensions to the Minister of Social Services and added to the club's report; it was interested in a survey of children of working mothers; it supported a move to establish another Child Guidance Clinic; it was concerned with establishing housekeeper services; it was keen to maintain the interest of citizen volunteers beyond the war period; the Commonwealth Department of Social Services invited it to make suggestions for the training and employment of invalid pensioners; it was keen to improve the lot of unmarried mothers; it objected strongly to the Recreation and Leadership Movement setting up a Standing Committee on Community Centres instead of working through the Council of Social Service; it urged the case for increased widows' pensions with the Director-General of Social Services; and it recommended a school social work service to the Education Department.

The Sydney almoner group had many similar interests but in addition it urged an improvement in state aid with surgical appliances; it made a significant contribution to a Public Health Sub-Committee of the National Council of Women and sent a memorandum on their recommendations to the Minister for Health; its members gave their services in an honorary capacity to the Medical Benevolent Association; it made a survey of the care and accommodation of cancer patients and was mainly responsible for a similar survey of tuberculosis patients in New South Wales; one of its leaders was a joint author of a Council of Social Service report on housing for the Commonwealth Housing Commission; it spent time considering various proposals for the nationalisation of medicine; it made recommendations for coping with the increased venereal disease among women and girls; and it was concerned about the lack of provision for chronic cases.

At the end of 1940, the Melbourne general group decided to adopt a more aggressive policy in social welfare matters. Its interests during the war included young offenders, unemployment and standards of living, the handling of truant children, repatriation problems, difficulties connected with women in industry and war work, the temporary placement of children, youth during the war, juvenile labour, the breast feeding of illegitimate children, the forming of a council of social service, Service regulations concerning pregnant women, the care of families not entitled to rehousing, a Children's Court clinic, the falling birth rate, increased venereal disease, the running of the central index, housekeeper services, allowances to dependants of people dishonourably discharged or in prison, and anomalies in Commonwealth unemployment and sickness benefit provisions.

As in Sydney, the interests of the general and specialist groups overlapped. Among the Melbourne almoner group additional interests were legislation for controlling venereal disease, a gift from Australian almoners to English almoners who were victims of air raids, the conditions at a convalescent home, the 'adoption' of a prisoner of war, the provision for the chronically ill, the care of male inebriates, national health plans, pensions of patients in mental hospitals, the lack of housing, and priority for housing on health grounds.

The activities of the two small new groups in Adelaide covered far fewer topics. The general group there did, however, take an interest in a 'Women for Canberra' move, the appointment of a qualified social worker to the Adelaide City Council, the changing of legislation on venereal disease, the establishment of a Youth Welfare Coordinating Council, the appointment of a psychologist by the Education Department, and the running of the central index.

The war was, then, a period when the qualified social workers in Australia took a keen collective interest in improving the community's social welfare services. At least in Sydney and Melbourne, their aims became much more widely known in social welfare circles and some government circles, but whether the general public was more aware of their existence is, however, difficult to decide.

In Sydney and Melbourne especially, educational opportunities for qualified social workers expanded. A few agencies – the Red Cross Society, the Family Welfare Bureau in Sydney, the Royal Melbourne Hospital, the Sydney Hospital – now had enough social workers to make staff development programmes effective, but still most social workers looked outside their agencies for their professional stimulation. The training bodies were too busy to provide refresher courses, except for those offered by the Sydney general training body in September 1941. It was to their associations that the qualified workers turned. Their social action frequently involved them in study, and association committees met to discuss professional skills. In addition, the general membership met frequently, often to hear speakers of some community or professional consequence.

No interstate social work conferences were held during the war; but the New South Wales Social Workers' Association did hold four residential weekend conferences; and the Victorian Social Workers' Association two, and also a one-day conference at Melbourne

University. Representatives of interstate associations sometimes attended these conferences, and so did American social workers attached to the American Red Cross in Australia.

As well as the educational activity of their own associations, the social workers in Sydney now had that of the New South Wales Council of Social Service – its public lectures, meetings, journal, and library. For all groups, the main professional stimulation through literature still had to come from abroad.

A small vigorous group of able leaders with a fair measure of experience were largely responsible for guiding the associations in their social action and were often its main instruments; also, frequently it was they who initiated or sustained the associations' educational activity. With experience, and sometimes with training in either Britain or North America as well, they derived their stimulation not only from each other and the demands of the local situation, but from American and British writings. The gap, in terms of experience and competence, between them and most of the social workers was, however, considerable. During the war there could be no dramatic improvement in the basic professional training, and marriage continued to weaken the occupational group, leaving a disproportionate number of inexperienced people in the profession. Yet it is likely that the fact that qualified social workers were almost all unmarried women, and the rather confined social base of the group, were not as restricting as formerly, for sex roles were changing and social differences were more tolerated under wartime conditions.

The war years provided qualified social work with a great expansion of opportunities, and to some extent they were seized. In 1945, Lyra Taylor asked the qualified social workers in Victoria a number of probing questions about their place in society. These were taken seriously and studied by the Victorian Social Workers' Association with the following result:

1. Does the progress in professional social work mean a lessening or loss of the service motive in social work? Answer: It does not mean a lessening of the service motive, but rather a refining and disciplining of it for the better understanding and service of mankind.

2. How far does the professional social worker identify herself and the professional interest with free enterprise groups from whom the money is derived? Answer: The general opinion is that professional social workers in Melbourne have not allowed their casework to be so influenced. Wider participation in the community's political and economic as well as social development is desirable, but the Association should not tie itself to any specific group.

3. Do you think there is some element of patronage in social work? Answer: There has been a marked element of patronage in past years, but this has been eliminated in modern professional work. This change of attitude is becoming more appreciated by the public as our work with all income groups increases.

4. What is the professional social workers' attitude towards this age of social planning and social control? Answer: Whatever the social framework of society, the social worker will judge it by the consequence to the individual – the effect on human personality. Social workers should judge the trend towards community planning from this professional viewpoint.[22]

Apparent in this is a new awareness of themselves as a group with a professional identity.

22    Victorian Association of Social Workers, Minutes, 4 April, 22 May, and 24 July 1945; Annual Meeting Minutes, 28 February 1945; Executive Minutes, 16 March 1945.

# CHAPTER 7

# Under University Control

The three general social work training bodies entered the war years in a precarious financial position, fearful that even the limited financial support they had previously received would shrink. Yet they could expect a greatly expanded demand for qualified social workers. From the first, each of these independent training bodies had had a firm connection with its local university, and had hoped to be taken over by it. This was now imperative if the Australian training movement was to have any chance at all of meeting war and post-war demands for qualified people.

## From Independent to University General Training Bodies

University education for social work had begun many years before in both Britain and the United States. In Britain, the general case for and against the development was crystallised by the mid-1920s.[1] The arguments against pointed out that a university's standard of scholarship was endangered when it undertook training for an occupation which had scarcely formulated its requirements, and which was frequently influenced by those without a university education. In addition, the quality of practical work could not be closely controlled, since it was spread over a wide variety of autonomous social agencies, and its quantity distracted students from the already broad range of subjects they briefly covered. To these arguments,

---

1   See Elizabeth Macadam. *The Equipment of the Social Worker*, pp. 50–7.

which were usually voiced in academic circles, were added those of some practising social workers who feared that a university training would become increasingly remote from professional practice.

The arguments used to support a university education for social work were varied. The rapidly growing occupational group engaged in social provision should belong in a new 'learned profession'. The university had a social responsibility to recognise this, because it was the main centre of relevant systematic knowledge, scientific and normative, and was in a position to preserve the essential unity of disciplines studying man and society. A university department could draw from many other university departments, and in turn it could make a significant contribution to them. Social work training was a way in which such studies could be of benefit to the community, and, because it needed to be identified with both the city and the university, it broke down the isolation and suspicion of town and gown, to the benefit of each. With its traditions of academic freedom and intellectual integrity, a university provided safeguards against sectional bias, to which social work training was peculiarly prone. Social work students had a demanding practical profession ahead of them, so that the value of study in a university was immense, for liberal attitudes and broad perspectives would be encouraged. Moreover, for social workers a university training gave employment mobility between fields of social work and a qualification of recognised and permanent status.

Swayed by the general argument, and by immediate circumstances which will be examined shortly, the universities of Sydney, Melbourne, and Adelaide in the early years of World War II took over general social work training from the New South Wales Board of Social Study and Training, the Victorian Council for Social Training, and the South Australian Board of Social Study. These universities were long-established institutions, predominantly British in tradition.[2] They were patterned on Scotland's non-residential universities governed by a combination of teachers and citizens, and were similar to many English provincial universities, but without their advantage of geographical proximity. A considerable portion of their not very large revenue came from the state government, which, though it generally refrained from direct interference in university affairs, determined some directions

---

2    The universities of Sydney and Melbourne were established in the early 1850s, the University of Adelaide in 1874. They are the oldest Australian universities.

of development by specific grants. Governments inclined to support the more 'practical' projects, which weighed against the development of the humanities and social sciences. Arts courses, when they were encouraged, were seen as primarily for training school teachers, and many evening students took them. The universities tended more to be collections of professional training schools than communities of scholars. Only a small minority of staff and students were women. The purpose of a university was not a subject widely discussed.

The dissatisfaction with the standards of the New South Wales Board of Social Study and Training which led to the establishment of a separate almoners' institute in Sydney continued in the late 1930s. A small but important group of overseas-trained almoners in the institute were concerned about the board's course which provided the first two years of the almoners' three-year training. They realised that the financial position of the general training body was becoming desperate and were aware, as was the board itself, that the only secure future for the general training lay with the university; but they wanted it under different personal direction.

Dr Grace Cuthbert, the New South Wales Director of Maternal and Infant Welfare and a member of both the general and almoner training bodies, captured the active interest of the Minister for Education, D.H. Drummond, who in turn consulted the leading almoners. At the beginning of 1939, he informed the Vice-Chancellor of Sydney University that he and the Minister for Health considered that there was an urgent need to put the training of social service workers on a satisfactory footing by placing it under university control. Money would be provided, but it was insisted that the present director should not be reappointed.[3]

The year 1939 was one of negotiation. In November, Helen Rees, who was in charge of almoner training, drew up for the Vice-Chancellor a comprehensive memorandum on the establishment of a university training body. This suggested both a postgraduate and undergraduate qualification, and pointed out that difficulties connected with the university's control of practical work, a minimum age for students, and the restriction of the course to those personally suited to practise

---

3    Hon. D.H. Drummond to Dr R.S. Wallace, 4 January 1939 (Fisher Library Archives).

social work, had not proved insuperable in overseas universities.[4] In February 1940, the Senate of Sydney University agreed that a Board of Studies in Social Work (the name was soon changed to Board of Social Studies) be established to institute an undergraduate diploma, the Minister for Education having indicated that £2,600 would be provided annually for such a course. Despite some opposition, the course was started immediately.

Although many of the personnel of the University's new board were also on the executive of the independent training body, and its students were accepted in mid-course, the Vice-Chancellor insisted that the new university body was quite unrelated to its predecessor. The chairman of the former board implied that the retiring director had been a victim of 'a whispering campaign of the most extensive and imposing character'.[5] When Aileen Fitzpatrick left the professional social work scene in Sydney, those associated with the training movement had been deeply divided and personal feeling had run high, something which the new training movement could ill afford.

The movement of general training into the university in Melbourne was much less troubled than in Sydney. After the first overtures to Melbourne University in the early 1930s, the matter lay dormant until April 1936 when the university representatives on the Executive of the Victorian Council for Social Training re-opened the question. After some months of debate, negotiations broke down because the training body could not guarantee that it would be financially self-supporting inside the university.

In May 1939, the Vice-Chancellor told the Victorian Council for Social Training that it was 'sponsoring a new professional career', and indicated that the university was willing to cooperate as fully as possible.[6] One year later, spurred on by the action of Sydney University, the chairman of the executive of the Victorian Council, Professor Boyce Gibson, began negotiations afresh. His memorandum for the Professorial Board was of central importance. It argued that the existing training was run by highly qualified and respected social workers. If the university provided accommodation, the training could

---

4    Memorandum on the Establishment of a University School of Social Study, November 1939 (Fisher Library Archives).
5    Professor Harvey Sutton to Dr H. Powell, 4 April 1940.
6    J. Medley, Address, Annual Meeting, Victorian Council for Social Training, 10 May 1939.

be self-supporting financially. University recognition was sought because of the saving on overhead costs, the increased likelihood of early government recognition, the greater convenience for the growing number of graduate social work students, and because the University of Sydney had already adopted training. The four problems cited, all of which appeared 'capable of adjustment', were that the existing diploma was sub-graduate, and that it was desired to retain the present training staff, the specially designed lecture courses, and the existing minimum age and selection on personality grounds.[7]

The Professorial Board decided in August 1940 that the training, unchanged, should be incorporated within the university under the control of a University Board of Social Studies. In January 1941, the Department of Social Studies began functioning within the university. The only condition of the transfer was that for three years there would be no cost to the university. The Victorian Council for Social Training stayed in existence until December 1943, primarily to finance the first three years of the new university department.

The most insecure of the three independent general training bodies, that in Adelaide, was the last to be absorbed by its local university. In 1938 it expressed itself categorically in favour of a university training for social work.[8] In 1940, worried about its financial survival, especially under war conditions, and spurred on by the developments in Sydney and Melbourne, the board requested to be taken over by the Adelaide University. The response was sympathetic – the board's syllabus was included in the University Calendar and university accommodation was provided from the beginning of 1941 – but the obstacle to full incorporation was finance. Sir William Mitchell and Professor McKellar Stewart explicitly stated they would support full incorporation if the board could show that it was self-supporting.

The Adelaide Board had been particularly disappointed by an unsuccessful approach for funds by the three general training bodies to the Commonwealth government in April 1940. A year later, it was again unsuccessful, this time after an individual approach. It also made an application to the Carnegie Corporation of New York, and sent

---

7    Director, Victorian Council for Social Training, to Dr J. Newman Morris, 24 June 1940, with the Memorandum attached.
8    The South Australian Board of Social Study and Training, Reply to Questionnaire of the League of Nations Social Questions Committee.

a deputation to the Minister for Education requesting an annual grant of £1,000 from the South Australian government to the University of Adelaide for social work training. In 1942, relief came at last when the state government provided the university with money to run the course. A University Board of Social Science was later established to supersede the independent South Australian Board of Social Study and Training.

## New Forms of Control?

In their size, composition, and actual membership, the three new university boards were roughly similar to the executive groups of the training bodies they replaced. This meant the representation of a polymorphous mass of agencies was eliminated. The new training bodies now came under the general surveillance of the university governing authorities, the Professorial Board, and the university's chief governing body, the Senate in Sydney, and the Council in Melbourne and Adelaide. The administrative and other requirements of the large complex educational institutions of which they were now a part set real limits to their freedom.

As they came to depend on a share of the general university funds, the ability of the training bodies to have their needs understood and accepted by authorities faced with many competing claims was of crucial importance to their development. In this, the standing of each board's chairman, and the amount of time and energy he was willing and able to give to its affairs, was a most important factor. Being professorial head of a university board was rather different from being head of an independent training body. Only if there were sufficient numbers of academically acceptable qualified social workers was there any chance of their controlling the training. As in the executive groups of the former general training bodies, the new bodies contained few qualified social workers, which meant that the director was still in a peculiarly vital position to determine the shape of the professional education. In the university's largely male, academic environment, it might be expected that the chairman's point of view would be likely to prevail over the director's in the event of conflict.

Although the new boards met rather less frequently than the earlier executive groups, they remained important, because they still had to decide on all policy matters, and this set very definite limits to any independent action taken by the director and chairman, either separately or together.

In Sydney, both the chairman and the director were changed when the training moved into the university. In Melbourne, Professor G.W. Paton[9] was the new board's chairman until mid-1943, when Professor Boyce Gibson again took the position. Jocelyn Hyslop remained the director, as did Amy Wheaton in Adelaide. The new chairman of the board in Adelaide was Professor J. McKellar Stewart[10] who retained the position until his death in 1953.

The new chairman and director in Sydney, upon whom fell the burden to nurture the university training body after such a troubled birth, were relative newcomers from abroad, Professor A.K. Stout[11] and Elizabeth Govan.[12] Both of these had recently been connected with the independent training body but had not taken an active part in its demise. Professor Stout continued as the board's chairman throughout the post-war years. His early association with the social studies course in Edinburgh University was valuable, and he was, in addition, a humanitarian with high academic standards, who saw a university's main function as the maintenance and advancement of learning.

The new Sydney board unsuccessfully advertised in Britain and America for a director who was a university graduate and an experienced qualified social worker. Its temporary appointment of Elizabeth Govan as acting director was extended, and she continued to direct the course until her resignation in mid-1945 to return

9    Knighted in 1957. Professor of Jurisprudence, University of Melbourne, 1931–51; Dean of the Law Faculty, 1943–51; Vice-Chancellor, 1951– ; Member of the Executive, Victorian Council for Social Training, 1933–37; Melbourne University Board of Social Studies, 1941–46.
10    Educated at universities of Melbourne, Edinburgh and Marburg; lecturer, Melbourne University; appointed Hughes Professor of Philosophy, Adelaide University, 1923; Vice-Chancellor 1946–48; died at 75; was not very active on the board's behalf.
11    Professor A.K. Stout, MA (Oxon.); son of the distinguished G.F. Stout; lecturer, University of Edinburgh, 1934–39; appointed Professor of Moral and Political Philosophy, Sydney University, 1939. He took an active interest in prison reform in New South Wales.
12    Elizabeth Govan, BA (Hons), MA, Dip. Soc. Sci. (Toronto University), BA (Oxon.). A Scottish Presbyterian background; barely into her 30s when appointed. Public relief work, casework with unmarried mothers and their children; an unhappy year as lecturer and tutor in casework for the NSW Board of Social Study and Training, 1939.

to Canada. Her administrative talent, complete reliability, and exceptional industry placed social work training on a firm footing in the university and helped the acceptance of professional social work in the community.

While these developments were taking place in the control of the general training, the almoners' institutes remained much as before. There were twice as many changes in the membership of the New South Wales Institute's executive group as in its Victorian equivalent, but this was of no great significance, for on the whole the same small group of people continued to control each institute's destiny. Katharine Ogilvie succeeded Helen Rees in 1941 and maintained the high quality of the New South Wales Institute's direction.

The formal machinery for cooperation between the three independent general training bodies, the Australian Council of Schools of Social Work, never really came into operation. The new university bodies had neither the time nor conviction to recast the council and it vanished; but the training bodies did not tackle their wartime problems in isolation from each other. Apart from other considerations, the war and estimated immediate post-war needs of certain Commonwealth government departments and of the Australian Red Cross Society demanded a joint approach.

Representatives of the general training bodies and of the Ministry of Labour and National Service met in Melbourne in July 1941. In February 1942, the director of the Melbourne general training body visited Sydney to discuss industrial welfare courses with the Sydney organising committee. She did this again in July 1943, and also discussed the Australian Red Cross Society's needs with the Sydney board's chairman and director. The following month the directors of the three university boards met in Melbourne to confer with the Director of Medical Services of the Australian Red Cross Society, and with representatives of the Commonwealth Department of Labour and National Service. In addition, they combined with the chairmen of the Sydney and Melbourne boards in a deputation to the chairman of the Universities Commission. In April 1944, the Sydney board appointed a committee to consider the present and future needs of its course, and suggested a conference between the three boards to consider common problems. This conference took place the following

August. The wartime discussion came to a climax a year later with the conference called in Melbourne by the Director-General of the Department of Post-War Reconstruction.

These interstate discussions in the war years were essentially of an *ad hoc* nature. They did not lay the foundation for regular discussion within the framework of an association of training bodies, as might have been expected for the post-war years.

## Training Standards

In her memorandum on establishing a university training body, Helen Rees said it was natural to turn to British models, but many aspects of American training should be considered, especially the care and thought given to instruction in professional technique and to the supervision of students in social agencies. At least in theory, the courses of the independent training bodies had already done this, and the transfer of the general training from independent to university control brought no immediate radical alteration in the content or length of the courses. They still consisted of academic work, made up of background and professional subjects, and a large proportion of fieldwork in the form of supervised work in social agencies and visits of observation. In Sydney and Melbourne in particular, there were changes in the background subjects but they were changes in emphasis. Teaching of social casework continued to dominate the professional academic part of the courses and the supervised fieldwork, but there was an increasing interest in group work.

The length of general training was periodically discussed during the war years. The acute demand for qualified social workers and the need for a longer training pulled in opposite directions and the two-year undergraduate courses remained intact. In July 1941, faced with the prospect of a great expansion of social work and the possibility of employing untrained people, the general training bodies considered shortening their courses. They decided that since newly trained social workers were so often placed in very responsible positions, no shortening of the courses should be contemplated. Instead, each body was to try to increase the number of its students.[13] The Melbourne board did in effect extend the length of its course when it decided that, from 1943, students would not be admitted until they had already passed two specified university subjects, but the almoners' institute was unhappy about the arrangement, and in practice it quickly had to be modified because of its effects upon recruiting.

Towards the end of the war, both the Sydney and Melbourne boards discussed a three-year course. This discussion covered provision of specialised training in the third year and its results lie in the post-war years. During the war, the two almoners' institutes continued to provide the only specialised professional courses, and their formal relationship with the new university training bodies was much as it had been with the independent training bodies. Because of the demand for the services of almoners in Red Cross and military hospitals, the Victorian institute decided that, from 1942, the training year would be shortened from 11 to eight months, but the experiment was not repeated. The New South Wales institute did not make even this temporary concession, but it did offer some educational help for social workers in medical settings.

Both the Sydney and the Melbourne boards provided sub-professional courses in industrial welfare during the war years. In addition, the Melbourne board from 1944 to 1948 offered a sub-professional youth leaders' course, out of which a professional specialisation in group work grew.

The need to train industrial welfare officers in Britain had brought government recognition of the British training movement during World War I. Prompted by overseas example, the Australian Commonwealth Department of Labour and National Service decided, near the beginning of World War II, that trained industrial welfare officers were needed to foster welfare work in government and private factories. In September 1940 Jean Robertson was appointed. In July of the following year, an emergency training course of six months was discussed with the social work training authorities, and in September, the Melbourne board ran the first course. In all, before the war was out, the Melbourne and Sydney boards each conducted five such

13   *Proceedings of the Conference of Representatives of Departments of Social Studies in Sydney, Melbourne and Adelaide, July 4th–6th, 1941.*

courses. Considerable official pressure was brought to bear on the boards to continue, but they considered the courses very inadequate, and eventually in August 1944 expressed strong opposition to their continuance.[14]

These industrial welfare courses were a mixed blessing for the training movement. Certainly they represented official recognition by the Commonwealth government who met all expenses connected with them, and they increased knowledge of the training bodies in government circles. They made a contribution to factory production and strengthened the idea of welfare activity within an industrial setting. Moreover, in Melbourne, they left a post-war residue in the form of a professional specialised course in personnel practice. On the other hand, they placed the staffs of the training bodies, and of fieldwork agencies, under strain and diverted attention and energy away from the diploma courses, and they also dislocated the diploma curricula. Although qualified social workers received substantial concessions, few actually did the courses. Finally, the quality of the industrial welfare students was extremely varied, despite careful selection.

No marked alteration occurred in the number and kinds of teachers who put the wartime curricula into effect. Each university training body, by the end of the war, had increased its staff, but not greatly, and the Adelaide body was by far the worst equipped. Apart from the limitation of finance, qualified staff had been very difficult to obtain, especially from abroad.

The Vice-Chancellor of Sydney University intended at first that its board should not rely to any great extent on part-time teachers, but several were later used because of a shortage of suitable teachers of the background subjects. Nevertheless, there remained a noticeable difference between the Sydney and Melbourne boards; in Melbourne a much higher proportion of the teaching was done by people employed outside the university, and this early pattern persisted throughout the post-war years.

---

14    *Boards of Social Studies of the Universities of Adelaide, Melbourne, and Sydney, Report of the Conference held in Sydney, August 16th–17th, 1944.*

A new development took place in Sydney with the appointment to the full-time staff of a teacher of one of the background subjects; this was W.D. Borrie, later Professor of Demography at The Australian National University, whose research work brought the department considerable credit. Quite apart from the obvious community need for social, including social work, research, and the advantage for students to have taken some part in a research project, research activity of staff members was important to the standing of the training bodies in the universities.

The staff members responsible for the classroom teaching in the professional part of the courses were under the same pressure to undertake research as were other members of university staff. In the first two decades of university training for social work in Australia, this key group of teachers, from lack of time, money, inclination, or training, produced very little research and even less of it was published. There is, however, no doubt that the university classroom teaching in the professional subjects was superior to the teaching in the 1930s.

The standard of supervision of students in the fieldwork was also higher because there were increasing numbers of well-qualified supervisors. In Melbourne the regular consultation between the supervisors themselves was continued, and this practice was adopted in Sydney, rather in contrast to pre-war practice. Developments in the same direction also began to appear in Adelaide; but there were factors keeping down the level of supervision. The social agencies were exceptionally busy. Further, marriage was making inroads on the number of experienced supervisors available. A careful assessment of the practical work in Sydney in 1945 pointed to a deterioration in the quality of supervision in the previous two years, mainly because a number of senior social workers had married. Recently qualified social workers were too much 'taken up still with their own development' to make good supervisors, it was asserted.[15]

Faith in the educational value of good supervision was particularly evident in Sydney, possibly because its main professional staff members were trained in North America. In 1943, to increase the

---

15   Sydney University Board of Social Studies, Minutes, 9 October 1945: Report on Practical Work.

number of practical work placements for students and to improve the quality of the supervision, the Sydney board paid half the salary of a senior social worker in the Family Welfare Bureau; and at the end of 1944 the full salary of a fieldwork supervisor working in the same agency. All supervisors were expected to give considerable time and thought to the students' work.[16]

In looking at the teaching materials available during the war, there is evidence of some improvement, and much hope for the future. Mainly to construct sound policy for the post-war reconstruction, impetus was given to inquiry into the nature of Australian society both by government and university departments. In June 1941, representatives of the Australian universities and of the Reconstruction Division of the Commonwealth Department of Labour and National Service met in Canberra to map out a programme of useful research, which included economic, social, political and legal questions. For the rest of the war, inquiry was restricted more by a shortage of qualified research workers than by a lack of money. The social work training bodies played only a small part in this research activity, but at least some of the material resulting from the total programme must have been immediately useful for teaching; and perhaps most important, the encouragement of local research related to social policy laid the foundations for future gains. The Sydney board in 1942 was strongly in favour of the establishment of a Chair of Sociology 'in view of the need for research and the training of research students in this field', but the University's Senate had decided no new chair should be advertised for the duration of the war.

For new material actually dealing with the social services, the reports of the Committee on Social Security should be mentioned. It was beginning to be realised, however, that the findings on social questions by parliamentary committees and Royal Commissions could be open to question.[17] The monthly journal of the New South Wales Council of Social Service was also a welcome addition to local social service material; but the books on social work used in the courses were still almost entirely foreign, and the casework books and articles were all American.

---

16   See Elizabeth S.L. Govan, Report on Practical Work. A memorandum given to supervisors.
17   See, for example, Norma Parker, *The Field of Social Research in Australia.*

Each of the new university bodies inherited its predecessor's small library. In Adelaide, the collection became fully incorporated in the general university library; in Sydney and Melbourne, it became the nucleus of a specialised collection of the general library held in the Department of Social Studies. The collections could grow only slowly during the war years.

Those responsible for arranging practical work now had a much wider range of agencies from which to choose. In particular, the establishment of family casework agencies was an important addition to the training equipment of the boards; but the opening up of new practical work was being offset to some extent by the inexperience of the qualified staff.

It seems, then, that during the war years, the teaching materials improved to some extent, but there was still much room for future progress. Changes also occurred in the student groups of each of the training bodies, which in turn influenced the nature of post-war qualified social workers.

Selection of students on grounds of age, education, and personal suitability, continued. Apart from the admission of public service cadets at 18 years of age in Sydney, each of the new university training bodies began with an entrance age of 20 years. Soon, however, all three, because of the wartime demand for qualified people, found it expedient to lower the age somewhat for the duration of the war. The educational requirements were much as they had been under the independent boards – a Leaving Certificate or general matriculation, with concessions considered for older applicants. In Melbourne, however, after a two-year transition period when the Leaving Certificate was still sufficient, all applicants were required to have matriculated, and in addition came the requirement of two prerequisite university subjects.

The acceptance of the principle that students for a course should be selected on personality grounds was a new departure for each of the universities. The selection was usually handled by a small sub-committee of the board which included the chairman and the director. In 1942, the Melbourne board decided to use psychological tests to assist in the selection of students. Both the almoners' institutes continued to have their own selection procedure, but hardly any of the general social work students were rejected for the medical social work courses.

Until midway through the war, student numbers were small, despite the urgent demand for qualified social workers; indeed, the Melbourne board, which had the highest standards of selection, was faced with an alarmingly low number of students. In the latter part of the war, special measures increased considerably the number of social work students in each city, but the Melbourne numbers remained very much lower than those of Sydney.[18] At this stage, the main check to greater numbers appears to have been limited practical work facilities. The device of a training body paying the salary of a fieldwork supervisor working inside an agency was not used extensively.

Of the utmost importance to the development of qualified social work in the immediate post-war years was the continuing pattern, during the war years, of the student body consisting almost entirely of women. In 1940, it seemed that the cadetships from the New South Wales Child Welfare Department, held by some of the Sydney board's students, marked the beginning of a breakthrough into public service, mainly male, circles; but early in 1942, despite the board's protests, the departmental cadets were called up for military service, and the cadetships were temporarily suspended. Although this particular scheme of financial aid to students was halted, in the second half of the war a variety of new financial aid schemes appeared, primarily designed to stimulate recruitment to the social work courses.

Towards the end of 1942, the Sydney board asked the manpower authorities that its women students be reserved from other forms of national service. The Director General of Manpower decided that if women were formally called up, 30 first-year students of the Sydney board, and 20 of the Melbourne board should be reserved for 1943. In the next two years, each of the boards had a reserved 'quota' of students.

In August 1943, a deputation to the chairman of the Universities Commission, established in the previous February, sought financial aid for the students of the three boards. The deputation was

---

18    For the output of the successful students of each of the boards, see Appendix.

strongly supported by letters from the Vice-Chancellors of Sydney and Melbourne universities, and from authorities connected with Commonwealth, state, municipal, church, and voluntary agencies. These testified to the work of qualified social workers, the current shortage, and the likely shortage in the future, and claimed that financial aid would have desirable effects on the size and quality of the student bodies. Although until then financial aid had only been given to students in degree courses, the Commonwealth government, on advice from the Commission, decided to extend the assistance to a proportion of the reserved women students in these diploma courses. But the government, despite the emerging government demand for qualified people, remained firm in its decision not to reserve male social work students.

The Australian Red Cross Society fully supported the move to obtain government aid for social work students. To increase the number of qualified medical social workers and psychiatric social workers in particular, the society offered a series of scholarships. In September 1943, it offered 12 for qualified social workers to do almoner training the following year, and it offered a further four to experienced qualified social workers to train abroad in psychiatric social work. In January 1944, it offered 16 for the two-year general diploma course in any of the three university training bodies, and the following year, a further 22. Scholarship holders, once trained, had to work for two years as directed by the society.

A few other scholarships became available to students, but the only other financial aid scheme of any size was that of the New South Wales State government to Sydney almoner students. In 1943, £1,300 was granted to the almoners' institute to assist social workers in need of outside aid to do the almoner course. These students had to be willing to work in a public hospital for two years after they qualified.

The various schemes of financial aid represented a significant recognition of the work of qualified social workers. In addition, such aid was responsible for social work students with much more varied social backgrounds. This was an important development, for it weakened the claim that qualified social work was a class activity, an extension of the voluntary welfare work of the middle and upper classes.

# THE POST-WAR YEARS

# CHAPTER 8

# An Improving Education for Social Work

In the post-war years the Australian social work training authorities, already alive to the British and North American training movements, became increasingly aware of the worldwide development of education for social work. Only five years after World War II, there were at least 373 schools of social work of various kinds in 46 countries, and the United Nations was trying to help them interchange information.[1]

The growth of the Australian social work training movement after World War II was not rapid, but by the early 1960s solid gains had been made. By then the minimum professional qualification was a three-year course provided by four universities in the four largest Australian cities. The pioneer almoners' institute in Victoria no longer existed; the almoners' institute in New South Wales remained, but without its training function. The three relatively long-established training bodies in the universities of Sydney, Melbourne, and Adelaide, had gained in strength and functions. They had recently been joined by the University of Queensland in Brisbane, and in Perth it had been approved in principle that the University of Western Australia should train social workers. The host cities and universities of the training bodies had grown to a size which could sustain a substantial development of social work education. Sydney now had over 2 million people, Melbourne almost this number, Brisbane and Adelaide well over half a million each, and Perth rather less than half a million.

---

1    United Nations, 'Directory of Schools of Social Work', *Training for Social Work – An International Survey* (1950), pp. 219–48.

# Comprehensive University Schools of Social Work

A feature of the post-war years was the development of university schools of social work with both general and specialist training functions, which naturally affected the two almoners' institutes. When in 1949 Melbourne University's Board of Social Studies became responsible for training in medical social work, the Victorian Institute of Hospital Almoners decided to disband; but to retain the interest, knowledge and influence of its members, especially the doctors, a Consultative Panel was established in May 1951 by the local almoners' association. The panel and the association met later that year, but was then inactive, and in 1954 the association dispensed with it. This severed the last formal link between the medical social work group and the medical profession upon whom it had leaned so heavily in its formative years.

For the greater part of the post-war period, the New South Wales Institute of Hospital Almoners continued largely unchanged in its structure and activities. When the Sydney University assumed full responsibility for training medical social workers in 1956, the New South Wales institute did not follow its Victorian counterpart into oblivion. It remained in existence to retain for medical social work the assistance of the institute's non-almoner members, and also to register qualified almoners and take an interest in the specialist training in the university.

When the universities assumed new social work training functions, changes were to be expected in the composition of the boards controlling the courses. Immediately after the war, the possible size of Melbourne University's Board of Social Studies was increased by eight, to include additional people connected with the specialisations to be offered in the third year. In the event, however, few such additions were made. In 1955, perhaps for the first time since the board was established, its membership regulations were closely examined. Eight possible places on the board were unfilled, specialisations were unevenly represented, only one organisation, the Australian Red Cross Society, had an official representative, and the practice had arisen of including full-time staff members. In the subsequent revision of the board's membership rules, teachers in the course and other university teachers were included, but representation of agencies was excluded. The board was to nominate not more than 10 additional members who were either fieldwork supervisors or persons otherwise interested in the work, and these were to include people who could speak for the major fields of social work. The 1956 board had over 30 members, an unwieldy number for effective decision-making.

For a decade after the war, the constitution of Sydney University's Board of Social Studies remained unchanged. Then came reorganisation connected with the inauguration of a postgraduate diploma. A Board of Studies in Social Work replaced the former board. It was exclusively a body of teachers and had a possible membership of 20. To enlist the aid of people outside the university an Advisory Council for Social Work was suggested. The board decided, however, not to form the council; instead, it would co-opt to any of its committees whose purpose was to assist the integration of the work of the social agencies and that of the department, any suitable persons either inside or outside the university. Except for medical social work, such committees were not formed.

There were a few changes in the Adelaide University's board before 1957, perhaps the most notable being the addition of a representative of the social workers' association. With the institution of a three-year course, the board, now called the Board of Studies in Social Studies was reorganised. Apart from not more than five people outside the university, all board members were now university authorities, teachers in the course, or other university teachers. In 1958 there were 23 members on the board.

Apparent in these various organisational changes was a further shift towards academic control. Although the qualified social workers became better organised professionally, and an increasing number of them were experienced practitioners and student supervisors, only a few were members of the boards. Communication with the professional field remained largely informal through student supervisors. Few of the practising social workers seem to have had the time, inclination, or opportunity to influence the planning of the courses. The inclusion on the board of the classroom teachers of professional subjects strengthened the chance of their courses having relevance to actual practice only to the extent that they themselves were close to professional practice. Generally, the background subjects remained heavily represented because of the practical difficulty of discriminating between them, and because the training gained strength within the university from its formal links with many departments. The few board members who had a good working knowledge of social work practice had the difficult task of preventing the social work course from becoming a pawn in the game of academic politics, a game often difficult to follow because of the highly developed powers of rationalisation of the participants.

The influence of the boards can, however, be exaggerated. During the post-war period there was a decrease in their activity. The detailed planning of the course usually rested with the director or with a sub-group of the board which included the director and the chairman. It is impossible to know the extent of power relations within each of the boards. Frequently the boards appear merely to have rubber-stamped decisions or suggestions made by the directors or chairmen; and yet, of course, the board's existence may have strongly influenced their nature.

A few of the pioneers of the training movement, such as Katharine Ogilvie and Amy Wheaton, continued in influential positions in the post-war years. In addition to these, six others may be mentioned for their positions of influence in the period: Norma Parker, J.A. Cardno, and Dr Morven Brown in Sydney, and Ruth Hoban, Professor R.M. Crawford, and Alison Player in Melbourne.

The first three at various times directed the university training body in Sydney, a contrast to the continuing directorship of Ruth Hoban in Melbourne, and of Amy Wheaton in Adelaide. The story of the Sydney directorship focused attention on the difficulty at this stage of obtaining as head of a university school of social work a person with both high academic standing and professional social work experience and ability.[2]

When Elizabeth Govan gave notice in July 1944 that she wished to return to Canada the following year, the Sydney Board unsuccessfully advertised for a director with both good academic and professional qualifications. So that a person of high academic standing might be obtained, the position was re-advertised at a higher salary and the professional qualification was not specified. In July 1945,

2    See Memorandum to Professor Stout, 19 March 1945.

Elizabeth Govan resigned, and Norma Parker, an experienced qualified social worker just returned from North America, was appointed acting director. The new director, J.A. Cardno,[3] took up his post in August 1946, and Norma Parker was appointed senior lecturer in social casework, to be responsible to the director for the supervision and control of the teaching of theory and the organisation of practice in social casework. It was a difficult arrangement whatever the personal characteristics of the people involved, but it was made even more difficult because the inexperienced new director felt unable to act with any confidence. This made the leading social workers impatient, for opportunities presented by the immediate post-war years were being lost. Eventually in March 1949, Norma Parker was again the board's acting director.

For more than five years the director's post was unfilled while the place of the Department of Social Studies was being reassessed. In 1955, at the time the university instituted a postgraduate diploma in social work, another academic director, Dr Morven Brown,[4] was appointed. He was responsible for the department's overall administration, and Norma Parker, now appointed Supervisor of Professional Training, had immediate control of the professional aspects of the course, both within the university and the community. Because this director knew the Sydney community and university scene, was familiar with social work, and also enjoyed a good personal relationship with the Supervisor of Professional Training, the arrangement worked; but in 1958, Dr Brown left to occupy the first Chair of Sociology in Australia (at the University of New South Wales), and again Norma Parker became acting director. In 1959 there was appointed another academic director, T. Brennan, a highly regarded British urban sociologist.

As an interim measure until a suitably qualified professional director was available, the choice of an academic director of a university school of social work could be well justified. It was, however, like having

---

3    J.A. Cardno, MA (double first-class honours), University of Aberdeen; BA (first class) (Cantab.); Board of Trade, 1941–44; Ministry of Information, 1944. A Scot in his early 30s.
4    Dr Morven Brown, PhD (London), MA, Dip. Ed. (Sydney); 1943–48, Lecturer-in-Charge of child welfare courses, Sydney Teachers' College; 1948–49, Australian Carnegie Fellow; 1949–50, Senior Research Fellow, University of London Institute of Education; 1952–54, Senior Lecturer in Education, Sydney University. His new status was Reader.

a physiologist as head of a medical school. The arrangement created difficulties and, long-term, the status and effectiveness of professional social work were affected.

Throughout the post-war period, Norma Parker[5] held the Sydney training body together. Yet her interest was not in administration; she was primarily a first-rate practitioner and teacher of social casework. Her position, experience, warmth, optimism, and stamina, combined to give her unparalleled respect and influence among Australian social workers in this period. After being a vigorous president of the New South Wales Social Workers' Association, 1940–43, in the immediate post-war years she played an important part in the formation of the Australian Association of Social Workers, and was its president, 1946–53. Among her many wishes was for Australia to have a national body representing the major social welfare agencies, and she did much towards the eventual establishment of the Australian Council of Social Service.

Turning to the Melbourne training movement, one person, Ruth Hoban,[6] was dominant in these post-war years. When Jocelyn Hyslop resigned at the beginning of 1945, Ruth Hoban became acting director. Within a few months Melbourne University's Board of Social Studies unanimously agreed she should fill the director's position. She was an active president of the Victorian Social Workers' Association from 1943 to 1945, but in the post-war period she devoted most of her attention to building up the standards, particularly the academic, of the professional education. This policy and the way it

---

5    Norma Parker, MA (Western Australia), Dip. Soc. Sci. (postgraduate; specialised in psychiatric social work), National Catholic School of Social Science, Washington, DC; 1931, social agencies in Cleveland and Los Angeles; 1932, Certificate of Victorian Institute of Hospital Almoners, first almoner, St Vincent's Hospital, Melbourne; 1936, first almoner, St Vincent's Hospital, Sydney; 1941–43, Assistant Director, Sydney University Board of Social Studies; 1943–44, first psychiatric social worker, Callan Park Mental Hospital, Sydney; 1944–45, Fellowship of the Commonwealth Fund of USA for study in Chicago; 1951–52, Fulbright travel grant and a Smith Mundt scholarship to study social research methods at the School of Social Service Administration, University of Chicago. Her original interest in social work was aroused in Perth by a progressive Director of Catholic Education and a psychologist with a Stanford University doctorate.

6    Ruth Hoban, B.Com., BA, Dip. Ed. (Melbourne). Daughter of a prominent Methodist minister, a leader in his church's social services. Five years' school teaching; one year of library work and economic research, Victorian State Electricity Commission; Certificate of Social Science and Administration (London); social worker, Victorian International Refugee Emergency Council, then the Victorian State Housing Commission; 1940, lectured in Economics to social work students; 1942, became full-time staff member, Department of Social Studies, Melbourne University; 1951–52, Carnegie Travelling Fellowship, Europe and USA.

was implemented did not go uncriticised. There were complaints that the training body was providing too few qualified social workers, that students were being overburdened, that the training authorities did not take into their confidence the people in the fields of social service, and that in general the training authorities had become separated from social work practice. Yet it was in Melbourne, largely because of the insistence on high academic standards, first by Jocelyn Hyslop then by Ruth Hoban, that the rightful place of the professional training in the university was never questioned in the way it was in Sydney and Adelaide. Moreover, it was in Melbourne that a real breakthrough in social workers' salaries came in the late 1950s, and this was largely because of the high level of the basic training. In 1957, Melbourne University recognised the soundness of Ruth Hoban's achievement by appointing her an Associate Professor, the highest academic rank achieved by any of the Australian social work teachers. In 1962, she resigned as the department's director to take up a university research position.

Ruth Hoban's final years as director were marred by an episode which was unfortunate both for the individuals concerned and the training body. It was alleged that in her absence on study leave, a Communist plot was hatched in the department. This received nationwide publicity by the *Bulletin*, and eventually the university instituted an official inquiry. The charges were found to be groundless, but meanwhile irreparable damage had been done to certain personal relationships.

No one in Melbourne rivalled Professor Stout's continuing chairmanship of the board in Sydney. Professor R.M. Crawford[7] was, however, the Melbourne board's chairman, 1948–50 and 1954–57, and throughout the board's existence was concerned with its work. This interest was of considerable value because of his standing within the university where he had built a strong history school.

---

7    Professor R.M. Crawford, BA (Sydney), BA (Oxon.), MA (Melbourne). 1930–35, schoolmaster; 1935–36, Lecturer, University of Sydney; Professor of History, University of Melbourne, 1937– ; 1942–44, First Secretary, Australian Legation, Moscow; 1958, married Ruth Hoban.

Alison Player[8] was Dorothy Bethune's successor in directing almoner training in Melbourne. In 1950 she again became primarily a practitioner, and from 1950 to 1952 she was president of the Australian Association of Almoners, and 1953–59 was the second president of the Australian Association of Social Workers (its third was Elizabeth Ward, also a medical social worker). Although originally trained in the tradition of the English almoner, Alison Player's experience in social casework in North America made her representative of a newer kind of Australian almoner, one who identified more strongly with the social work profession as a whole, and who placed an emphasis on casework in the practice of medical social work. Her personal qualities inspired general confidence, among her colleagues and in the community.

So far, attention has been concentrated on the three cities with training bodies since the 1930s. For about 20 years, on and off, a small group in Brisbane contemplated following the lead of these southern cities but not until 1956 was a social work course started.

In the early post-war years the main pressure for a social work course at the Queensland University came from the newly formed Queensland Council of Social Agencies and from the National Council of Women. Later the pressure was continued by the social workers' association and by leading interstate social workers such as Norma Parker and Lyra Taylor. Money for the university to run a course, and adequate supervision of students in their fieldwork, were the two main problems to be overcome. Eventually, in 1954, the University of Queensland decided to train social workers.

When the training began two years later, only 10 qualified social workers were employed in the whole state, an alarming situation for those responsible for supervision standards in the fieldwork of the new course.[9] In the beginning, the training was to be conducted by

---

8    Certificate of the Victorian Institute of Hospital Almoners, 1935; almoner at Geelong and District Hospital; almoner at Alfred Hospital; almoner experience in UK then USA, 1939; 1940, almoner at Alfred Hospital; 1941–44, Director, Family Welfare Bureau, Sydney; 1945, Directress of Training, Victorian Institute of Hospital Almoners and Chief Almoner, Royal Melbourne Hospital; March 1946 – July 1948, study and observation in UK and USA; 1949, part-time lecturer in medical social work, Melbourne University Board of Social Studies, and part-time associate almoner, Royal Melbourne Hospital; 1950, Senior Almoner, Alfred Hospital; 1957, Deputy Superintendent, 'Turana', a Children's Welfare Department institution; 1958, married Hamish Mathew; later returned to child welfare work.
9    See Hazel Smith, 'Social Work Training in Queensland', *Social Service*, Vol. 8, No. 6, May–June 1957.

a Department of Social Studies within the Faculty of Education and under the general direction of Professor F.J. Schonell. A Board of Social Studies representing different faculties was to watch over the course.

When the small group of qualified social workers in Perth formed a professional association immediately after the war, they stated their intention 'to help in the eventual promotion of a course in Social Studies at the University of Western Australia'. Without a local school, the growth of professional social work, as in Brisbane, was very slow. Many positions for qualified social workers went unfilled, were filled by untrained people, or were filled temporarily by qualified social workers, from interstate or abroad. In 1954, only 12 qualified social workers were in employment throughout the city. The following year their association was forced to become more active in promoting a school because an in-service training course for officers of the State Child Welfare Department was established at the Technical College, and the association feared that, unless a university school of social work were founded, professional social work status would be given to people with this sub-professional training. In the next four years, its Standing Committee for Professional Education urged the case for a school, and by the end of 1959 the Professorial Board and Senate had approved in principle that the University of Western Australia should train social workers. Once finance was available, a Board of Social Work was to control the course which was likely to be at a postgraduate level.

When this course was established, the only capital city[10] without a university school of social work was Hobart, a city about a quarter of the size of Perth. The concentration of population in the capital cities was such that, in future, new schools of social work were likely to develop in the second universities emerging in the largest of the capitals, rather than in the nation's other, smaller, cities; but as yet there was no association of university schools of social work which could provide guidance to any newcomers.

In 1948, the social workers' professional association considered suggesting to the then three schools of social work that an Australia-wide body should be considering training standards, but nothing was done. In August 1955, the Melbourne school took the opportunity

---

10   Apart from the small but rapidly growing national capital.

of a national conference of the professional association to call representatives of the schools together. The view was expressed that fairly frequent communication between the schools was valuable, but that a formal organisation was unwarranted since it could only be for an exchange of ideas and information. In 1956, representatives of the Sydney and Adelaide schools met. Shortly afterwards all four schools were represented at a meeting in Melbourne with the social workers' association, who had considered it had not taken enough responsibility for professional education as a whole. In future, similar meetings were to be held at the time of each biennial conference of the professional body. Those responsible for this development were mindful of the comprehensive American Council on Social Work Education which had begun to operate in 1952.

## Changing Curricula

The recasting of the social work courses which accompanied the various organisational changes in the Australian training movement in these post-war years should be seen against a general reassessment taking place overseas. Major studies in both Britain and the United States, quadrennial international surveys by the United Nations, and widespread discussion in the professional journals were available to Australian social work teachers — to clarify or confirm their thinking, to suggest new solutions to similar problems, and to break down their sense of isolation.

Shortly after the war Ruth Hoban singled out five developments which were behind much of the replanning of courses that was taking place: the growing emphasis on the need for preventive social work, the realisation that basically all social work is the same, the realisation that valuable social work knowledge can be taught in the class room as well as in the field, the recognition of the need for the development of the student's personality, and the recognition of the need for social research. [11]

---

11    Ruth Hoban, 'Education for Social Work', *Proceedings of the First Australian Conference of Social Work*, Sydney, 1947, pp. 87–94.

The main points at issue during the post-war years were the length and level of the training, the place and nature of specialisation (by method, by setting, or both), selection among specialisations, the amount of fieldwork and its timing, and the use of specially designed background subjects. Local pressures inside and outside the universities as well as general trends determined the actual balance maintained by the individual schools between these interrelated factors.

In 1947, the Melbourne school extended its diploma course to three years. At no stage in the protracted preceding discussions had a post-graduate training been suggested, even as a long-term goal. Under the new curriculum, social biology and social history were included, and since these were accepted as degree subjects, the combined degree and diploma could still be covered in four years. After two years of general social casework, students could now choose in their third year between medical social work, family casework, group work, and personnel practice. Why these particular specialisations?

The almoners' institute had closely examined the proposals of the Board of Social Studies, and generally favoured university training as long as an almoner's course would not be lengthened or the specialist training standards lowered. The board's plans included some reduction of fieldwork in the almoner student's third year, but the institute had eventually agreed that the better planning and coordination of the total training would maintain standards, and in May 1945 it had decided to relinquish fully its training function.

The second of the specialisations offered, family casework (including child welfare), was more closely linked with the preceding two years of the course than were the other specialisations, for family agencies were the traditional casework setting. In effect, this was the choice for the general practitioner.

The third and fourth of the specialisations offered, group work and personnel practice, were mainly developments from sub-professional courses run by the board. In response to fairly long-standing pressure, a one-year youth leadership course had been started in 1944. At the end of 1947 when 73 students had entered the course, the board decided it should end the following year. Emergency conditions no longer existed and the students had proved of disappointing quality, which meant that group work was suffering from poor leadership, and some of the more responsible group work posts remained unfilled. In future the board was to concentrate on a group work specialisation in the full professional diploma. Diploma students had already learnt something of group work, but now this new specialisation meant that some would be trained specifically as group workers, albeit on a casework base. The development was in line with the accelerated growth of professional education in group work which took place in the United States in the 1940s.

While the final emergency industrial welfare course was in progress in 1944, the Commonwealth Department of Labour and National Service had urged the Board of Social Studies to provide a one-year course, especially designed for ex-servicemen and women, in industrial welfare. The board had done this, but had also set up a committee to consider the future of such training. In August 1945 the board endorsed this committee's view that it should be a third-year specialisation in the full diploma course. In the subsequent discussion of a curriculum, the chief question was the amount of basic social work training the students specialising in personnel practice should do. In some large overseas companies a qualified social worker was part of the personnel team; in Australia, where companies were smaller, the personnel officer usually had other duties as well as social work. The question as to whether one person could in practice combine social work and management had not received much attention.

Notably absent amongst the specialisations offered was psychiatric social work. The board had considered that such training should come only after experience in general social work and as yet there were too many practical difficulties in its way.[12]

The 1947 reorganisation of the Melbourne curriculum was its most comprehensive, but there were others. Five trends are discernible in the following decade – the increasing number of combinations in which diploma students could also take degrees, some reduction in the proportion of fieldwork in the total course, the provision of a research degree, the movement of the diploma itself towards a degree, and the shift to a more fully generic course.

---

12   In 1950, the Minister for Health sent to London a senior social worker who, on her return, was to assist the board to train psychiatric social workers, but illness upset the plan.

The main features in chronological sequence were: in 1949 the total fieldwork in the course was reduced from 12 and a half months to 11; two years later, it became possible for the diploma to be taken with an Honours Arts degree, in psychology, in philosophy, or in history, and a combined diploma and commerce degree was opened to all specialisations, not only to personnel practice. In addition, a new course, 'The Philosophy and Method of Social Work', was introduced in the third specialised year to encourage students to identify with the profession as a whole rather than with a particular setting.

The introduction, in 1953, of examination papers in the professional subjects, Social Work I, II, and III, indicated their increased academic standing. During the same year the teaching staff of the Department of Social Studies discussed the future of the training, and the board adopted their conclusions. Social work was seen as a discipline in its own right with a developing body of theory which justified the establishment of a degree course (if this seemed wise on other grounds), and also a provision for advanced studies and research in social work.[13] One result of the discussion was to make available to graduate social work students a Master of Arts degree supervised by the department.

From 1954, the department offered only two courses. One was for personnel officers; the other was mainly a generic social work course in which the only specialisation was either social casework or social group work as part of Social Work III. In 1956, the amount of fieldwork in the third year of the course was reduced because of the burden on students. In the following year the question as to whether the diploma should become a full degree was discussed again.

By the late 1950s, these developments had produced an improved curriculum. The academic content was now generally acknowledged to be of degree standard, but there was less certainty about the quality of the fieldwork. The amount packed into the course placed a heavy load on students, and unless there were to be further inroads into the fieldwork requirements, the extension of the course to four years appeared to be warranted. The trend towards the same basic professional training for all social workers based on common method and philosophy had closely matched American developments,

---

13    Melbourne University Board of Social Studies, Minutes, 23 November 1953.

but some, particularly among the medical social workers, were still unconvinced that generic training produced better professional practice.

Although by the late 1950s, the Sydney board provided a curriculum similar to Melbourne's in its length and level, the route it had followed since the war was markedly different, mainly because of its wish for postgraduate training and the instability of its directorship. In 1944, the board agreed with its policy committee that the ultimate aim should be a postgraduate diploma, and that a three-year diploma course including specialisations could be introduced as a transitional stage. In 1945, the board considered the latter development desirable, and it resisted pressure to provide various new *ad hoc* one-year courses – in industrial welfare, youth leadership, and housing management. The following year, through its curriculum committee, the board effected a better integration of the existing lecture courses and eliminated overlapping in some subjects, but it would make no major changes until the new director arrived and until university plans for a degree in social sciences were settled.

Between October 1946 and April 1948, the long-term development of the social studies course was considered by a committee of the board. It eventually recommended a postgraduate course, with specialisation, to begin in 1949, and a three-year undergraduate diploma for an indefinite interim period. The board, however, decided to concentrate for the present on an undergraduate three-year diploma. The Senate subsequently approved in principle a three-year course with specialisations in the third year, but it could not be instituted because of a general shortage of university funds. Meanwhile, in 1949, there was one development for which many people had worked over a number of years: this was the introduction of Principles and Practice of Group Work as an alternative to Social Case Work in the second year.

A new phase in the discussion of the future of the Sydney course began early in 1950. The Vice-Chancellor saw the appointment of a new director as closely bound up with this question, and appointed a powerful committee, consisting of seven professors (including the redoubtable John Anderson), Norma Parker and Katharine Ogilvie, to advise him. Its report, presented the following year, was a landmark in the academic acceptance of social work education in Sydney. Asked to comment on the extent to which the university should contribute to the training for social work, the committee recommended that it should assume full responsibility. Largely because of insufficient funds, the committee's main curriculum recommendations were not implemented until 1955, but in 1954, part responsibility for training medical social workers was accepted, in preparation for full responsibility in 1956. For a decade this development had been discussed with the almoners' institute, but prevarication over the university's course had delayed it.

The 1955 curriculum change was dramatic but not unexpected. A two-year postgraduate diploma in social work, with specialisation in the second year in medical social work, psychiatric social work, family casework and child welfare, and social group work, was introduced. The existing two-year diploma of social studies was to be retained for a further three years. Because the new postgraduate course attracted hardly any students, a crisis developed in the training movement in Sydney.

In 1957, the board's director undertook a full appraisal of the situation.[14] He gave nine main reasons for the shortage of postgraduate students. In practically every field there was a shortage of trained social workers. Social work training via Arts took five years, via Economics six years, but psychologists, applied scientists, and many teachers could become professionally qualified in three years. Some intelligent people well suited for social work did not have the particular type of academic interest and application required for a degree. In relation to comparable professions, social work salaries and status were still low, and although better and longer training could assist these, it could not do so rapidly. Social work students could receive Commonwealth government financial assistance, but this compared unfavourably with grants to student teachers. The cost of a long course and the low level of salaries deterred women students, many of whom were destined to work professionally for only a relatively short time. That there were so few opportunities for advancement was a particular obstacle with male students. Uncertainty about the future of the courses had hindered recruitment. Finally, social work training at a postgraduate

---

14   In an unnamed typescript document.

level was at a competitive disadvantage, for many of its possible students, particularly the best students, were often drawn off into other disciplines at an earlier stage.

The director stated that unless an alternative to the postgraduate diploma was provided, it seemed that important agencies would be forced to look elsewhere for trained staff. The old diploma was condemned as being unworthy of a university. A four-year course for a Bachelor of Social Work degree had much to commend it, but it was against the university's traditions and also was still unlikely to have sufficient students. A three-year undergraduate diploma was therefore favoured.

Guided by the director's study, a sub-committee of the board decided that the situation demanded a complete reconstruction of the social work training. The old diploma course was extended for a further year until 1959, when a three-year diploma was at last instituted. In the new diploma, teaching in professional subjects did not begin until the second year. In the third year, which extended to April of the following year, there was a choice between social casework and social group work in Principles of Social Work II. Those who did the former studied generic social casework, and then chose between three casework specialisms, medical social work, psychiatric social work, and family and child welfare. Sydney University's Department of Social Work was now more than ready for a period of stability and consolidation. In the early 1960s, the Vice-Chancellor was able to testify that the course was now of a graduate standard.

The post-war improvement in university social work courses was not confined to the two largest cities. Until the early 1950s, the Adelaide course appears to have been in a university backwater; but then came a Vice-Chancellor keen to eliminate sub-graduate diploma courses,[15] and some academic newcomers who challenged the right of the social science diploma, in particular, to be in the university. In November 1952 matters were brought to a head when the Board of Studies in Social Science sought from the council, through the university's Education Committee, a full-time lecturer in group work. The outcome was a committee appointed by the University Council to investigate the scope and nature of the work and the staffing of the Department

15   A.P. Rowe, *If the Gown Fits*, p. 51.

of Social Science. Illness held up the committee's work, but so did its lack of relevant knowledge. Evidence was gathered from social work training bodies and professional associations throughout Australia and from overseas publications. From the documents Amy Wheaton prepared at the time, it is clear she had fears for the fate of the training she had sustained for so long. She herself favoured a four-year degree course which included professional education, but she realised that this was unacceptable in the university even though there were precedents, such as clinical medicine.

The committee's eventual resolutions were approved by the University Council in November 1955. The department's name was changed to 'Department of Social Studies'. From 1957 the diploma was extended to three years, although graduates in Arts or Economics could complete it in two; and in the final year, specialised training in medical social work was offered. The status of the department's head was raised, and it seemed that social work training in the university was about to enter a new phase.

A.P. Rowe has said that a university should have imparted to first-degree men:

i.  professional knowledge which will be more or less immediately useful in their chosen spheres;

ii.  an understanding of the fundamental principles of their professional knowledge, so that they can adapt themselves to a changing world;

iii.  a lifelong desire to keep abreast of advances made in their professional fields;

iv.  a background of general education, including a knowledge of the history of their subjects, of work in related fields, and of the place of their work in the whole fabric of society; and

v.  the almost indefinable results of discussion and friendship with fellow students in the process of leading full university lives.[16]

This coincides well with the aims of the reformers of social work education in post-war Australia. A four-year professional degree appeared to be the next move in their attainment. The example had

---

16   Ibid., p. 205.

already been set in 1957 when the University of Queensland offered a four-year Bachelor of Social Studies degree, as well as a three-year diploma.

Different conventions, trends and regulations in the various universities affected the courses and each school had its own problems and opportunities. When the schools met in 1955, they agreed that rather different approaches were probably not harmful, and that experimentation was beneficial. It could be argued, however, that in these later post-war years, there had developed a far deeper understanding of what was needed for a minimum professional education for social work, and experimentation tended to be within agreed limits. Although it is true that comparative studies of Australian curricula had still not been undertaken, neither were studies of the relevance of the education for actual professional practice.

The reward of the post-war struggle for full university recognition was security for the schools of social work in their universities. They had still a long way to go before they enjoyed the reputation of the schools of the established professions, but they had weathered a crucial period in their development. As small units in large, mainly indifferent or unfriendly, educational institutions their patience and endurance had been tested. For the sake of the growth of a genuine social work profession, it was as well that their university hold was made secure.

## Teachers, Teaching Materials, and Students

Changes in the curricula of the schools were only one aspect of the improvement in education for social work in the post-war years. Better teachers and teaching materials also played their part. Each school increased the number of its full-time staff (in Sydney the increase was from two to eight), and this allowed staff members to improve their teaching; but the background subjects were still often given by people outside the school, particularly in Melbourne; in Sydney and Adelaide, more from other university departments. During these post-war years, all the university departments with which the schools were connected expanded, but their large student numbers made individual teaching difficult, and left teachers with little time for research.

In the immediate post-war years, the Australian Red Cross Society offered each of the three schools financial assistance to increase their teaching facilities. At this time in particular, suitably qualified social work teachers were difficult to obtain, and throughout the whole period a shortage persisted both overseas and in Australia. This meant that the Australian schools often had to resort to makeshift arrangements in the professional subjects in the course. Some overseas social workers did spend periods teaching in Australia, and their contribution was valuable. The increased number of Australian social workers who gained significant academic appointments in the 1950s was a sign of the coming-of-age of the Australian training movement.

Although the uncertain quality of the teaching in fieldwork was still a bar to a degree course, supervision standards received increasing attention during these post-war years. The period opened with a supervisors' conference in Adelaide addressed by interstate speakers. In the next few years the Sydney and Adelaide schools in particular, with their increased student numbers, were hard-pressed to find suitable supervisors. The former had much greater resources, however; some of its fieldwork supervision was done by staff members or by social workers paid by the school for the time they spent on supervision in their agencies. The relationship between the Sydney school and the agencies that provided fieldwork supervision was generally close and healthy. From 1945 the school conducted courses on supervision, and from 1948 it instituted regular meetings between fieldwork supervisors, students, and classroom teachers.

In Adelaide and Melbourne more development of supervision standards took place in the 1950s. The Adelaide effort, because of staff changes, was intermittent. The Melbourne school attempted a systematic development of student units in a few selected agencies, each unit run by a social worker responsible for classroom teaching on the professional side of the course, but most of the supervision was still done by honorary supervisors in a wide variety of agencies. In 1953 the social workers' association arranged discussions on students' supervision, and the following year the school instituted a course for new supervisors. The school's staff made frequent visits to agencies to discuss supervision problems, and in addition, an annual supervisors' conference was arranged, whose papers produced the beginning of an Australian literature on student supervision.

During the post-war years it is likely that the teaching in the fieldwork improved, but even in Sydney and Melbourne by the early 1960s, much of it was still being done by relatively inexperienced social workers. The structure of the young profession made this difficult to avoid, unless supervision was to be done mainly within student units run by experienced social workers paid by the schools.

There is no question that the teaching materials in the background subjects improved to some extent. Early in the post-war years, the facilities available for teaching the social sciences to undergraduates were found to be inadequate in every Australian university, and in some, grossly inadequate.[17] Even after the general improvement, sociology still lagged behind. An increasing amount of what could be broadly described as sociological research was undertaken within university departments, but Australian universities were reluctant to form departments specifically responsible for sociological teaching and research.[18]

In these post-war years, then, Australian teaching materials in the social sciences became increasingly available. Much the same could be said of the teaching materials in the professional section of the course. An Australian social work literature began to appear, although very slowly. Moreover, as putting the 'social' back into 'social work' became the conscious aim of American professional writing, American literature became more relevant for Australian teaching. Because of English and local influences, Australian social work, even in Sydney where American influence was strongest, had never been in tune with the extreme psychiatric orientation found in some of the earlier American literature.

The Sydney school had the best library facilities, in sharp contrast to those of the Adelaide school. In general, the number and size of Australian social work and social science collections increased markedly, although the cost of overseas, especially American, literature was restricting.

---

17    Australian National Research Council, Committee on Research in the Social Sciences, The Teaching of the Social Sciences in Australian Universities, 1947.
18    S.F. Nadel, Sociological Research in Australia, January 1953. Not until the late 1950s did any university have a full department of sociology.

The choice of those responsible for selecting fieldwork placements for students was greatly widened by the spread of professional social work in these post-war years. Because of changing staffs and the relatively short period in which many of the agencies had employed qualified staff, only a few of the agencies, however, could have been illustrations of well-established professional practice. In Sydney there was apparent declining interest in visits of observation as an educational method in the fieldwork.

Even if, by and large, the curricula, the teachers, and the teaching equipment of the schools did improve, what of the students who took the post-war courses? In the immediate post-war years, the number of students, especially in Sydney and Adelaide, increased very considerably, and they included a small group of men, many of them ex-servicemen on Commonwealth Reconstruction Training Scheme grants.[19] The Sydney group was by far the largest, partly because the New South Wales Public Service Board resumed its child welfare cadetships, and because, from 1945 to 1947 men took an evening course. The Board of Social Studies agreed to run this one three-year evening course to allow Child Welfare Department officers to become fully qualified. Relations between the board and the department became strained, however, over the fieldwork these officers were required to do. In the 1950s, the number of cadetships dwindled, and the Child Welfare Department turned to a sub-professional course that had been established at the Sydney Teachers' College.

If the Director-General of the Commonwealth Department of Social Services had consistently recognised the value of fully qualified administrative staff,[20] the number of men students would have increased, but as it happened, apart from the ex-service group after the war, the Child Welfare Department group in Sydney, and a few clergymen, hardly any men chose social work as their professional career, a dismal record after the high hopes of the post-war reconstruction period. Not until the late 1950s in Victoria were the prospects of advancement sufficient for social work to begin to attract

---

19   See Appendix for the number and sex of successful students over these years.
20   Sydney University Board of Social Studies, Minutes, 27 February and 7 March 1946. F.H. Rowe to Miss N. Parker, 3 June 1949.

men students. Under a new Director the New South Wales Department of Child Welfare and Social Welfare firmly re-established cadetships in 1963.

In the post-war years the amount of government financial aid available to university students was increased. First, there was the Commonwealth's assistance to ex-servicemen and women and its continued assistance to civilian students; and then, from 1951, its fairly extensive scholarship scheme. This general financial aid increased the number of students, and it also opened to able students a wide choice of subjects with which social work found it difficult to compete in terms of status, salary, and advancement. In Melbourne and Sydney a few agencies provided assistance to social work students, usually on the condition that they were bound to work for them for two or three years after they qualified. Both the Victorian Hospitals and Charities Commission and the New South Wales Hospitals Commission were forced, about the mid-1950s, to adopt such measures to obtain medical social workers (and the latter attached no bond to its aid). Unless such financial aid schemes were attractive enough to add to the total number of social work students, they merely competed internally with each other for recruits. The various post-war schemes of financial aid, did, however, continue the process of broadening their social base.

Some guide to the social background of people qualified by the Sydney university school of social work up to 1957 is given in Table 1.

Table 1 [21]

|  | Female | Male |
|---|---|---|
| Attended a non-Catholic private school | 117 | 8 |
| Attended a Catholic private school | 69 | 9 |
| Total attended a private school | 186 | 17 |
| Attended a state school | 120 | 30 |
| Information not available | 105 | 17 |
| Total number qualified | 411 | 64 |

Though the information is incomplete, and the numbers are small, it seems reasonable to make these comments. Since in the period covered by these figures only about one child in every four attended

---

21   Compiled from student records in the Department of Social Work.

a private school in New South Wales, private schools were heavily over-represented among the women social work students but not as much among the men students. These are patterns one would expect. Generally a far greater proportion of students from private schools continued to university education than did students from state schools, and possibly there was a higher incidence of people with welfare motives amongst the higher income and church groups, both of which tended to use private schools. The lower proportion of male social work students from private schools is to be expected. It is different for men because of social work's weak career inducements in the higher socioeconomic groups, and also because a higher percentage of the men received financial aid which presumably allowed a larger proportion of state schools to be represented.

Since, during this period, out of every five children attending a private school about four attended a Roman Catholic school, it is apparent that Roman Catholic schools were under-represented. This is contrary to views sometimes expressed during the period, yet it could be expected because many in the lower socioeconomic groups were attending Roman Catholic schools.

Each of the schools of social work in the post-war years attracted a few first-class students. Most of the Melbourne students combined a degree with their professional qualifications; in Sydney, a considerable proportion did this; in Adelaide, a lesser proportion. When higher standards were sought in the Sydney and Adelaide courses in the later 1950s, the quality of their student bodies could be expected to improve, bringing them into line with the Melbourne school, and certainly this improvement took place in Sydney.

One other feature of the post-war student bodies should be mentioned. The schools of social work had their share of the Asian students who attended Australian universities in this period. The Sydney school became concerned about the cultural relevance of its diploma course for these students, the difficulties they had in adjusting to university study in a strange country, and their consequent high failure rate. After careful study, it instituted in 1955 a special course adapted to their needs. Having drawn for so long on British and American social work experience, the Australian training movement now had the opportunity to make, in turn, some contribution to the needs of less developed countries.

The various developments in these post-war years added up to an improving education for social work. By the early 1960s, each of the schools was ready to follow the Melbourne school's example of a great increase in the number of its students aided by demographic factors, and with improved salaries and status, this expansion was likely. In 1958, before this wave of expansion had begun, the total cumulative output of the Australian social work training movement since its inception is shown in Table 2.[22]

Table 2

|  | Female | Male |
|---|---|---|
| New South Wales | 483 | 70 |
| Victoria | 212 | 23 |
| South Australia | 180 | 23 |
| Total | 875 | 116 |

About 1,000 qualified social workers was a small number in view of the size of the population and the extent of its social provision – especially when only between a third and a half of the qualified social workers were employed as such.

The university schools of social work were still without serious competition from other narrower training schemes. A 1960 study[23] found that at least 300 people were undertaking various sub-professional courses, usually geared to the work of a sponsoring organisation, but only a small proportion of these were matriculated students, and, apart from those in the New South Wales Child Welfare Department, there was no evidence that the status conferred by such courses was as high as that obtained through the full professional qualification.

22   See also Appendix.
23   Australian Association of Social Workers, Courses in social welfare work offered by organisations other than universities.

# CHAPTER 9
# The Employment of Qualified Social Workers

In Australia the post-war years were marked by vigorous economic growth, full employment, sustained inflation, substantial population growth, much of it through an immigration programme, increases in the government, especially the Commonwealth government sector of the economy, and political stability at a national level. Each had significance for the country's social provision.

## Meeting Basic Social Needs

When in 1948 the United Nations Universal Declaration of Human Rights declared the right of everyone to a standard of living adequate for the health and well-being of himself and of his family, Australia was well on the way to achieving this. The older achievement of fair minimum living wages had been extended by the new social policy of the war years. Now, as a matter of national policy, full employment was to be maintained, and all Australians were to have some security against the financial hazards of life. When the Federal Labor Party went out of power in 1949, its main unfinished social service business was the health services. Its Liberal–Country Party successor, which was still in power in the early 1960s, introduced a number of limited health services; it also introduced child endowment for the first child, in 1950, and extended the range of other benefits.

As Table 3[1] shows, federal government expenditure on social security measures grew steadily until, in 1960–61, it was more than six times that of 1945–46.

Table 3: Commonwealth Government Consolidated Revenue Expenditure on Social Security (£m).

| | Years ended 30 June | | | | | |
|---|---|---|---|---|---|---|
| | 1946 | 1949 | 1952 | 1955 | 1958 | 1961 |
| Social Services: | | | | | | |
| Age and invalid pensions | 27.0 | 41.7 | 59.8 | 88.0 | 121.6 | 157.9 |
| Child endowment | 18.0 | 24.3 | 46.6 | 52.5 | 58.7 | 74.3 |
| Widows' pensions | 3.2 | 4.4 | 5.6 | 6.9 | 9.8 | 13.5 |
| Unemployment benefits, maternity allowances, sickness, special and funeral benefits, and the rehabilitation service | 3.8 | 4.2 | 4.8 | 6.8 | 11.8 | 12.1 |
| Sub Total | 52.0 | 74.6 | 116.8 | 154.2 | 201.9 | 257.8 |
| Health Services: | | | | | | |
| Hospital benefits | 1.1 | 5.9 | 6.7 | 9.3 | 10.8 | 20.7 |
| Medical benefits | | | | 4.2 | 7.1 | 10.0 |
| Pharmaceutical benefits | | 0.1 | 7.3 | 9.4 | 12.9 | 20.5 |
| Pharmaceutical benefits for pensioners | | | 1.4 | 3.8 | 5.3 | 11.5 |
| Nutrition of children, tuberculosis allowances and campaign, | | 0.2 | 5.4 | 8.4 | 9.5 | 10.1 |
| Sub Total | 1.1 | 6.2 | 20.8 | 35.1 | 45.6 | 72.8 |
| War and Service Pensions and Widows' Allowances | 14.1 | 20.1 | 33.6 | 44.5 | 58.9 | 73.5 |
| Total | 67.2 | 100.9 | 171.2 | 233.8 | 306.4 | 404.1 |

In 1954–55, social security expenditure replaced payments to or for the states as the largest item in the federal budget. In 1960–61, it accounted for a quarter of the current federal expenditure and absorbed about three-tenths of total taxation, or alternatively over three-quarters of income taxes on individuals.

This vast increase in Commonwealth money payments to categories of people assumed to be in need of outside assistance reduced markedly the relief activity of state governments, non-government agencies, and of individual families and citizens; but the need was by no means eliminated. The greatly increased expenditure reflected a rising cost of

1    From C.P. Harris. 'How Much More Social Security Can Australia Afford?' *Australian Quarterly*, Vol. XXXII, No. 4, 1961, p. 60.

living and increased numbers of beneficiaries as a result of the greater population and the broader terms of eligibility, rather than increases in real benefit levels. Many beneficiaries still needed supplementary assistance to reach even an austere minimum living standard, some needed assistance while waiting for their benefit to be determined, and there were still some ineligible for Commonwealth benefits. As yet no system of supplementary assistance had been established within the Commonwealth's social security services.

Wherever they worked in these post-war years, the qualified social workers had to be familiar with the Commonwealth's provision and also with other sources of relief, but only occasionally was relief-giving their main function. No person with a social work qualification directly administered the Commonwealth's social security programme. The administrators at all levels came from the general public service pool without any special educational preparation. Theirs was often difficult work and their status was not high. The main department, the Department of Social Services, was a relative newcomer among Commonwealth government departments. Its minister was not a senior one despite the size of the department's expenditure. It tended to be political expediency and Treasury dictates rather than welfare needs which brought about social service changes, partly because the department's senior officers were not experts in social welfare matters and the department was still somewhat remote from the rest of the social welfare services.

Although they did not administer social service benefits, qualified social workers were employed by the Commonwealth Department of Social Services in a separate social work and research section. According to the section's head, Lyra Taylor, in 1947, they were to provide a skilled casework service for the department's beneficiaries, to make the department's administration as humane as possible, and to form a useful instrument for social progress by assembling evidence on social questions.[2] The following year, the department's Director-General asked an experienced American social worker to report on the section's work.

2    Lyra Taylor, 'Social Work in the Statutory Agencies', *Proceedings of the First Australian Conference of Social Work*, Sydney, 1947, pp. 28–30.

In the resultant report,[3] it was stressed that social security measures should be of the maximum benefit to the recipient and society. It was claimed that the department's files showed innumerable instances of beneficiaries or potential beneficiaries who could benefit from a social worker's help, and these were not confined to just a few categories. The acceptance of social work within the department was found to range from enthusiastic cooperation to active hostility and obstruction. Difficulties cited were the failure to refer suitable cases, the denial of the existence of social problems, interference with a social worker's handling of a case, the intrusion of others into social casework, and certain mechanical impediments such as lack of privacy for interviewing. The section was considered grossly understaffed. To play its part in the expansion of the department's rehabilitation programme, and at the same time to maintain its existing work, at least 50 social workers, twice the existing number, were needed. Moreover, the central office of the section needed to expand to carry out its many-sided programme effectively.

About a decade later, however, the section was still much the same size. When Lyra Taylor retired in 1959, the attitude that a monetary payment was a sufficient solution for problems of social maladjustment was said to be changing.[4] To no small extent this was the achievement of her section in the department; but many of the hopes centred around the Commonwealth Social Services Department had gone unfulfilled. In 1960, Lyra Taylor described as a major deficiency in the social services, 'the lack of sufficient numbers of suitable people trained for social work and for social services administration'. She doubted that Australia was using her few trained social workers as effectively as possible, and in this connection mentioned the attitude towards and discrimination against women which persisted in Australia's public life.[5]

---

3    Dorothy Sumner, Report on Professional Social Work and Research Activities in the Commonwealth Department of Social Services to the Director-General of Social Services, March 1948.

4    Ronald Mendelsohn, 'Social Services', in R.N. Spann (ed.), *Public Administration in Australia*, p. 136.

5    Lyra Taylor, 'Deficiencies and Gaps in Social Services', *First National Conference of Social Welfare, May 1960*, p. 32.

The increased interest by government authorities in the health of individual Australians during the post-war years took a number of forms. The Commonwealth government provided free certain lifesaving and disease-preventing drugs on medical prescription; from 1960, the range of drugs was greatly extended but a small charge was imposed. In 1948, in conjunction with the states, it began a very successful national campaign against tuberculosis. Two years later, again with the cooperation of the states, it instituted free milk for school children. In 1951, it introduced the pensioner medical service for recipients of social service, repatriation pensions, or tuberculosis allowances, which provided for them and their dependants free drugs and consultations with a general medical practitioner.

The Commonwealth government, immediately after the war, subsidised the fees of patients in approved hospitals. From 1951, there was a further payment if the patient belonged to an approved hospital insurance organisation. Reflecting the political party in power, this voluntary insurance principle was again used when the Commonwealth government introduced a medical benefits scheme, in 1953, under which it supplemented insurance payments by approved private organisations. The coverage of the hospital and medical benefits schemes was, however, far from complete, and frequently those most vulnerable were not insured.

During this post-war period a wide range of social security measures gave people some protection against the financial hazards of illness. In many cases, the vicious circle of poverty and ill-health, which had taken up so much of medical social workers' time, was broken; but in some it remained. Moreover, many people still needed outside assistance to make full use of the new provision.

The post-war climate was generally favourable to a large expansion of medical social work. In 1949, a visiting teacher of medicine, Professor F.A.E. Crew of Edinburgh University, predicted that soon the quality of a hospital's service would be assessed by the degree of integration between the work of its medical and almoner staff.[6] The growth of medical social work in Australian hospitals was, however, comparatively slow. Opportunities were missed because qualified people were not available, or they were lost, at least temporarily,

---

6    New South Wales Institute of Hospital Almoners, *Annual Report 1950*.

because of the turnover of staff and the professional inexperience of social workers appointed. It is true that towards the end of the 1950s, compared with 1946, there were almost twice as many almoners in civilian hospitals in Victoria, and almost three times as many in New South Wales; but in view of the near-desperate staff position in civilian hospitals at the end of the war, and the population increase, this did not represent great development.

In 1946, eight Sydney, and six Melbourne hospitals, and hospitals at Newcastle and Geelong, employed qualified almoners. Towards the end of the period the figures were 15 in Sydney, 12 in Melbourne, two in Newcastle, and three in country districts in Victoria.

Outstanding among the new post-war almoner employers in either state was the Royal Prince Alfred Hospital in Sydney. In 1948, Joan Lupton, originally an English almoner, was appointed to establish a modern almoner department in place of its existing social service department. Despite staffing problems, the new department grew steadily until in 1958 it was employing 11 social workers. Joan Lupton's contribution to professional social work in Australia was significant. Unlike most of the other early leaders, her influence was not so much in the training movement as in the professional field. Increasingly in these later years, practitioners of her calibre were needed for senior positions and for the adequate representation of the practising social workers with the training authorities.

In the states which had no medical social work training, social work in hospitals remained relatively undeveloped. In South Australia and Western Australia there was some extension of almoner work, but as late as 1957 no Queensland general hospital employed a social worker. Only in 1958 was the first almoner appointed at Canberra's single hospital.

Not all the medical social work in these post-war years was done in hospitals. There were appointments with certain handicapped groups, and with ex-servicemen, and a few other social work positions primarily in a medical setting became available, but this development was not, as yet, extensive.

The fairly slow growth of Australian medical social work was both a cause and a result of the comparatively slow recognition by the Australian medical profession of social and psychological factors in health and disease. The post-war Australian medical social workers accepted as far as they could a broad responsibility for these neglected areas of medicine, but what they were called on to do often did not match their ideal functions. One of their leaders, Alison Player, after visiting North America in 1954 reported that medical social work in America was more advanced than in Australia – in terms of knowledge, skill, and general professional maturity, and particularly in terms of its community status and recognition. It attracted people of ability, she said, who in turn demonstrated convincingly the part medical social work could play in the treatment and prevention of ill-health.[7]

The training of qualified social workers in Australia was designed to make them aware of the psychological, as well as social, implications of the cases they handled; but the absence of further training to equip them specifically for psychiatric work severely restricted its development. In 1951, there were only about six qualified psychiatric social workers throughout the country, as well as a few other qualified social workers in psychiatric settings. Generally, social work in the nation's mental health services was much less developed than in its general health services.

With Victoria's Mental Hygiene Authority leading the way, Australia's mental health services in the 1950s began the transition 'from custody to treatment, from asylums to hospitals and from in-patient to non-residential care'. In the mid-1950s, the Stoller Report defined the nature, size and cost of Australia's mental health problem.[8] Amongst the many deficiencies found in the mental health services was a shortage of trained professional staff. Referring to social workers, the report said that they were badly needed in all states, but the chronic shortages had led to inertia. In the later 1950s, Commonwealth government finance helped capital building projects, mental health associations became increasingly active, the general public became more aware of mental health problems, and psychological medicine gained ground in the medical profession. Some of the leaders in this new mental health movement stressed the need for social workers in a community's mental health services. For instance, in 1959, W.H. Trethowan, Professor of Psychiatry at Sydney University,

---

7    Report Submitted to the Australian Association of Almoners.
8    Alan Stoller, with the assistance of K.W. Arscott, *Report on Mental Health Facilities and Needs of Australia.*

stated that social workers had an invaluable and essential part to play in modern psychiatric diagnosis, in working with patients' relatives, and in carrying forward rehabilitation measures.[9] Two years earlier, Dr J. E. Cawte recommended that the South Australian government consider establishing a Social Service Division in its Mental Hygiene Department. This would not only provide a social work service in the mental hospitals, but would also supervise community facilities – family care schemes, licensed nursing homes, halfway houses – for treating mentally ill patients outside the hospitals. From observation overseas, he concluded that such a division would need to have reasonable autonomy. It would work 'in close liaison with the medical profession in the total handling of the patient population, but it should not be dominated by individuals with training in other fields'. Salaries would need to be 'commensurate with the skill and value of the profession of psychiatric social work'.[10]

So far attention has been concentrated on social provision to meet the basic social needs of material welfare and health.[11] Provision for five other such needs, housing, employment, education, recreation, and family welfare, will be mentioned.

Without sufficient low-cost housing, the social security programme was not only incomplete, it was likely to be jeopardised. Before World War II, both state and Commonwealth governments assisted home purchase and some states became interested in slum clearance. In the post-war period, the housing shortage, the greater emphasis on home ownership, and the numbers employed in the housing industry, all encouraged housing to be seen as ultimately a government responsibility, and increasingly a federal government responsibility. In 1945, the Commonwealth government undertook to supply state governments with finance mainly to provide more low-cost housing for people in lower income groups, and a scheme of rental rebates was introduced. When a new agreement was made in 1956, because a different political party was in power, there was greater

---

9    W.R. Trethowan, *Report to the South Australian Association for Mental Health*, p. 7.
10    J.E. Cawte, *Report on the Principles of Operation of Mental Health Services Overseas with Recommendations for South Australia*.
11    What is considered 'basic' to human living does, of course, differ from society to society, and from time to time within the one society. Basic needs can be defined as those which are already met for the majority of the society.

emphasis on home ownership and no provision for rental rebates. The continuing housing shortage meant that slum clearance projects were delayed.

Inadequate or expensive accommodation was a frequent problem of social workers' clients in these post-war years. Very few social workers, however, worked directly with the various government housing programmes, despite the fact that, at the beginning of the period, the Commonwealth government housing authorities had stressed the need for good management on the states' housing estates, and for trained personnel to carry out all management. One of the problems in New South Wales was whether it was possible to combine property management and helping with individual, problems.

In the mid-1950s, the Brotherhood of St Laurence, in conjunction with the Victorian Housing Commission, began a notable social work experiment with a group of 'problem families' in a government temporary housing area. By 1960, through intensive social casework and group work, there was some progress in helping the families to manage their own affairs and to attain standards necessary for a Housing Commission house.

Apart from a period in 1952–53, and again early in the 1960s, the post-war full employment policy was very successful, and a useful part in this success was played by the Commonwealth Employment Service within the Department of Labour and National Service. This was a national employment exchange which tried to match men and jobs. To assist in this, it employed psychologists, whose aptitude testing had been used so extensively during the war, and at first it seemed that social workers would also be an integral part of the new agency. Social workers lent by the Australian Red Cross Society demonstrated the usefulness of social casework within the service, but hardly any social workers were appointed.

For the employment of handicapped people, the Commonwealth Employment Service did cooperate to some extent with medical social workers in hospitals and other establishments, and with the social workers engaged in the Rehabilitation Service of the Commonwealth Department of Social Services. This last service was a civilian programme which developed from ex-service rehabilitation in 1948. Its main object was to assist beneficiaries of the department to gain employment and become economically independent. Much of the time of the social workers in the social services department was spent on its rehabilitation programme. Towards the end of the post-war period in New South Wales, it was recommended that more social workers should be employed in both government and non-government agencies concerned with the rehabilitation and employment of handicapped persons.[12]

Generally the post-war growth of personnel work in Australia was not closely linked with social work. The few social workers who worked in industrial environments often found themselves with a variety of functions difficult to combine. In the United States, some trade unions employed social workers and social work help was not associated with the management. In the late 1940s, the Sydney Metropolitan Branch of the Federated Ironworkers' Association appointed a social worker, but this proved to be the only appointment.

Social workers were vitally concerned that the basic need for education be met, for on this depended so much of the community's welfare. Often they themselves saw their task as primarily educational – to help clients, administrators and other professional people to gain insight into the forces of social and personal breakdown, and to understand how to combat them. The employment of social workers by specifically educational authorities was, however, still extremely rare. A few worked at a preschool level, but a school social work service did not develop at a primary and secondary level, nor did the growing counselling services at a tertiary level become the responsibility of social workers. That social as well as psychological factors could interfere with students' educational progress was increasingly realised, but because there were so few social workers in schools, and psychologists had already been accepted, social factors tended to take second place.

When helping individuals and families the post-war social workers sometimes found their work hampered by a lack of suitable group recreation facilities. The Commonwealth government, through its

---

12   E. Marilyn Stacey and S.M. Barker, *A Survey of the Employment Problems of Physically Handicapped Persons in New South Wales*, pp. 111–3.

National Fitness scheme, stimulated government and non-government recreation programmes and brought some coordination in their work, but its main focus was the physical health of the young.

The training of social workers who specialised in group work aimed to provide them with the ability to help any group to make the best use of all its resources in running its affairs. At this stage the fully qualified group workers were still usually to be found in youth clubs, although a few did work with adult groups.

In the late 1950s, it was said in Sydney that the confused environment facing adolescents, the need to learn to take responsibility, and the need to assimilate newcomers, required youth workers 'with a philosophy, an understanding of youth and direction in their work'. Keeping youth off the streets by merely entertaining them was not enough. Voluntary leadership training schemes had increased, but the need for paid, fully trained people was only gradually being recognised, partly because youth work agencies were poor financially. The professional youth worker's status and salary were still fairly low, even though the work was, it was claimed,[13] as important as teaching and often more demanding because of the long hours. In New South Wales, with the increased government and public interest, the 1960s promised to be a period of considerable development in youth work, but whether this would include a substantial growth of paid, university-trained group workers was uncertain.

In meeting the needs already considered, the post-war social provision relieved the Australian family of some of the responsibilities it had formerly carried. Yet in much of the provision, for instance, dependants' and maternity allowances, widows' pensions, child endowment, and housing policy, the family unit was recognised as being worthy of special maintenance. Many writers pointed to changes in the structure and functions of the family in Western society. In the first collective study of marriage and the family in Australia,[14] it was suggested that the Australian family was becoming more specialised, but that it was no less important as a social institution. It was stressed that the newer

---

13    Betty Battle, 'Current Trends in Youth Work', *Social Service*, Vol. 10, No. 1, July–August 1958, pp. 13–4.
14    A.P. Elkin (ed.), *Marriage and the Family in Australia*.

democratic partnership form of marriage was more demanding than the former authoritarian form, particularly with regard to emotional maturity, responsibility and adaptability.

Wherever they worked social workers were concerned with the social relationships of their clients, especially their family relationships. The post-war growth of specifically family welfare agencies was, however, slow. Although restricted by finance, some church family agencies employed qualified social workers, in particular, the religious-inspired Brotherhood of St Laurence in Melbourne. Service and ex-service family agencies continued to employ social workers, but theirs was a special, although large, clientele. Only in Sydney and Melbourne were there non-sectarian, civilian general family agencies with fully qualified staff, and these were restricted by a shortage of funds. Immediately after the war, the services of the Sydney Family Welfare Bureau were opened to all members of the community; and the transformation of the Charity Organisation Society of Victoria into a modern family service agency, the Citizen's Welfare Service of Victoria, began in 1948.

Among the problems family agencies handled were marital ones. Alison Player in 1952 insisted that marriage counselling could not be separated from the whole of family counselling, and that this work was, therefore, not in a field separate from social work.[15] Beginning in 1948 in New South Wales, however, a marriage guidance movement largely based on British models spread throughout the country. Its counselling work was done by voluntary lay counsellors backed by an array of experts. The counsellors were trained by courses which inevitably were short, narrow, and scrappy, compared with the full professional education for social work. Some qualified social workers were concerned over the development since cases including disturbed marital relations were often as complex as any they handled. Two of them described as 'nonsense' the contention of Dr David Mace, the high priest of the movement in Britain, that marriage counselling was too strenuous for people to do more than a few hours of it each week.[16]

---

15  'Marital Conflict', Papers of the Social Work Institute, August–September 1952, *Forum*, Vol. VI, No. 4, p. 22.
16  L.J. Tierney and S.H. Lovibond, 'A Review of "Marriage Counselling" by Dr David R. Mace', *Forum*, Vol. III, No. 4, March 1950.

In all states there were qualified social workers associated with the Marriage Guidance Councils, but generally they remained apart from the movement. Separate from questions about the quality of the counselling activity, professional social workers, because they were almost all unmarried women, were not in any case well placed to affect the movement.

The influence of the National Marriage Guidance Council was evident when the Commonwealth Attorney-General introduced his uniform divorce legislation in 1959. When speaking of his proposal to subsidise approved marriage guidance organisations, he said the work would best be done by trained volunteers. Later, after considerable further discussion, he publicly declared[17] that ideally the counsellors would be fully qualified social workers if they were available.

Agencies designed to meet the society's basic social needs naturally found themselves dealing with categories of people who fell below accepted community standards of well-being. There were, in addition, agencies created to help particularly vulnerable groups. A few social workers were employed specifically to assist physically handicapped groups; others, in the late 1950s, to help groups of aged people. Special mention should, however, be made of employment of social workers with agencies concerned with the welfare of ex-servicemen, of migrants, of children, and of legal offenders.

## Helping Special Groups

Much of the post-war social provision for ex-servicemen and women was administered through the Commonwealth Repatriation Department. As with the Department of Social Services, no one with a social work qualification administered the provision, but the department, with the aid of Red Cross, began employing a few medical and psychiatric social workers soon after the war. Except for the Family Welfare Bureau of the World War II Services Welfare Fund in South Australia, easily the largest social work employer among service agencies in each state was the Red Cross Society.

---

17    In a lecture on marriage guidance at St Mark's Library, Canberra, 1960.

By 1960, Australia's population had grown to over 10 million. The net gain from post-war migration exceeded 1.25 million, some 60 per cent of whom were of non-British European origin. The broad social implications of the post-war migration still remained largely a matter for speculation, although the subject was beginning to be studied seriously. Many of the qualified social workers, however, became aware of individual difficulties in these post-war years. Almost all worked in agencies which included migrants among their clients. In addition, from 1949, the Commonwealth Department of Immigration decided to offer its own migrant social work service in each state, and within five years it was employing almost as many social workers as the Department of Social Services; but this was not a permanent development. At the end of the period under review, the department, despite some disapproval in social welfare circles, cut back its social work staff so that migrants would use the social agencies available to the rest of the population.

Of all the state government child welfare departments, the New South Wales department enjoyed the highest public reputation during the post-war period. Yet most of its officers were still inadequately trained, and the field officers were asked to carry huge case loads, which made casework almost impossible and held in check the department's preventive work and much-needed expansion of its foster home programme. Further, most of its few fully qualified personnel resigned during the 1950s.

The Victorian state government began to move into a progressive phase in its child welfare programme in the second half of the 1950s. A new development was the opening up of responsible administrative positions to people with a social work qualification. At the end of the period this trend was extended by the creation of a Social Welfare Department which incorporated all the existing social welfare services run by the state government. It had divisions for family welfare (covering the work of the former Children's Welfare Department), youth welfare, prisons, research and statistics, training, and probation and parole.[18]

---

18   Victorian Legislative Assembly, *The Social Welfare Act 1960.*

Qualified social workers made little, if any, impact on government child welfare services in the smaller states. In Queensland the position was particularly underdeveloped. As late as 1957, there was no juvenile probation service, no trained social workers were employed in the state's child welfare services, policemen often reported on adopting homes, and the majority of dependent children not suitable for adoption were kept in institutions. Generally throughout Australia, as late as 1960, government child care programmes still left much to be desired, and non-government, often church, provision, was frequently worse. The child welfare field in each state still awaited social work leadership.

Provision for the underage legal offender was usually part of each state's child welfare system. In some states, however, voluntary probation officers were still largely used. The 1956 Barry Report[19] in Victoria recommended an increase in the number of professional probation officers, and commented that the system of honorary probation officers now appeared to be outdated.

In the 1950s there was a new consideration of the treatment of adult legal offenders. In 1951, the New South Wales Adult Probation Service was established as an independent branch of the Department of the Attorney-General and of Justice. At its head was a qualified male social worker, who saw the service's work as essentially social work, although of course in an authoritarian setting. To allow effective work to be done, caseloads were strictly limited. The continued expansion of the service outstripped the available qualified male social workers, and it was necessary to resort to in-service training.

A parallel development in the correctional field in New South Wales, as part of a series of reforms in 1951, was the appointment of parole officers in the Department of Prisons to provide a casework service for prisoners and to help them become re-established in the community after their release. In the second part of their work they were greatly assisted by widely representative civil rehabilitation committees. As with the probation service, caseloads were kept within bounds. In 1959, all seven of the parole officers were qualified social workers,

---

19   *Report of Juvenile Delinquency Advisory Committee to Chief Secretary of Victoria*, pp. 56–7, 93.

but then, faced with the need for expansion and with no qualified men available, the service was forced to accept people with less appropriate educational qualifications.

The development of professional adult probation and parole services was rather later in Victoria and took a different form. In 1957, a professional section was established within the Penal Department to perform both probation and parole functions. The section expanded quickly, and again, because there were not enough qualified male social workers, an in-service training scheme had to be instituted. The people who undertook the training were university graduates, yet the head of the section wrote in 1959 that the arrangement was in no way a substitute for a full diploma of social studies course. In particular, it failed to develop attitudes in the direction of recognised social casework principles.[20] Unlike their New South Wales counterparts, the Victorian officers carried hopelessly heavy caseloads.

In addition to these developments in the two largest states, a small adult probation service headed by a qualified male social worker began in South Australia in 1954, and in 1959, an adult probation and parole service was started in Queensland.

This development of adult correctional work was important to the future of professional social work in Australia. To the heads of these new services this was very properly a field of professional social work. Yet the shortage of qualified staff was likely to restrict the work's expansion, or alternatively it would expand with people with a lesser training which would separate the correctional field from social work, to the detriment of both. Moreover, because most of the clients were men, and salaries were relatively good, this field was likely to drain the few qualified males away from other fields where they were urgently needed; and this division of the profession on sex lines would hinder its broad development.

To this point, two main groups of social agencies have been considered — those concerned with meeting basic social needs, and those concerned with the needs of special groups. One other important group remains, the coordinating social services.

---

20   Hamish E. Mathew, 'Adult Probation and Parole Services in Victoria', *Australian Journal of Social Work*, Vol. XII, No. 2, December 1959, pp. 21–6.

# Coordinating Social Services

Through regular cooperation with colleagues in many different fields of social provision, the qualified social workers themselves acted as coordinating agents. In addition, they usually strongly encouraged agencies specifically designed to achieve coordination; but the growth of general coordinating bodies was slow. A struggle to form a national social welfare body, which amongst other things would give Australia official status with the International Conference of Social Work, occupied most of the post-war period. The main problem was that the ministers and officers of the Department of Social Services and leaders in non-government social provision held different views on what should be such a body's role, its finances, and the degree of government participation and control in its affairs. When the Australian Social Welfare Council (later, the Australian Council of Social Service) was eventually formed in 1956, it was without full government cooperation, and in the early 1960s its existence was still precarious.

At a state level, both the New South Wales and Victorian Councils of Social Service employed qualified social workers as their executive officers, but in terms of the size of the communities they were serving, they remained comparatively weak. The similar organisations developing in the smaller states were even weaker. None of the councils of social service was connected with a community chest. As yet joint fundraising was not widely used, despite the parlous financial condition of many of the voluntary agencies, but there was increasing interest in the subject. Again, there was obvious lack of conviction about the usefulness of a Central Index.

A significant new development in the post-war years, at least in the larger states, was a rising number of limited coordinating bodies outside the framework of the councils of social service. In 1961, there were at least 22 such bodies in Victoria. This was not yet a developed employment field for qualified social workers.

Another feature of these years was the growth of general community-serving men's organisations, such as Rotary, Lions, and Apex Clubs, and Junior Chambers of Commerce. Sydney Rotary Club set an example to these organisations when in the late 1950s it appointed a qualified social worker to make its welfare sponsorship more effective.

Another social work appointment which was partly a community organisation one was with the South Melbourne City Council immediately after the war. Towards the end of the period other municipal bodies in both Sydney and Melbourne began to follow suit, although not always with qualified people.

Generally there was some post-war movement towards coordination, but it was hampered by the lack of a tradition of government and non-government partnership in social welfare programmes, the financial weakness of most voluntary agencies, the general shortage of qualified social workers, and the particular shortage of those specifically equipped for community organisation positions.

## The Broad Scene

Occasional surveys for special purposes gave a glimpse of the developing employment pattern for qualified social workers. In 1954 one such survey for a Current Affairs Bulletin revealed the overall picture shown in Table 4.

Table 4: The Employment Distribution of Qualified Social Workers in Australia, 1954.

| | |
|---|---|
| Commonwealth government departments: | 56 |
| Social Services | 25 |
| Immigration | 21 |
| Repatriation | 8 |
| Labour and National Service | 1 |
| Interior | 1 |
| State government agencies: | 89 |
| Child Welfare | 40* |
| Mental hospitals or clinics | 22 |
| Education | 10 |
| Child guidance clinics | 6 |
| Probation and Parole | 5 |
| Health | 3 |
| Housing | 2 |
| Labour and Social Welfare | 1 |
| Local government agencies: | 6 |
| Total employed in government agencies: | 151 |

| Non-government agencies: | 217 |
|---|---|
| Hospitals | 96 |
| Family welfare (including Red Cross) | 42 |
| Physically handicapped | 14 |
| Ex-service | 13 |
| Recreation | 11 |
| Industry | 8 |
| Children's services (kindergartens etc) | 7 |
| Health associations | 6 |
| Universities, councils of social service, etc. | 20 |
| TOTAL | 368 |

* 33 in New South Wales

It was apparent from this that since the early war years there had been a pronounced trend towards employment in government agencies, a trend which would have been much stronger if more qualified men had been available. The survey also showed that over 90 per cent of the qualified social workers were employed in the three cities with training bodies.

A much more intensive survey in New South Wales, which contained about half the qualified social workers then employed in Australia, was undertaken two years later.[21] The 184 people covered by this 1956 survey worked under no less than 54 different titles. It was difficult enough, without this further impediment, to identify a social work professional group in the wide variety of social work settings. In all, they were working in 53 different agencies, 40 per cent of them in 14 government agencies.

Of the social workers who had qualified since 1940, the study found that, mainly because of marriage, only about a third of the women remained in social work employment, and, because of better opportunities for advancement elsewhere, only a half of the men. The existing group in employment was very largely unmarried women, and about half of these were 30 years of age or older.

---

21    Sydney University Department of Social Work, Survey of Professional Social Workers in New South Wales, 1956.

Most of the men were married and the great majority of them worked in government agencies. None of them had had a professional experience of more than 10 years. The proportion in the whole group with a long professional experience was comparatively small. Two out of every five had had less than five years' professional experience, and four out of five less than 10 years. Two-thirds of the total group had, however, had experience in other employment before taking the social work qualification.

The study revealed that the women had a much greater tendency to move from agency to agency than the men. This tendency had aggravated staff situations already unstable because of professional wastage.

Most of the social workers were shown as being primarily engaged in social casework, but it was also apparent that there was not much division of labour within areas of professional activity, and most of them were engaged in two or more of casework, administration, community relations, group work, and research.

The conditions of work were far from ideal. Most of them worked overtime, some long and often; and almost none were paid for it. In many instances, especially in government agencies, caseloads were impossibly large which made effective work difficult, and threatened the professional identity of the caseworker. Not everyone had privacy for their interviewing, and less than a half had adequate secretarial assistance.

As a group their qualifications were by no means confined to the basic two-year diploma. Almost two-fifths had an additional social work qualification, usually an almoner's certificate, and almost a third had university degrees. Yet it was found that the additional educational qualifications counted for little in salaries received.

The salary picture provided the obvious explanation for the failure of professional social work to attract and hold large numbers of able men and women, particularly men. Almost 90 per cent received less than £1,200 a year; almost three-quarters, less than £1,000 a year; and about a third, less than £800. Male levels were higher. The state public service salaries were better than the Commonwealth's; non-government agencies usually followed Commonwealth rates or were lower. Of those with more than 10 years' professional experience, only one-tenth received more than £1,050, and this was mainly when they were engaged in teaching social work.

In general, the social workers' salaries compared unfavourably with those of teachers and psychologists, both at the beginning and after some years of service. In the late 1950s, however, the salary scene began to change, especially in Victoria where the three-year minimum professional qualification had existed for some years. There, salaries of qualified social workers in the state public service became fully competitive with those of other professional groups, and new opportunities for advancement into administrative positions greatly extended possible financial rewards.[22] As well-paid, administrative social welfare positions became available, however, there was a danger that the more experienced qualified social workers would be drawn away from practising and teaching casework, group work, or community organisation. For balanced growth, professional social work needed roughly equal financial rewards for first-rate, experienced people in all its fields.

At the end of the post-war period qualified social workers were still very unevenly distributed both in fields of social provision and geographically. This could only be rectified if increased numbers, especially men, became available, and to some extent this depended upon employment conditions able to compete with other professions with comparable training and satisfactions. If the other states followed Victoria's lead, and salaries became based upon the new three-year professional qualification, if salaries were no longer linked with inappropriate occupational groups like medical ancillaries, and if senior administrative positions became available, the 1960s could begin a new era for the employment of qualified social workers in Australia.

---

22   £4,000+ p.a. was quoted as a possible salary for a qualified social worker in Victoria in 1961. See 'Summary of Salary Scales', *Proceedings of the 7th National Conference of the Australian Association of Social Workers*, p. 49.

# CHAPTER 10

# Towards Effective Professional Organisation

If social work was to be a profession worthy of the name, it was important that qualified social workers throughout each country combine in a single, effective, overall professional association, rather than remain isolated, either geographically or in specialist associations. To bring this about members had to identify with the national body and there had to be adequate provision for specialist interests inside it.

Again it was American social work which gave the lead. In 1955, four well-established specialist professional associations, two embryonic specialist groups, and the long-established general association, were all absorbed by the new National Association of Social Workers. Provision was made within the new association for specific interests, and by 1958 there were sections concerned with group work, medical social work, psychiatric social work, school social work, and social work research, and committees on community organisation and international social welfare. To be a member of the association, it was necessary to hold a degree from a graduate professional school of social work accredited by the Council on Social Work Education, and for membership of a section there were further qualifications. The association at the beginning of 1957 had roughly 22,500 members in 143 chapters.[1]

The stage of professional organisation reached by British social workers was very much less advanced. They remained organised in a number of specialist associations, some of which, such as the Association

---

1    Nathan E. Cohen, *Social Work in the American Tradition*, pp. 283–5.

of Psychiatric Social Workers, and the Institute of Almoners, insisted on a full professional qualification for membership, but others were far more open.

The wide variety of British training schemes and much less emphasis on a generic professional training and a social work profession, made it difficult to organise a united national professional association. The British Federation of Social Workers was plagued by a shortage of money and by disagreement over membership requirements. After becoming almost moribund, it was replaced in 1951 by the Association of Social Workers of Great Britain. Amongst other aims, the new association was 'to promote unity of interest and purpose between specialist groups'. Full membership was opened to individuals with a recognised training. In addition, associations of specialists, for whom professional training based on a university course of social studies was an approved way though not necessarily the only way, of entering their particular field, could become affiliated. In 1959, when it had eight affiliated specialist associations and 320 individual members, its chairman described it as still a small body. There were indications, however, that a need was now felt for a strong, informed, national coordinated body which could deal with training and employment questions and could make a significant contribution to social policy.[2]

Three outstanding changes took place in the way in which qualified social workers in Australia were organised professionally: the establishment of a national general association with branches in each state, the closing of the association to unqualified people, and the absorption of the well-established almoners' association by the general national body, a development similar to that in America, although, of course, on a very much smaller scale.

---

2    F.E. Waldron, 'The Association of Social Workers', *Case Conference*, Vol. 5, No. 7, January 1959, pp. 183–6.

# A National Comprehensive Professional Association

In 1945, 1946, and 1947, general associations of qualified social workers were formed in Queensland, Western Australia, and Tasmania, matching the earlier development of general associations in the three states with training bodies. As the war came to a close, a national general association to parallel the almoners' association began to be discussed seriously, not only to unite professional social workers throughout the country, but also because of the growth of national and international social welfare programmes. On the initiative of Norma Parker who urged speed in establishing a national body that might carry some weight in Australian government circles, a constitution was drawn up, and was adopted after interstate conferences in Sydney in June, and in Melbourne in September 1946.

The aims of the Australian Association of Social Workers were those of a fully developed national professional association, but whether it could be an effective body depended upon its mode of organisation, the nature of its executive officers, its financial resources, the characteristics of its general membership, and the extent to which qualified social workers were distracted by other professional loyalties.

The association's constitution was far from settled during these post-war years. At first it was experimental, then came the need to conform to the Commonwealth Arbitration Court's requirements, and later the need to provide for special groups within the association; but the broad structure and machinery remained largely unaltered. The governing body was a federal council consisting of seven office-bearers and two delegates from each branch. Apart from questions on membership, the division of responsibility between it and the state branches was left vague. Throughout the whole period, the federal council met only at half-yearly intervals, and it became customary for the federal executive officers to refer most matters by correspondence to state branches; further, when the council did meet, it frequently wished to have its decisions confirmed by the state branches. This meant federal action was usually slow and much of each branch's time was absorbed by federal business. By the end of the period no solution had been reached in the problem of making federal council decisions more rapid and confident, while retaining the active interest and approval of the general membership.

The federal council was in Sydney from 1947 to 1953, in Melbourne from 1954 to 1958, and again in Sydney from 1959, and these two central states had provided its chief officers.

The organisation of the Australian Association of Social Workers at branch level during these post-war years varied widely, because of differences in the size of branches, and also because of a general tendency towards unstable organisational forms. The larger the branch, the more the association's affairs were carried on through committees, the most important being an executive committee, or the committee of management as it came to be called. In both the New South Wales and the Victorian branches, a great number of sub-groups existed for varying periods and under a variety of names and terms of reference. Periodic attempts to regularise the relations between these groups and the executive group failed. Even when rules were drawn up for the purpose, they appear to have been either unknown by later conveners of the sub-groups and executive officers, or ignored by them. In general, there was recurring uncertainty about the roles of the executive and other sub-groups in relation to each other and to the general membership. Right at the end of the period, both the Victorian and New South Wales branches began to make a determined effort to rectify this.

Another administrative problem, this time encountered in all states, concerned the role of branch representatives on outside organisations such as the Council of Social Service, the National Council of Women, the Good Neighbour Council. Branches did not as yet have an established policy on the subject, although in the late 1950s, the two largest branches were giving some thought to it.

Problems of organisation naturally were more complex in the larger branches, but throughout the whole association they were rarely handled successfully. A certain degree of flexibility was desirable, but this was not a conscious policy, and in any case it could well have been argued that an organisation so liable to changes of membership needed stable organisational forms and adequate records. Older members were often aware that certain problems of organisation kept recurring, and many members were dissatisfied with ineffectual discussions on association machinery. Because records were defective, non-existent, or inaccessible, and of a lack of awareness of the past among the many newcomers, there was little building from an established position.

An explanation of the administrative weakness of the association was, in part, that most members and executive officers had no particular interest in broad policy and administrative issues because they were women and also because they were mainly caseworkers. If many of the members had a sense of only short-term commitment to the work, this too would lead to a concentration on day-to-day details.

A strong factor in the association's effectiveness was the nature of its executive officers at both a federal and branch level. Often presidents and secretaries were inexperienced, and sometimes they had little knowledge of the branch's affairs. Throughout the whole period, the association relied upon changing, honorary, spare-time officers. The load borne by the officers, particularly the secretaries in the larger branches, became overwhelmingly heavy in the 1950s. Either the branch's work or the officer's own professional work was, therefore, likely to suffer. As they were unpaid as well as overworked, it was difficult to call the officers to account if they were inefficient, and as an experiment in 1956, the Victorian branch employed, part-time, a married woman member as its secretary.

In the early 1960s all the federal executive officers were still honorary, yet as early as 1947, the federal president had said the burden of the association's work at a federal level was becoming intolerable.[3] In 1949, part-time clerical assistance was employed; three years later the federal executive officers argued strongly for the appointment of a permanent full-time executive secretary, and the outcome was a money-raising scheme by a committee in the New South Wales branch. After four years of toil this yielded the equivalent of only a year's salary for a well-qualified, full-time, executive secretary.

Not only did the association now need salaried services, but it also needed, at least in the largest states, premises of its own – to provide a tangible witness to the existence and serious intention of the association, to give a sense of continuity and permanence to the social

---

3    Presidential Address by Miss Norma Parker, 15 August 1947.

workers themselves, and, not least important, to provide a permanent home for the association's records. In 1960 the New South Wales branch began to think seriously about acquiring premises of its own.

By the end of these post-war years, it was apparent that the only realistic long-term solution to the association's inefficiency was considerably increased membership fees,[4] yet there was still hesitation to take this step for fear that it might discourage membership of the association. The initiative lay with the association's members since they were its only source of income.

The movement of the New South Wales general association in 1945 towards an association exclusively for qualified social workers was carried to its conclusion by the founders of the Australian Association of Social Workers. After June 1947, only qualified social workers were to be admitted to membership. When the constitution was recast to meet the Arbitration Court's requirements, it was specified that membership was open to professionally employed social workers holding a qualification from a school of social work approved by the federal council. Usually it was considered desirable to have as associate members qualified social workers not professionally employed, but there continued to be doubt over their legal position. Occasionally in the smaller branches in particular, the admission of unqualified people with limited rights was suggested, but normally there was strong opposition to this.

For membership qualifications, the federal council automatically accepted those of the Australian schools of social work. British and other overseas qualifications sometimes presented a problem, however, since some were academic rather than professional in character, and others were only specialised in scope. In the mid-1950s, the federal council sought the guidance of the Australian schools in setting admission standards, and towards the end of the period, the trend was in the direction of raising them.

---

4    By 1960 the subscription in the larger branches was £5 a year, and rather less in the smaller ones. Just before the federal council was formed in 1946 subscriptions were: New South Wales and Victoria, £1 1s; South Australia 10s 6d; Queensland 5s. At first 5s of each branch's membership fee was paid to the federal council, in 1949 this became 10s, and in 1952 was raised to £1 10s.

In 1949, the association had roughly 300 members, In 1958, the number was 360, three-quarters of whom were in New South Wales and Victoria (43 and 32 per cent respectively), and the branches in Queensland, Western Australia, and Tasmania were very small (each 4 or 5 per cent). The future distribution according to branches was likely to be altered by the foundation of new schools of social work, increased student numbers in Victoria, and the possible establishment of new branches at Canberra and Newcastle where small groups of qualified social workers began to meet during the 1950s.

Although the actual proportion fluctuated according to the attention given to fostering membership, the great majority of qualified social workers in employment in the various states were members. The low proportion of professionally experienced people, and the wide variation in the degree of professional commitment found amongst social workers in employment was likely, therefore, also to be found in the association's membership.

Because there were so few qualified men social workers, the association's membership remained largely of women, and for the most part its officers were women. This made it easy for outside bodies to dismiss the association as 'just another women's organisation', especially when in four states its branches were affiliated with the National Council of Women.

The extent to which the qualified social workers were distracted by other professional loyalties from participating in the general association depended largely upon the activity of the Australian Association of Almoners (in 1949, 'hospital' was dropped from its title). Its branches in New South Wales and Victoria were roughly a third the size of the local branches of the general association and they met with about the same frequency. The almoner group in South Australia was proportionately rather larger, but it met less often. In addition, a tiny branch in Western Australia survived briefly in the late 1940s. In the period 1947–57, the central council of the almoners' association met between four and eight times a year. It was in Adelaide 1946–48, Melbourne 1948–52, and Sydney 1952–59.

During these years, the two associations cooperated quite frequently at federal and state levels. Many almoners belonged to both, and leadership of the general association was often in the hands of an almoner. Its first three federal presidents were qualified as medical social workers. The climate in the post-war years was favourable to an even closer relationship between the general and almoner groups. The post-war emphasis on a generic professional education stressed the common core of all social work. Further, the absorption of training for medical social work by the university schools and the emergence of other specialist interests within the broad professional discipline encouraged social workers to think in terms of a common association which would cater for specialist interests inside it.

Eventually, in May 1958, after over a decade of intermittent discussion, the Australian Association of Social Workers made provision for special groups, at a branch level, of members with distinctive professional interests. The arrangements were such that specialist interests could have wide scope within the association, although they were under the general surveillance of the branch's committee of management. By the end of 1958 a Medical Social Work Group had been formed in both New South Wales and Victoria, each group having identical objects and almost identical terms of membership. The disbanding of the Australian Association of Almoners in March 1959 marked the end of a phase in the development of professional social work in Australia. The substitution of 'medical social work' for 'almoner' signified a wider professional identification, and a general levelling up in the standards of social workers in other than medical settings.

The need to accommodate special groups within the Australian Association of Social Workers presented it with yet another organisational problem. For the association to be efficient in its purposes, it now, more than ever, needed greater continuity of membership and executive officers, better records, more stable functions, paid staff, and proper accommodation.

## Protecting Social Workers' Interests

The poor employment conditions experienced by most of the qualified social workers since the war was partly a commentary on their ineffective attempts to improve them. What they did manage, however, perhaps partly to the detriment of short-term gains in employment conditions, was to keep clear of various industrial groups who might break up their unity or lower their prestige. One solid post-war achievement was registration with the Commonwealth Arbitration Court (from 1956, the Conciliation and Arbitration Commission), which provided some safeguard to their corporate existence; but by 1964 the second step of seeking an award had not been taken, even though much of the discussion before registration had concentrated upon this.

The experience of three different groups of qualified social workers in the immediate post-war years brought the question of registration with the Arbitration Court to the notice of the Australian Association of Social Workers. First, in South Australia, almoners were handicapped in their negotiations with the state Public Service Board because there were no recognised employment conditions for social workers. Next, a group in the Commonwealth public service were required to join a union to obtain full salary rights even though there was none with the appropriate interests and status; and then the almoners in New South Wales were threatened by absorption into the inappropriate Homes and Hospitals Employees' Union. The matter was brought to a head in 1949 by the claim to industrial authorities that the Federation of Scientific and Technical Workers could cover social workers in industrial matters.

To help carry a unanimous federal council decision to take the first steps towards registration, the case was put to the general membership in a detailed memorandum. It was argued that the professional status and skills of social workers could only be protected by suitably defined employment conditions. The individual discussion of the past on these questions had proved ineffectual. Some social workers interested in new developments had taken posts which were underpaid, but it was doubtful whether they served the interests of social workers or their clients if they continued to accept this. Unless recruitment figures could be increased by improved status, salaries, and working conditions, 'a period of frustration and stagnation [appeared] inevitable for professional social work in Australia'.

To counter doubts about the propriety of a professional group registering as a trade union, the memorandum pointed out that, unlike medicine and law, but like teaching and nursing, the social work profession did not consist primarily of self-employed persons; further, when doctors were in government employment, they had sought industrial protection. In Australia, trade unionism was widely accepted as desirable for employed persons, and in general agencies employing social workers would welcome regulated conditions of employment.

Registration would prevent the inclusion of social workers in unions foreign to their interests, but would not prevent them joining another union if they so wished. If some but not all of the association's members registered as a union, this was likely to cause bitterness and dissension in the profession, since only a small group would be spending their efforts and money for the benefit of the whole.[5]

The memorandum's arguments were convincing, and in September 1950 the general membership of the association very firmly endorsed the federal council's decision to seek registration. After a series of delays, in 1955 the association became registered with the Commonwealth Arbitration Court – as an organisation of persons 'usually employed for hire or reward in or in connection with the industry of professional social work'.

The association did not press on to seek a federal award for a number of reasons. It was deterred by the possible cost, the difficulty of explaining much of its work because of its intangible nature, the fear that an award might prevent some voluntary agencies from employing qualified staff, the possibility that state groups might seek state awards, and finally, general uncertainty about industrial matters. The association could have received assistance on the last point if it had accepted an invitation to affiliate with the Council of White Collar Associations (later the Australian Council of Salaried and Professional Associations), but it decided to remain independent.

Although the Australian association did not seek an award, from its beginning it took some responsibility for members' employment conditions. In the immediate post-war years, an increasing number of agencies, particularly government ones, sought from it information about salaries and working conditions, and the need for an authoritative statement such as the British Simey Report was felt. In 1949, a federal committee of the association sent to each branch a statement on possible employment conditions, and then began a study of actual

---

5    Executive Officers, Australian Association of Social Workers, Memorandum on the Registration of the Australian Association of Social Workers as a Trade Union, 15 May 1950.

conditions in New South Wales. It did not report until 1952, and the study was not extended as originally planned; but the association did begin an inquiry through another New South Wales committee into the employment of men social workers. This found that the main male employment opportunities were within government agencies which could pay a suitable salary, and recommended that more cadetships be offered, and that administrative posts be opened to qualified men. The findings of both this and the earlier general New South Wales study were fruitless.

In the later 1950s, there was increased interest in employment conditions in the two largest branches of the association. In 1955, a Personnel Practices Committee was established in New South Wales to keep itself informed on social workers' employment conditions, but by 1957 it was without a convener. In 1956, a Status and Salaries Committee was set up in Victoria to achieve some coordination between the various groups of association members who were negotiating about salaries, since 'what [happened] in one group [had] a vital effect on others'. It was slow to become effective, however. It was in fact the success in 1958 of a sub-group working through the professional division of the Victorian Public Service Association which made Commonwealth government and voluntary agencies re-examine their salary levels.

Medical social workers' salaries continued to be linked with those of inappropriate hospital groups; but there was a new departure in 1959, when the New South Wales branch of the Australian Association of Social Workers negotiated with the Hospitals Commission on behalf of the medical social workers. It argued, with some success, that their salaries should be related to those of social workers in other fields and not to those of other hospital groups. The branch declared its policy was now to work for equitable salaries for all social workers, and it hoped employers would accept this. Yet to do this effectively, in one branch or throughout the association, up-to-date knowledge of the employment conditions, and ways of altering them, was needed, and it was doubtful whether changing honorary spare time services could meet this need. Also, while the association remained relatively inactive industrially, social workers in government employment were induced to join public service bodies, which reduced the association's possible area of industrial cover.

Periodically during these years, the subject of the use by unqualified people of the term 'social worker' was discussed, but as yet the qualified social workers could claim no monopoly on the title. Moreover, some of them were not comfortable with it, because of its 'charity' overtones and non-professional sound. Until the title 'social worker' was used exclusively and normally for a qualified person performing social work, the public image of the social worker was likely to be very blurred, or a false one as far as qualified social workers were concerned.

The question of a written code of ethics for Australian social workers was raised in 1954 when a Queensland Red Cross official demanded access to social workers' case records. Subsequently the federal council of the social workers' association asked branches to consider the subject. Two important points arose in the resulting discussion: the level of generality of a code, and its degree of relevance for actual practice. In August 1957 the association agreed to use, although without any interpreting or enforcing machinery, an experimental code for a set period.

This code reflected the philosophy and general principles of professional social work. It spoke of the worth of every individual and men's mutual responsibilities to each other, the need to respect clients' confidences and their right to make their own decisions, the need to balance individual and community interests when these conflict, a responsibility to have self-understanding and to understand others, a duty individually and collectively to increase professional competence and use it for the community's good, an obligation to act with professional and moral integrity and to enhance the standards and prestige of the profession.[6]

## Social Action

Turning from the negotiations on salary and employment conditions to the post-war efforts of qualified social workers to improve the community social welfare, it is apparent that, compared with the war years, there was some waning of interest. Many and diverse factors at different times held their collective social action in check

6    Australian Association of Social Workers, Interim Code of Ethics, August 1957.

– the continued concentration on casework in their training and practice, the inexperience and employment instability of many of them, their lack of specialised knowledge in many areas of social policy, fear of political involvement, identification with employing agencies rather than with the professional group, fear of losing cooperation in social welfare and professional circles, lack of a tradition for social policymakers to use specialist opinion – especially when it came from women – the ability of some of them to change their own agencies' policies from within, and so on.

Frequently action taken by the qualified social workers was not publicised, which meant that they appeared far more timid and complacent about social provision than in fact they were. Nevertheless, the following challenge issued to American social workers in the 1930s could well have been issued to Australian social workers in the 1950s.

> Do social workers believe that any other profession is better able to speak authoritatively of need for, and method of, achieving maintenance of normal family life, protection of children, prevention of delinquency, extension of public social services including public health and medical care, creation of social group activities, or improvement of housing conditions? To the extent that the solution of these problems is within the competence of any profession, it is certainly within that of social work.[7]

The variety of their community interests is illustrated by a glance at the activities of the New South Wales branch of the general association. The interests of its members, arranged roughly in the chronological order in which the branch became involved in them, were as follows: the extension of medical benefits to sick, age and invalid pensioners in their homes, women's employment problems, various issues connected with migrants' welfare, marriage guidance, fostering interagency cooperation, compiling a resource file on leisure-time activities, publishing a newsletter for the local Council of Social Service, radio talks on social welfare topics, the needs of country people, the care of the aged, recreation for special groups, the use of the central index, the non-payment of pensions to patients in mental hospitals, the welfare of unmarried mothers and their babies, the welfare of pensioners' children, support of the local Council of Social Service, 'The Call to the Nation', the employment of the physically handicapped, the inclusion

---

7    Esther L. Brown, *Social Work as a Profession*, p. 186.

of family casework services in a list of parent education facilities published by the Minister for Education, contributions to the Lord Mayor's Flood Victims Appeal Fund, supporting the Australian Social Welfare Council financially, preventing sensational newspaper articles on social work cases, cooperation with the Department of Education, the Australian Rheumatic Council, and the New South Wales University of Technology in various surveys, promoting and supporting the New South Wales Association for Mental Health, housing needs and the Commonwealth–States Housing Agreement, anomalies in legislation relating to deserted *de facto* wives, the relationship between state and federal children's allowances, support of the Psychiatric Rehabilitation Association, the housing position of marginal families, the New South Wales Child Welfare Act, evidence to a committee preparing legislation on the care of the intellectually handicapped, and letters to the press about pension anomalies and hospital benefit payments.

Similar lists, though rather shorter in the smaller states, could be given for each of the branches of the general association and for each of the three branches of the almoners' association; but it must be remembered that frequently these interests were not spread throughout the whole group and often were shared by outside groups, that the amount of time spent on each, and the degree of effectiveness of any action taken, varied greatly, and also that this list covers about 15 years of endeavour in the largest of the groups.

## Educational Opportunities

The post-war improvement in education for social work was not confined to basic training. An increasing number of educational opportunities became available to the qualified social workers, especially in New South Wales and Victoria, and if they were medical social workers. These opportunities were provided by the training schools, some employing agencies, other social welfare organisations, overseas experience, and by their professional association.

The training schools helped many practitioners to increase their skill and knowledge by their greater concentration on standards of student supervision. In addition, both the Sydney and Melbourne schools provided occasional refresher courses. In the mid-1950s, there was a significant new development in Sydney when an autonomous

Committee for Post-Graduate Study, consisting of people from the school and the professional association, was established. In the following years, it sponsored various lectures and discussion courses, and in 1961 brought out a new publication, *The Australian Journal of Social Issues.*

Another aspect of this post-war period was a growth of staff development programmes within agencies employing qualified social workers. Two national agencies, the Commonwealth Department of Social Services and the Australian Red Cross Society, paid particular attention to this. Each had its library, its staff meetings, and its national staff conferences. Moreover, the social work section of the department regularly sent to agencies, associations, and social workers throughout the country, selected journal articles, and general and specific bibliographies of material in its library. By the end of the period it was customary in most agencies to set aside working time for professional staff development.

The growing number of coordinating bodies in particular fields of social welfare often provided the qualified social workers with opportunities to learn. To cite just one instance: by 1958 the Australian Advisory Council for the Physically Handicapped had held nine conferences. In addition, addresses, discussion, study, and occasional research, on a wide variety of social welfare topics, were undertaken by the various councils of social service. By now the journal of the New South Wales council was well established, although a similar publication in South Australia lapsed after a trial period. In the 1950s, both the Victorian and New South Wales councils held state social welfare conferences; but there was no national social welfare conference until 1960 because of the delay in establishing a general national body.

This delay also meant that for the greater part of the period, Australia had no official representation at the International Conference of Social Work. The Australian Association of Social Workers was represented, sometimes only after considerable effort, at each of the Conference's post-war meetings — at the preliminary discussions at Brussels and the Hague, and at the Fourth Conference in Atlantic City, in 1948; and at the subsequent biennial meetings held in Paris, Madras, Toronto, Munich, Tokyo, Rome, and Rio de Janiero. Some of the association's members became acutely aware of Australia's international social welfare obligations, especially to the under-developed countries. Directly and indirectly, many qualified social workers also benefited from other conferences held overseas during the period.

Qualified social workers often went abroad after the war. The federal president of the general association commented in 1950 on the migration overseas, especially of more senior people, in search of professional education and experience.[8] In the early 1950s, it was estimated that about 40 Australian social workers were away – seven in the United States, one in Canada, and most of the others in Britain.[9] This pattern was to be expected while entry into the country, money problems, and employment, were far easier in Britain than in North America, and, in addition, of course, there was a general inclination for Australians to visit Britain. Both the general and almoner associations concerned themselves with overseas opportunities for their members, and especially notable was the establishment by the general association in 1956 of machinery to give professional endorsement to social workers who sought to work and study in North America.

The post-war educational opportunities most generally available to the qualified social workers were those provided by their own professional organisation – through meetings, seminars, study groups, conferences, and journal. The general membership in each branch of the general association and of the almoners' association met regularly. Association business absorbed some of their time, but the greater part of it was usually spent in listening to and discussing addresses by members of their work and experience, or by non-members, such as visiting social workers, doctors, psychologists, nurses, government officials, and university teachers.

Occasionally, usually when an overseas social worker was visiting, branches of the general association held refresher courses and seminars. To help qualified social workers from interstate or abroad, orientation programmes were also provided by some of the social work groups.

8    Norma Parker, Report to Federal Council, 9 December 1950.
9    T.H. Kewley, 'Social Work and Training in Australia', *Social Welfare*, January 1952.

To give close attention to a subject, to provide opportunities for many members to participate, and to allow for specialised interests, various study groups were formed in the branches, especially the largest branches, of the general association. With encouragement from the federal council, most of the branches tried, usually through study groups, to prepare for the association's national conferences. All branches in 1954 reported difficulty, however, in arousing members' interest in pre-conference study groups, and by 1957 there was little preparation for the association's national conference, except in New South Wales.

The founders of the Australian Association of Social Workers agreed that one of its first activities was to hold a conference. From 1947 to 1957 at two-yearly intervals at Sydney, Melbourne, and Adelaide in rotation, the association held national conferences. At times, because as yet there was no national body to run a social welfare conference, pressure was placed upon the association to make its own conference much broader in scope. Occasionally it did invite outside speakers and opened some of the sessions to the public, but the conferences were kept mainly for the professional development of qualified social workers. Members of the fourth conference decided that the national conferences of social work should widen the horizons of the association and of individual social workers, help develop a common body of knowledge and purpose for Australian social work, and provide educational and personal stimulation.[10]

The Australian Association of Social Workers did not hold a conference between 1957 and 1961 so that its members could give their maximum support to the first National Conference of Social Welfare. This conference was in no way a substitute for the association's conferences, but once it was established, the association could concentrate wholeheartedly on its members' professional development in its own biennial conferences.

The association's national conferences had an important public witness aspect. The publicity they received in the press, and amongst employers, contributed to the general recognition of qualified social workers as a distinct national occupational group with professional

---

10    Australian Association of Social Workers, *Proceedings of the Fourth Australian Conference of Social Work*, Sydney, October 1953.

aspirations. But with the growth in the number of conferences of social welfare interest it was important to think clearly about the function of each, to avoid too much overlapping and to make each a worthwhile occasion.

The general, though slow, improvement in the amount of social science and social work literature in Australia in these years did help to spread knowledge gained by local experience but little of what was produced was printed in a permanent form. The first move towards a national professional social work journal was made when, in September 1945, the New South Wales Social Workers' Association began publishing a monthly *Social Workers' Digest*. When the Australian association was formed it was suggested that it should take over the publication, but though a national journal was considered desirable, the question was postponed and soon afterwards the *Digest* lapsed.

The next move was in Melbourne when the Public Relations Committee of the Victorian branch of the general association began a slim two-monthly publication called *Forum*. Early in 1949 it became a quarterly, and in mid-1949 a joint publication with the Victorian branch of the almoners' association. In 1950, on the suggestion of its Victorian branch, the Australian Association of Social Workers decided to develop *Forum* into a national journal concerned with professional social work. The Australian Association of Almoners, who had themselves been showing interest in a journal, agreed to join in the venture, but the main responsibility rested with the general association.

At first the new *Forum* had financial problems, but these were solved in 1955, when the membership fee of the general association was increased to include a subscription to the journal. Problems of control and responsibility were settled the previous year by a federal council decision that the committee which published *Forum* should be one of its standing committees even though its members were drawn from and nominated by one branch. At the same time, issues settled down to two a year, mainly because of cost and the dearth of contributors.

For a variety of reasons, very few of the members of the association made contributions to the journal during the 1950s, and many of these had to be solicited, or were a record of papers given on other occasions. Editors, therefore, could not be very selective and description rather than analysis predominated. *Forum* did, however, slowly improve both in form and content, and in 1959, a change of name to *The Australian Journal of Social Work* was considered justified. It was now intended to make the journal a truly national professional publication. Some four years later, its format was again improved and it promised to become a quarterly.

There were, then, expanding educational opportunities for social workers during this period, and many of them were provided through the professional association; but whether individual social workers made full use of the opportunities depended on where they lived, where and how long they worked, their financial resources, and their sense of professional commitment.

The ideal to which the qualified social workers in Australia appeared to be moving was an Australia-wide association containing all qualified social workers, an association which catered fully for both general and specialist needs; one which provided a wide range of educational opportunities, alone and in conjunction with other bodies; an association which was effective in its community activities, both in its independent action and in combination with other groups; and one which protected the interests of its members through raising their status and salaries, through defining their areas of professional competence, and through sponsoring a common ethical code.

# CHAPTER 11
# The Social Work Profession

Returning to the characteristics listed in the introduction as describing the established professions, to what extent in the early 1960s were these demonstrated by the occupational group which has been the subject of this study?

1. Members of the profession and the rest of the community recognise that it is a distinct occupational group with certain rights and duties.

Most qualified social workers in Australia now considered that they belonged to a distinct occupational group. They possessed a university qualification, similar in broad outline from place to place and over time. The only high-level specialised training which had existed, in medical social work, was now fully integrated with the general social work course. The majority of social workers belonged to a common professional association which had recently absorbed the specialist almoner association. Almoners, the most united group among qualified social workers, were now identifying themselves firmly with the whole group. Apart from organisational changes in their training and their professional association, a sign of their identification with all qualified social workers was their use of the term 'social worker' rather than 'almoner' or even 'medical social worker'.

In the community there were a growing number of people in social welfare, university, and other professional circles, who were aware of social workers as a distinct occupational group with at least some corporate solidarity. This awareness was, however, much stronger in the larger states. The extent to which social workers' clients realised they were using the services of a distinct and responsible occupation group varied greatly.

Although there was some measure of recognition, among members themselves and in important sections of the community, that this was a distinct occupational group with collective responsibilities, a number of factors were holding back a greater degree of recognition. Members worked in a wide variety of agencies and often not under the title of 'social worker', or with the same-named qualification. Sometimes to gain acceptance in the early stages and to meet some genuine need, they assumed work other than that for which they had been trained. Their relationships, particularly with people from other professions, were frequently determined as much by their personal characteristics, their sex, age, and personality, as by their professional competence. Teamwork between the various professions tended to be haphazard because of changing personnel, the relative newness of some of the professions, and very different ideas about the relative roles of each. A clear demonstration of competence as a profession was likely to be reduced when social workers did not stay in one position for any length of time, when they were inexperienced, and when they carried large case loads.

There was no legal bar to anyone attempting to practise social work. Because of the general shortage of qualified social workers, and the continued reliance by numerous agencies, especially in the smaller states, on unqualified or semi-qualified labour, there were still many outside the group claiming to practise social work. Yet the attitudes, skills, and knowledge of these people were different from those of the qualified social workers. Where there were substantial numbers of qualified social workers, their work tended to be called 'social work', and the work of others was called 'welfare work' or some other name.

By and large, Australian communities were not alive to their social problems or thought they could be bought off, and so did not connect any professional group with them. The qualified social workers did not publicise their work to any great extent; for many of them this smacked of self-advertisement. The limited effectiveness of their professional association also held back community recognition of them as a distinct occupational group with collective responsibilities.

But the group could be widely recognised throughout the community without necessarily having the social standing accorded to the established professions. Many of their predecessors enjoyed a high social status, partly because they worked voluntarily, but perhaps more important because they already belonged to the higher socioeconomic groups. The grounds on which the new occupational group could expect social recognition were that its work was useful, responsible, and difficult, and it required a preparation comparable with that of the established professions. The recently improved salaries were a sign that such arguments were beginning to carry weight with employers and that future status would be linked with such factors.

2. A general common purpose, for example healing the sick, guides the members' work, and this is in reasonable accord with the goals of the wider community.

Through their professional education and organisation, qualified social workers had learned to pursue a common purpose. Briefly stated, it was to help individuals, groups, and communities, to make the most constructive use of themselves and their environment in the solution of their social and personal problems. This was a humanitarian purpose, strongly based on a democratic philosophy.

This aim was not usually in conflict with the goal of economic efficiency advocated by many in this increasingly industrialised society. Repeatedly it was stressed that social work was good business. Social and personal problems were impediments to the nation's economic productivity. Moreover, so much in terms of money, time, and effort, was spent on social services in the modern society that any improvement in their more effective application was likely to be an economic saving. The helping of individuals and groups to help themselves when possible was well in accord with the business community's formal emphasis on individual independence. Generally, in Australian communities the extent to which human values were placed above others varied, but social work's aims were at least in reasonable accord with the goals of a society which increasingly recognised social rights.

3. There are shared intellectual techniques which are acquired only after prolonged training at a tertiary educational level, and these require originality and judgement, not routine application. The development of technique is a recognised responsibility of the group.

From their education at a tertiary level, qualified social workers had learned to apply certain techniques in helping with social and personal problems. They had learned how to practise social casework, social group work, and community organisation. These techniques required thought and judgement. Any rule-of-thumb application of them was likely to have disastrous consequences, and this was generally recognised. For many social workers, lack of professional experience was limiting the quality of their practice.

There was some awareness of a responsibility to maintain and develop the techniques of social casework, but there was not very much systematic study of technique under Australian conditions. Very much less time was spent on developing and maintaining social group work and community organisation as techniques for achieving the purpose of social work.

> 4. The fundamental knowledge, or theory, at the basis of the group's practice is capable of being set forth systematically, is scientifically based, and is at a level of difficulty requiring tertiary education. The group recognise a responsibility to define, develop and systematise their theory and are free to do so. This is a direct responsibility with regard to their own clinical or practitioner experience. For the part of their theory borrowed and adapted from other groups, it is the indirect responsibility to support the work of those groups.

The theory of social casework was by now systematically set down, but again this did not apply so much to group work and community organisation. There was no doubt that students needed to be at a tertiary level to grasp existing theory. As with the application of the technique, the maintenance and development of social casework was much more evident than with the other two methods, but still there was little examination of casework theory in the light of Australian conditions.

With regard to that part of social work knowledge borrowed and adapted from other disciplines, social workers drew heavily from psychology and the social sciences, and although the subjects themselves may have been systematic, those parts relevant to social work practice in many instances still needed to be systematised. Moreover, the social sciences in Australia, especially sociology, were under-developed;

in some states less than in others. Social workers looked favourably upon any extensions of these disciplines, but usually did not actively press for their extension.

5.  The group conform to certain standards of behaviour, because their practice involves them in private affairs, and they are experts advising non-experts.

Persons practising social work knew about details of a private and sometimes intimate nature. Further, they possessed and used information not known by their clients. Through their education and professional association there was some agreement on what was proper professional behaviour. How much their actual behaviour conformed to this is difficult to tell. An ethical code was being made explicit, but questions of its implementation still had to be answered.

6.  In their dealings with their clients, service to the clients and the community rather than gain to the practitioner or the group is stressed in the group's ethical code.

Perhaps no group of people stressed more, both in theory and practice, that service to their clients and the community was their intention. The fact that social workers did not rely upon their clients' fees for their livelihood released them from a self-regarding pressure found in other professions.

7.  The group accept collective responsibility to use their knowledge for the benefit of the community, over and above services to individual clients.

Individually, many social workers felt a responsibility to use knowledge gained from professional practice to benefit the community; indeed, many would have seen this as an integral part of their professional practice. Collectively, mainly through their professional association, they assumed similar responsibilities. Social action was still part of the Australian social work tradition, even though it had undergone fluctuating fortunes. Singly and together, social workers were consulted by a variety of individuals and community bodies about social problems and ways of combating them. The extent of consultation was limited, however, by such restricting influences as ignorance of the collective existence of qualified social workers, parochialism, and suspicion of expertise in social welfare circles, the relatively small numbers of qualified social workers, and the disproportionate number of unmarried women, and inexperienced members in their ranks.

On each of these features, then, Australian professional social workers scored at least to some degree. Whether their existing composite score was sufficient to warrant calling them a profession depended on personal choice, attitude, and knowledge of other professions. Whatever the judgement on this, there was still plenty of room for further development of professional social work in Australia.

# CHAPTER 12
## Contemporary Issues

The previous chapters have given an historical analysis of the development of professional social work in Australia. They were written in an attempt to give present-day social workers an account of the tradition to which they are heirs, and to make known to others an historical story of considerable significance for human welfare. This final chapter discusses what appear to be the main contemporary issues facing the Australian social work profession.[1] Not all of these are 'issues' in the sense that they are matters of widespread lively concern, but they are all suggested by the analysis of the development of the profession and by observation of the current scene. The profession can, at least partly, mould its future according to its own values if it consciously weighs the advantages and disadvantages of the various courses lying ahead.

Briefly, the issues which demand discussion are these: Will men as well as women engage in the profession? Is the basic professional education to be raised to a graduate level and what of postgraduate education? Is social casework to remain the dominant social work method? Are social work services to remain available to only a small section of the community ? Does social work need better modes of organisation? Finally, should the profession have far greater numbers? Clearly these are interrelated questions, but for clarity they will be discussed singly.

---

1    It is written in mid-1964. Some of its discussion has already appeared in R.J. Lawrence, 'The Future Role and Development of Social Work in Australia', *Australian Journal of Social Work*, Vol. XV, No. 2, December 1962, pp. 1–7.

# A Mixed Profession?

In recent years, mainly on the grounds of equality of opportunity and waste of intellectual talent, arguments have been put forward to open up to women all areas of university education and the established professions. The story of this book is an oddity in that it tells of the establishment of a new profession largely by women, and much of its character has stemmed from this fact. That the social work profession has developed as far as it has in a not very encouraging male environment has been due to the general validity of its arguments for professionalism in social work, to the personal ability of a small group of its leaders, and to the standing of the few men associated with, though not part of, the profession. It no longer has to fight for survival, but it does face difficulties if it wishes to make a full contribution in the fields in which it claims to have special competence. Not the least of its problems is the continuing preponderance of women.

The advantages claimed for men qualified social workers over women are many. They have a greater sense of professional commitment in the early stages of their career. They provide essential employment stability in social agencies. They stay in the profession longer. They are not hampered by community attitudes to professional women. They rely less completely upon their work for social and personal satisfactions because they have a family and home of their own. They are more likely to gain recognition of qualified social work in public service circles. They are less likely to accept inadequate employment conditions. They are keener to insist upon independent and equal status with the established professions. They can more easily bridge the gap between government and non-government agencies. They take a broader view of individual problems. They are generally more aware of the father's part in family life. And so on. Although some of these claims may be challenged, either in terms of their accuracy or their importance, together they contribute a powerful case for a great increase in the number and proportion of men social workers in the profession.

This has been the trend in the social work profession in the United States and it can be regarded as a long-term trend in Australia. But how long-term? There is nothing automatic about it. Attitudes and actions inside and outside the profession will determine the pace and the strength of the trend.

There is little apparent hostility on the part of the present-day women members of the profession to men as their colleagues; in fact, many state this as a need, but generally they have not acted as if it were a vital problem. It is not easy for women to recruit men for a social work career. They can, however, influence the attitude of employers and others to men social workers and ensure that they do not promote a professional image related to their own sex. Those men already in the profession have a special responsibility in recruitment activities. As will be discussed later, social work as a possible career has usually not been represented, or at least not strongly represented, when most young men are choosing a career. At present many go into fields such as teaching, the church, medicine, and psychology, who are really more interested in social work than in these other professions.

At present men social workers remain very unevenly spread in fields of social work. There may be some good reasons for a preponderance of one sex over the other in particular situations, but no field may be seen as 'belonging' to one or other sex – either male adult correctional work to male social workers or medical social work to female social workers. There are many reasons why the male qualified social workers in the adult correctional field in New South Wales are not active members of the professional association, and why the probation field, and at least temporarily the parole field, has only tenuous links with professional social work. One appears to be that they regard the existing profession and its association as a women's organisation which is not very interested in militant industrial action or in new 'male' fields of work.

Any division of the profession on sex lines, whether in fields of employment or in thinking about professional matters, is likely to interfere with the effective performance of social work's tasks. This does not mean that an awareness of sex roles is unimportant in assessing realistically the position of a professional worker, but it is professional competence not sex which should count. Neither sex has a monopoly on the personal qualities considered desirable for social work practice.

Though men students may be a better long-term investment for the profession than women, it would be undesirable to have an undue emphasis on male recruitment. This would encourage sex antagonism in the profession, and would lead to a great waste of talent in work in which able women have already gained widespread acceptance.

All that is being argued here is the need for a better sex balance in the profession. What the optimum should be is a complex question, at least partly influenced by general cultural changes in the community, but it is evident that at present there are not enough men.

## Graduate Education?

The social work education scene in Australia leaves no room for complacency. Until each of the courses has achieved, and is worthy of, degree status, and is offering postgraduate opportunities, the profession's basic educational facilities leave it vulnerable.

Why is the degree label so important? Is it not sufficient to have, as at present, the diploma courses of the same duration as an Arts degree and the same academic entry requirement of matriculation? And anyway, do not a substantial proportion of the social work students do an Arts degree as well as the professional diploma and are therefore university graduates? There are good reasons – inside the universities, in the profession, and in the general community – for the basic professional education of social workers to be at a degree level and to be labelled as such.

A completely new university climate in the 1960s was brought about by the post-war population bulge hitting tertiary education, by concern over the relatively small proportion of the national income devoted to institutions of higher learning, and a new Commonwealth government general interest in tertiary education. As never before, the role of the university and the technical college is being examined. One obvious way of relieving pressure on the universities is to off-load sub-graduate courses onto technical institutions.[2] This is sensible if these courses are technical in nature, that is, if they are concerned primarily with the application of certain techniques.

Is social work education technical in nature and therefore amenable to a transfer from the universities to technical colleges? The distinction between technical education and more fundamental education is not easy to draw, but it is clear that those who have designed the curricula of the Australian social work courses have been solidly on the side of a broad professional education similar to that of the so-called 'learned' professions. Even though the length of the courses has been very restricting, they have not made the courses primarily applied in character. The strong connection with Arts faculties, although this has had its disadvantages, has ensured an emphasis on 'background' subjects and the teaching of the principles and techniques of social work has used a body of knowledge at least partly integrated with the 'background' disciplines. Whatever the outcome, the intention has been education rather than training for the profession.

Since of all the professions this one is most directly involved in questions of human welfare, it has to be the most explicit in its moral justification.[3] It has to develop a tradition of criticism – of its own work and of the community's social welfare services. Because of the complexities of human beings and their social systems, it can only do this after a fairly lengthy preparation which has stressed the university values of free inquiry and intellectual integrity and capacity.[4] By recognising a professional preparation as a degree course, a university indicates its acceptance that this is and should be a learned profession.

The University of Queensland has decided to discontinue its three-year Diploma in Social Studies, and in future all new students will enrol for its four-year Bachelor of Social Studies degree.[5] After a very uncertain start involving modifications to a Diploma of Sociology,

2    The Committee on the Future of Tertiary Education in Australia, which is about to report, is very likely to have views on this.
3    See R.J. Lawrence, 'The Function of Professional Social Work in Australian Social Administration', *Proceedings of the 7th National Conference of the Australian Association of Social Workers*, 1961, pp. 3–10.
4    See R.J. Lawrence, 'Has Australian Social Work a Critical Tradition?' *Australian Journal of Social Work*, Vol. XVII, No. 2, May 1964, pp. 26–30.
5    Commonwealth Office of Education, Training in Social Work in Australia, May 1964.

it now appears that social work education at the University of New South Wales will take the form of a four-year Bachelor of Social Studies degree. These are not dramatic new developments, they are the logical outcome of the history of social work education in this country. As yet the old-established social work courses at the universities of Sydney, Melbourne, and Adelaide continue as diplomas, despite the fact that the Vice-Chancellors of the first two have testified that their social work courses are of graduate standard, and the Victorian Public Service Board has accepted the Melbourne University diploma as the equivalent of a full degree qualification. Because of the substantial fieldwork requirements it is doubtful whether these three-year courses warrant being called a degree. If they were extended to four years, there would be no doubt about the quantity of their academic content and little about its quality. As has been mentioned, a large proportion of social work students already spend at least four years on their university education anyway. They might better spend the extra year making their professional qualification a degree rather than on general education. For many reasons, arrangements for combining a social work diploma with an Arts or some other degree have been flexible. A social work degree qualification would allow some flexibility in the curriculum, but one could expect to develop a greater measure of social work relevance in all sections of the student's course.

That social work education should be guided by social work functions would seem to be almost axiomatic.[6] It is easy to assume that much human knowledge and experience has at least a rough relevance for social work, and also to take an all-embracing approach to the functions of the social work profession. This presents special hazards when a social work curriculum is designed. The 1956 study of social work employment in New South Wales stopped short of a full analysis of social work functions as actually performed. For many reasons much more needs to be known about social work functions in Australian society, and important among these reasons is that the initial professional education should be relevant.

If there is too big a gap between current teaching and practice, all interested parties suffer. There should be no strict dichotomy in people's thinking about theory and practice, for all so-called practical

6    Herbert Bisno, 'The Use of Social Science Content in Social Work Education: Some Problems and Possibilities', *International Social Service Review*, No. 8, March 1961, p. 46.

people are making theoretical assumptions, and further, the value of theory is eventually assessed according to its usefulness in real-life situations. The development of social work theory is a joint enterprise between people in social work practice and people in social work education and there must be no rift between the two. Developed professional subjects in a degree course will tend towards a generic treatment based upon empirical study, and should give students a grasp of professional social work functions, of those which may be performed by other than qualified social workers, and where qualified social workers fit in with other professional groups. Other subjects in the degree course should preferably be designed so that they are related to social work and to other subjects in the course.

One of the advantages of a degree social work course is that it provides a basis for a postgraduate qualification. For some years, Melbourne University has offered a Master of Arts degree specialising in Social Studies to graduates with an Arts degree and the Diploma of Social Studies, but this has been little used. A candidate for the University of Queensland's Bachelor of Social Studies may enrol as an honours student and may go on to a Master of Social Studies degree. This would seem to be a suitable model for the other social work courses to follow. The profession badly needs local opportunity for formal higher study – to extend its most able students, to produce a group with Australian research experience, and to provide the social work teachers of the future.

The American pattern in which basic professional education is postgraduate has still not much support, especially in view of Sydney University's almost disastrous experience with it in the mid-1950s. The University of Western Australia is, however, thinking in terms of a postgraduate diploma, although it will be guided by the person appointed to establish its school of social work. Recently, too, the University of Adelaide has introduced a one-and-a-half-year postgraduate diploma. Whatever the local reasons for this, it does not seem educationally sound. In particular, the professional teaching and learning, although intensive, extends over much too short a period to be effective, and the Sydney school, with far greater teaching resources, found the provision of two streams of professional teaching at different levels a very difficult arrangement.

Although to make all the social work courses full degree courses immediately would not constitute a drastic change, it is difficult to know what effect this would have on student numbers. They could in fact increase because of the greater status of a degree qualification in a community which is becoming qualification-conscious, and because of the greater professional opportunities offered by such a qualification. One result and an inducement to increased numbers would be for the salaries to come into line with those in Victoria. With most public service authorities a degree carries far more weight than any undergraduate diploma. If social work employers had to pay more for their social work employees, it might make them more thoughtful about their most effective use. A degree qualification should give them assurance of a more even quality of performance than prevails at present. It should also place social workers in a stronger position when cooperating with other established professional groups.

Those who talk about the need for different levels of training in social work can be talking about a number of different things. They may mean what has been discussed above – the need for further formal education beyond the basic professional qualification. This is a need recognised in the established professions. They may, however, mean a need for training people who will be performing social work functions but who are not able, for a variety of reasons, to undertake the full professional training. Or again, they may be using 'social work' to cover all social welfare, and may be referring to a need for special training for people engaged in the various kinds of social welfare work.

The profession can be expected to give every encouragement to special training schemes for workers in social welfare performing clerical, simple administrative, and highly specific tasks, so that they will be more efficient. Usually this is done by in-service training, although agencies could sometimes profitably combine in at least some of this type of training. But what should be the profession's attitude to training schemes which are in effect sub-standard professional courses, for example the courses provided for marriage guidance counsellors? Should the social work profession lend its educational facilities and prestige to such developments, or should it actively discourage them? If the profession has conviction about the necessity for the length and level of its basic training, it cannot look disinterestedly upon such developments. What the profession can do is to point out that these people are performing social work functions and that the relevant preparation for this work is provided by the social work courses in the universities. If these people are not capable of handling the basic professional preparation, should they have the right to practise? This is essentially a moral, not a legal question.

The question of different levels in social work will be returned to when the availability of social work services is discussed.

## A Variety of Social Work Methods?

Most qualified social workers are still engaged in social casework, but many of these also employ other methods to further the community's welfare, and there are a few social workers primarily engaged in these. The profession does demonstrate some awareness that social work's goals can be achieved in a variety of ways other than through helping individuals one by one or family by family.

In 1963, a New South Wales seminar on group work undertaken by social workers revealed a rather unsuspected range and variety of work, much of it undertaken in traditional casework settings such as family agencies, prisons, rehabilitation centres, and psychiatric clinics. This seminar has begun a local examination of the social worker's function in relation to various kinds of groups. The outcome will be clearly relevant to the extent and nature of the teaching on group techniques in the basic professional education. Most courses have some teaching in this, but it is not as highly developed as casework.

There are still very few qualified social workers employed in community organisation positions, although most social workers are familiar with community organisation principles and they occasionally have a chance to apply them when they spend some of their time in working towards a better adjustment between community resources and community welfare needs. A much greater emphasis, both in social work education and practice, on community organisation as a social work method could pay large welfare dividends. The Australian social welfare scene badly needs professional help to become better organised. There is little doubt that in terms of its purposes much of it is not very efficient – it lacks regular evaluation, much of it is excessively paternalistic, much of it has a narrow view of its responsibilities, and considerable potential community resources are as yet untapped.

A 'community development' movement has tentatively begun in Australia. In the last decade, partly because of the ineffectiveness of wholesale external financial assistance to less developed countries, the subject has received a great deal of international attention. Its emphasis is on helping communities to change and develop in ways which they themselves desire. This is, of course, easily recognisable as the social work approach in community organisation, which, however, has generally been a social work method used in an urban environment where living levels are relatively high and social services relatively developed. It has been largely applied to social welfare organisation, whereas community development has usually been concentrated on the rural areas of less-developed countries, and has been concerned with improving the community's living standards in general. The close relationship between the professional social work method of 'community organisation' and the principles and techniques of 'community development' has been discussed in international forums.[7] In Australia, as yet few social workers could contribute to such a discussion. The community development movement here has received its stimulus largely from agricultural extension work and adult education. As the movement extends its interest to urban community development, the social work profession has an especially important part to play because of its knowledge of this kind of environment.

Social welfare administration as a social work method is beginning to receive specific attention. This is not surprising because a group of senior social workers administer social casework agencies, a small, though growing, number of qualified social workers administer other social welfare programmes, and all social workers, because they are employees, work within an administrative context. Moreover, as revealed in a recent survey,[8] the teaching of organisational or administrative theory for people in many fields – business, industry, education, and the public service – is becoming common in Australia. There is, however, some confusion arising from the term 'social administration'. This, as an identifiable university subject, is essentially concerned with the historical and present development

---

7     See e.g., United Nations Department of Economic and Social Affairs, *Training for Social Work – Third International Survey*, 1958, pp. 74–101.
8     By Perth Technical College, reported upon in Cecil E. Carr, Elephants and Trainers, Canberra Seminar on Administrative Studies, 1963.

of collective action for the advancement of social welfare.[9] It is not primarily concerned with administrative structures and processes as is 'social welfare administration'.

The most influential piece of social welfare research undertaken in recent years has been the survey of civilian widows in Australia.[10] Its main research worker was an experienced English social worker, who received considerable help from the local social work profession; The local scene provides little money for this kind of research, but it is also severely hampered by a shortage of both social scientists and well-qualified social workers to undertake it. The same is true of social work research, that is, study related more closely to the profession's actual functions. The profession must become more research conscious if it wishes to further its social welfare goals and improve its effective professional performance.

There are signs that the profession is trying to work out its proper role in relation to another social work method – social action. Through its professional association it has set up a standing committee on the study of Australian social welfare, one result of which should be better informed social action. In addition, the association is giving serious thought to setting down principles to guide its social action.

The final method by which social work may achieve its goals is through teaching people who will be engaged in casework, group work, community organisation, social welfare administration, research, and social action. Some educational principles are similar to social work principles, but teachers in the social work courses, as in most other university courses, have rarely had any formal instruction in educational methods. Well-qualified (that is from a subject point of view) teachers are so few that thought could be given to this. It would also be more advantageous if fewer social workers in the field had to teach students, while those who did were used more intensively.

Although social workers of the future are unlikely to confine themselves to only one aspect of their work, the profession and its clients would benefit from more specialisation. Individuals need to perform fewer functions than at present, and could be more evenly

9    D.V. Donnison, *The Development of Social Administration, An Inaugural Lecture*, 1962.
10   Jean Aitken-Swan, *Widows in Australia*.

spread amongst the various social work methods, and each method needs to be more closely connected in professional education and practice with a developing body of knowledge.

The social work profession has to be on its guard against encouraging a hierarchy amongst its methods. First-rate practitioners are needed to concentrate on each method and they should be paid accordingly. One possible danger is that as relatively highly paid administrative positions become available, social welfare administration will be seen as the highest form of professional life and will drain experience and talent away from other fields.

Whatever the future holds in terms of social work methods, social work practitioners will still need to have an abiding concern for the welfare of the individual, perhaps the sort of concern which can only be imparted by at least some supervised social casework experience.

## Wide Availability?

The availability of the services of the social work profession and the extent of the need for them throughout the community is a subject worthy of study, even if it concentrated only on the direct professional service of social workers to people with personal and social problems. Such a study would need to consider the number and experience of available qualified social workers, their location geographically and in types of agencies, their hours of work, the size of their job, the attitudes of various social groups to social work help, the public images of the social worker, the attitudes towards and knowledge about social work of potential referral sources, the incidence of problems amenable to social work assistance, where people seek help at present, the role of other professional groups, the role of non-professional services.

From general observation, Australian social work services continue to be concentrated in the hearts of the larger cities, especially those with established social work schools, the number of available qualified people is small, and the degree of public acceptance of professional social work is hindered by false images or by ignorance of its existence. Again from general observation, it seems that the kinds of personal and social problems social workers are trained to help with are widespread throughout Australia's 11 million people. A recent pilot study of general medical practice in New South Wales supports this.[11] Modern social workers have been professionally educated for the complex task of helping people with their social and personal problems. It is naive to expect that in the near future all Australians, wherever they live and whatever their socioeconomic group, will have access to social work assistance and will feel free to use it, but this could well be a long-term goal to bear in mind. An odd feature of the profession's position is that it needs to become more available up the socioeconomic scale and possibly to introduce fee paying, as has happened in the United States, while the older established professions need to become more available down the socioeconomic scale, and possibly depart to some extent from fee paying.

There are some indications that the social work profession is becoming alive to the question of availability. In both New South Wales and Victoria there has been serious discussion on the decentralisation of social work agencies in the urban metropolises,[12] country districts in Victoria are becoming interested in employing social workers; in South Australia there is a new unconventional street work youth service; some agencies are working staggered hours to reach their clientele more effectively; and, as will be mentioned in the final section of the chapter, the question of numbers coming into the profession is receiving some attention. Yet these are only beginnings.

One important aspect of the question of availability is the most effective use of existing qualified social workers. Partly because of the underdeveloped state of social welfare administration as a subject, social work job analyses which isolate professional social work functions from tasks requiring less or different skills are rare in Australia. It is very likely that a full-scale employment analysis would show the wasteful situation of many Australian social workers who have to undertake tasks auxiliary to their main functions and skill which would be more economically performed by other workers. In some overseas agencies, welfare assistants, social aids, or case aids have been appointed to work under the direction of the qualified social workers. They may undertake receptionist duties and do some early

11    Preventive Medicine Committee of the Australian College of General Practitioners (NSW Faculty), *Social Work and Medical General Practice: A Pilot Study*, 1961.
12    See 'Social Work and the Local Community', *Australian Journal of Social Work*, Vol. XV, No. 1, June 1962; and Family Welfare: A guide for developing local services, a report by a committee of the Victorian Branch of the Australian Association of Social Workers, 1963.

and other interviews where information or a service is required but not social diagnosis or treatment, they may make various arrangements for clients, they may undertake straightforward 'welfare' visiting where greater skill is not required, they may take responsibility for various administrative procedures, they may undertake play group and other allied work.[13] These things require social work attitudes and simple interviewing skill, but they do not call for social work skill, and it would seem to confuse the issue to describe as social workers those people who do them.

If auxiliary social work is performed by others, there is a greater likelihood that the qualified social workers can demonstrate their professional skill and for this to be recognised as such. The Australian social work profession is, however, uneasy about this development, and certainly much of its effectiveness would seem to depend upon the quality of professional practice and direction the social workers can provide.

There are still Australian social work employers who do not provide sufficient clerical help for recording, correspondence, and filing, adequate office accommodation, or reasonable transport facilities, all of which contribute to an uneconomical use of a social worker.

The complex question of inter-professional boundaries has an important connection with the subject of availability. Ideally the education of all professional groups should include knowledge of cooperative relationships with complementary professions. Social workers frequently work in teams with other professional people or consult them, and their education specifically recognises this. Some professional education, however, neglects this important aspect of practice, and moreover, there is a noticeable trend, despite, or perhaps because of, an age of growing specialisation, for individual professional groups to talk about considering and treating 'the whole person'. The social work profession, whose education and experience make it expert in personal social relationships and the use of community resources, can find itself excluded by this kind of thinking. Of course a shortage of social workers may induce other professional workers to undertake social work, in much the same way as a shortage of psychiatrists has

13   United Nations Department of Economic and Social Affairs, *Training for Social Work: Third International Survey*, pp. 71–2.

induced some psychiatric social workers to undertake a psychiatrist's functions. Such expedients should, however, be recognised as such and the foreign though allied functions should not be incorporated into the proper practice of the profession.

## Better Modes of Organisation?

The most appropriate organisation depends upon the numbers and the aims of the people involved. Informal organisation relying upon individual personalities may be an appropriate form when numbers and aims are few. As described in previous chapters, social work in Australia has been moving towards more formal modes of organisation, in keeping with the continuous responsibilities it assumes. The two most substantial achievements are a nation-wide general association to which all qualified social workers in employment may belong and provision for special groups within the association. But the Australian Association of Social Workers, at both branch and federal levels, requires much more settled and efficient machinery if it is to fulfil its purposes effectively. It also needs greater membership interest, particularly in New South Wales, and a more stable membership. The profession's leaders should take the initiative in achieving greater interest, higher fees, salaried executive officers, and adequate accommodation. A higher proportion of men, and deliberate action to retain the membership of women when they marry, would ensure a more stable membership.

Amongst other things, a better organised professional association could become much more effective in looking after social workers' industrial interests. At present the association's federal council is examining the extent to which its members have joined other organisations, the public service associations, to achieve better working conditions. The association has not been strong enough or effective enough industrially to prevent this development. It must, however, continue to take an active interest. It could still have an important coordinating and servicing role in relation to various negotiating groups, and a direct role for those, mainly in non-government agencies, who have still not joined forces with other much larger and richer industrial organisations.

A crucial aspect of organisation is, of course, communication. The Australian Association of Social Workers has always provided important channels of communication between qualified social workers – through its meetings, its committees, its conferences, and its journal. Despite some recent improvement, the *Australian Journal of Social Work*, which is in a key position, has a long way to go before it nationally covers developments in all the profession's fields, discusses and reports social policy and social service changes, informs members regularly of the association's activities, and has a considerable proportion of the profession contributing articles. This kind of journal could only be sustained with far greater support from association members and this could partly be achieved by a reorganisation of the management of the journal so that all the profession's major areas of interest are systematically covered.

The better organisation of social work involves more than that its practitioners should be better organised professionally. Each of the schools of social work needs to have settled means of communication with its local field, with the professional association, and with other schools, but most of this still remains on an informal level in this country. Unless the various responsible bodies establish regular machinery for mutual discussion, misunderstanding and confusion are increasingly likely because of the growing numbers of people and the probable establishment of new schools of social work.

In addition to the organisation of the educational authorities, there is the organisation of the fields within which social workers are employed. Some mention has already been made – in the discussion on community organisation, social welfare administration and the identification of social work's functions – on the great amount of room for better social welfare organisation. A recent event which holds out hope for the future strengthening of the general coordinating body, the Australian Council of Social Service, was its third national conference on 'The National Income and Social Welfare'. This achieved high-level participation and, if it is adequately followed up, may have placed this body onto a new level of effectiveness.

Organisation may become an end in itself, yet without it in a complex society gains are likely to be only fragmentary and temporary. Australian social work needs to concentrate far more on cumulative achievement. Moreover, where there are reasonably settled ways of doing things, clear lines of communication and recognised allocations of authority, there is less likelihood of highly personal conflict between people engaged in social work. Such conflict not only interferes with the job but is poor publicity for a profession which specialises in human relations.

One invaluable gain from better organisation could be the compilation of relevant statistical information – in relation to the profession and social work education. Without this, planning tends to be very haphazard.

## More Social Workers?

The final major issue which demands discussion is the question of the numbers in the social work profession. Much of the previous discussion is connected with this issue. Complex social work organisation needs substantial numbers to spread social work services more evenly among the social work methods, to spread them geographically and into new groups of clients, and to lighten the load on many existing services and to allow greater specialisation. Without them, the amount of first-class talent will be insufficient to provide Australian social work with its leadership in social work theory and practice. Community recognition and acceptance can only come when substantial numbers are engaged in the work.

In 1962 the Department of Social Work at Sydney University held a seminar with social work employers to discuss the shortage of social workers, and recently the Victorian branch of the professional association was studying the subject in cooperation with the Victorian Council of Social Service and Melbourne University's Social Studies Department. Apart from changing the level of social work education and redefining social work jobs, which have already been considered, there are in fact three main ways of increasing the numbers of social workers available for social work employment – increase the numbers entering the social work courses, minimise student wastage, and minimise professional wastage.[14]

---

14    See R.J. Lawrence, Statement prepared for a Seminar at the Department of Social Work, Sydney University, held on 24 May 1962.

The most dramatic example of the effect of improved career opportunities on social work recruitment, especially male recruitment, has been in Victoria – although the recent great increases in Melbourne are also a result of the general rapid rise in university student numbers, and the previously small Melbourne social work student numbers must be remembered. The main responsibility for improving career opportunities rests with social work employers, but the professional association has a part to play and the social work schools need to bear in mind actual employment positions. Improved opportunities could include better initial and eventual employment conditions, greater ease of transfer to provide greater promotion and variety, more policy-making and senior administrative positions open to members of the profession, higher professional status within some agencies and in the community, and the removal of the traditional notion that social work is women's work.

More attractive and extensive schemes of financial aid, a responsibility of social work employers and the government, may increase the number of social work students. The present trend of scholarships and Cadetships which tie students in advance to particular agencies is, however, undesirable. No potential social work student should be debarred because of finance from undertaking the course. Insufficient government assistance has left the way open for employers to remove a money bar to professional social work education, but at the cost of severely restricting the professional choice of those students who must rely upon outside help. Consideration should be given to the establishment of general cadetships in both federal and state public services, so that students are not tied to a particular department. This would also encourage the respective public service boards to examine and compare the social work positions available in different parts of the public service.

Schemes of financial aid which allow older matriculated people either already in social agencies or in other work to become full-time social work students should be seriously considered. Usually such people, if they become students at all and if it is permitted by the school, undertake the social work course on a part-time basis. A substantial proportion of part-time students has been a distinctive feature of Australian universities, but existing evidence indicates that the chances of a part-time student to complete a university course are much less than for a full-time student. Moreover, the quality of the passes he achieves are likely to be lower and his extra-curricular experiences poorer than those of the full-time student.[15] He in fact represents a wasteful employment of educational resources which are increasingly scarce in relation to the demand for them, and some Australian universities are beginning to recognise this.

At particular points of time, for example when a large government department adopts the idea of full professional social work training for many of its staff but cannot release them for full-time study, there may be a strong case for temporary part-time social work education. The arguments against part-time study, however, apply here at least as much as in other university courses, and perhaps more, because of the spread of reading required, the difficulty of fulfilling the considerable fieldwork requirements, and because good fieldwork supervision is particularly scarce under existing arrangements and therefore should be conserved.[16]

Many people in the past have claimed special advantages for the recruitment to social work of the older person rich in life experience. It is difficult to generalise about this, but long experience may mean that there is more to unlearn, and the reasons why a person has not found a satisfying niche in some other work may require close examination. Entry of suitable people into the profession at a later stage should certainly be open, and a potential recruitment source is with educationally qualified, married women past their mid-30s who wish to become qualified for a professional job.[17] But this cannot and should not be the profession's main source. Social work has to compete with the established professions at the point where most talented people are choosing a career, that is, in their late teens.

Systematic attention is beginning to be given to regular social work recruitment, especially in New South Wales, and employers, the professional association, the schools of social work, the general community employment agencies, and the state and independent schools must all play their part in this. Social work as a career for young men is not, at present, often considered, and because of the

---

15    D.S. Anderson, 'The Performance of Part-time Students', *Vestes*, Vol. VI, No. 4, December 1963, pp. 286–95.
16    The development of student units in the field under direct university supervision is still slow, although it is likely to be hastened by the pressure of numbers.
17    See Norman MacKenzie, *Women in Australia*, pp. 333–5.

favourable demographic situation and the expanding opportunities for social work it is now an ideal time to attract more students. Recruitment should not be seen, however, only in terms of increasing numbers. Whatever the current student and employment situation, all potentially suitable people should know about social work, as they should know about all the other careers for which they may be suited.

Once students have entered the social work courses, there is the problem of reducing student wastage. Much of the dramatic new deal for social work employment in Victoria promised by the greatly increased student numbers has not eventuated because of a high drop-out rate.[18] Student failure rates are a general university problem, most acute where numbers are high. Schools of social work with expanding student numbers may well give careful thought to this matter.

The question of professional wastage could be tackled on three main fronts: a very much larger proportion of men in the profession, the improvement of career opportunities which not only will help recruit people but will retain them, and the encouragement of married women who are qualified social workers to return to social work.

All these issues call for a great deal of cooperative thought, study and action on the part of the social workers themselves, their professional association, their employers, their professional schools, and people in the wider community. Out of this could come a substantial, well-qualified and organised social work profession, engaged in by both men and women, and providing a variety of widely available services. But it will not just happen.

18   E. Hamilton-Smith, The Scarcity of Social Workers, an address to the 1964 Annual General Meeting of the Australian Association of Social Workers (Victorian Branch).

# Appendix

**The Yearly and Cumulative Output of Qualified Social Workers by the Australian Training Bodies, 1931–58**

| | New South Wales | | | | | | Victoria | | | | | | South Australia | | |
| | Board of Social Study and Training[1] | | | Institute of Hospital Almoners | | | Council for Social Training[2] | | | Institute of Almoners[3] | | | Board of Social Study and Training[4] | | |
| | F. | M. | Comul. Total | F. | M. | Comul. Total | F. | M. | Total | F. | M. | Comul. Total | F. | M. | Comul. Total |
|---|---|---|---|---|---|---|---|---|---|---|---|---|---|---|---|
| 1931 | 2 | | 2 | | | | | | | 3 | | 3 | | | |
| 1932 | 5 | | 7 | | | | | | | 4 | | 7 | | | |
| 1933) | | | | | | | | | ) | | | | | | |
| 1934) | | | | | | | 3 | | 3) | 7 | | 14 | | | |
| 1935) | 8 | | 15 | | | | 10 | | 13) | | | | | | |
| 1936) | 5 | | 20 | | | | 2 | | 15) | 6 | | 20 | | | |
| 1937 | 13 | | 33 | | | | 3 | | 18 | 2 | | 22 | | | |
| 1938) | | | | 5 | | 5 | 4 | 1 | 23 | 2 | | 24 | | | |
| 1939) | 12 | 1 | 46 | 3 | | 8 | 7 | 1 | 31 | 2 | | 26 | 5 | | 5 |
| 1940 | 8 | | 54 | 3 | | 11 | 7 | 1 | 39 | 6 | | 32 | 2 | 1 | 8 |
| 1941 | 8 | | 62 | 2 | | 13 | 4 | | 43 | 8 | | 40 | 4 | | 12 |
| 1942 | 12 | 1 | 75 | 7 | | 20 | 7 | | 50 | 5 | | 45 | 3 | | 15 |
| 1943 | 9 | | 84 | 6 | | 26 | 5 | | 55 | 8 | | 53 | 7 | | 22 |
| 1944 | 11 | | 95 | 3 | | 29 | 8 | | 63 | 2 | | 55 | 2 | | 24 |
| 1945 | 29 | 1 | 125 | 3 | | 32 | 8 | | 71 | 5 | | 60 | 8 | | 32 |
| 1946 | 38 | 2 | 165 | 13 | | 45 | 7 | | 78 | 4 | | 64 | 6 | | 38 |
| 1947 | 42 | 6 | 213 | 12 | | 57 | 13 | | 91 | 8 | | 72 | )25 | | 63 |
| 1948 | 53 | 9 | 275 | 16 | | 73 | 11 | 1 | 103 | 11 | | 83 | )20 | 3 | 86 |

The Yearly and Cumulative Output of Qualified Social Workers by the Australian Training Bodies, 1931–58

| | New South Wales | | | | | | Victoria | | | | | | South Australia | | |
| | Board of Social Study and Training[1] | | | Institute of Hospital Almoners | | | Council for Social Training[2] | | | Institute of Almoners[3] | | | Board of Social Study and Training[4] | | |
| | F. | M. | Comul. Total | F. | M. | Comul. Total | F. | M. | Total | F. | M. | Comul. Total | F. | M. | Comul. Total |
|---|---|---|---|---|---|---|---|---|---|---|---|---|---|---|---|
| 1949 | 36 | 9 | 320 | 11 | | 84 | 9 | 1 | 113 | 18 | | 101 | 21 | 7 | 114 |
| 1950 | 25 | 13 | 358 | 10 | | 94 | 9 | | 122 | | | | 14 | | 131 |
| 1951 | 22 | 7 | 387 | 6 | | 101 | 9 | 7 | 138 | | | | 14 | | 145 |
| 1952 | 24 | 5 | 416 | 6 | | 106 | 10 | 4 | 152 | | | | 4 | 2 | 151 |
| 1953 | 25 | 1 | 442 | 7 | | 113 | 10 | 1 | 163 | | | | 9 | 2 | 162 |
| 1954 | 16 | 3 | 461 | 12 | | 125 | 12 | | 175 | | | | 9 | | 171 |
| 1955 | 20 | 1 | 482 | 5 | | 130 | 7 | 2 | 184 | | | | 4 | 1 | 176 |
| 1956 | 12 | 3 | 497 | 12 | | 142 | 5 | 2 | 191 | | | | 10 | 2 | 188 |
| 1957 | 26 | 5 | 528 | 11 | | 153 | 11 | 1 | 203 | | | | 8 | 1 | 197 |
| 1958 | 22 | 3 | 553 | 5 | | 158 | 17 | 1 | 221 | | | | 5 | 1 | 203 |
| Totals | 483 | 70 | 553 | 157 | 1 | 158 | 198 | 23 | 221 | 101 | - | 101 | 180 | 23 | 203 |
| University-Trained | 430 | 69 | 499 | | | | 158 | 20 | 178 | | | | 166 | 22 | 188 |

Sources: Annual Reports and University Calendars.

Note: Except for the first 14 trained by the Victorian Institute of Almoners, the general social work course was a prerequisite for the almoner courses. Therefore, the output of the general courses plus these 14 gives the total number of qualified social workers.

(Footnotes)
1 Sydney University Board of Social Studies from 1941.
2 Melbourne University Board of Social Studies from 1942.
3 Institute of Hospital Almoners from 1933.
4 Adelaide University Board of Social Science from 1942.

# Bibliography

## I. Official Publications

### Commonwealth of Australia

Department of Social Services, *The Commonwealth Rehabilitation Service*, April 1957.

*Full Employment in Australia*, Canberra, 1945.

Official Year Books of the Commonwealth of Australia.

Stoller, Alan, assisted by K.W. Arscott. *Mental Health Facilities and Needs of Australia*. Canberra, 1955.

Parliament:

*First, Second, Third*, and *Fourth and Final Report* of the *Royal Commission on National Insurance*. Melbourne, 1925 and 1927.

*First, Second, Third, Fourth, Fifth, Sixth, Seventh, Eighth*, and *Ninth Interim Report from the Joint Committee on Social Security*. Canberra, 1941–46.

### Victoria

Parliament:

'Notes and Recommendations as to Hospitals and Other Philanthropic Institutions and Organisations based on Investigations in New Zealand, Canada, the United States, and the British Isles', by R.J. Love. *Parl. Pap.* 1927, Vol. II, No, 45.

*Report of Juvenile Delinquency Advisory Committee to Chief Secretary of Victoria*. Melbourne, July 1956.

## International Labour Office

*Approaches to Social Security – An International Survey*. Montreal, 1944.

## United Kingdom

Beveridge, Sir William. *Social Insurance and Allied Services*. Cmd. 6404. HMSO, London, 1942.

Ferguson, Sheila, and Hilda Fitzgerald. *Studies in the Social Services*. HMSO, London, 1954.

Titmuss, Richard M. *Problems of Social Policy*. HMSO, London, 1950.

## United Nations

Bureau of Social Affairs: *Training for Social Work – Second International Survey*. New York, 1955.

Department of Economic and Social Affairs: *Training for Social Work – Third International Survey*. New York, 1958.

Department of Social Affairs: *Training for Social Work – An International Survey*. New York, 1950.

# II. Newspapers and Periodicals

*Advertiser*, Adelaide, 1935–38.

*Age*, Melbourne, 1933–35, 1938.

*Argus*, Melbourne, 1929, 1933–35.

*Australian Journal of Social Work, The*, Melbourne, 1958–64.

*Australian Women's Weekly,* 1935.

*Current Affairs Bulletin*, Sydney, 1948–60.

*Forum*, Melbourne, 1947–58.

*Herald,* Melbourne, 1929, 1934.

*Medical Social Work in Australia,* Sydney, 1946, 1948.

*Social Service,* Sydney, 1942–60.

*Social Service Record, The,* Adelaide, 1947–50.

*Social Workers' Digest,* Sydney, 1945–47.

*Sydney Morning Herald,* 1929–30, 1937.


# III. Articles, Books, Pamphlets

Abbott, Edith. *Social Welfare and Professional Education.* Chicago, 1942 ed.

Abbott, P.D., and L.O. Goldsmith. 'History and Functions of the Commonwealth Health Department', *Public Administration,* XI, September 1952.

Aitken-Swan, Jean. *Widows in Australia: A Survey of the Economic and Social Condition of Widows with Dependent Children.* Council of Social Service of New South Wales, Sydney, 1962.

Anderson, D.S. 'The Performance of Part-Time Students', *Vestes,* VI, 4, December 1963, pp. 286–95.

Australian Association of Social Workers, Victorian Branch Committee, *Family Welfare: A guide for developing local services,* 1963.

Bell, Moberly. *Octavia Hill.* London, 1942.

Birch, A.H. *Federalism, Finance and Social Legislation in Canada, Australia, and the United States.* Oxford, 1955.

Bisno, Herbert. *The Philosophy of Social Work.* Washington, D.C., 1952.

Borrie, W.D. 'The Growth of the Australian Population with Particular Reference to the Period Since 1947', *Population Studies,* XIII, 1, July 1959.

—. *The Peopling of Australia.* George Judah Cohen Memorial Lecture, University of Sydney, 1958.

Bostock, John, and Edna Hill. *The Pre-School Child and Society: A Study of Australian Conditions and Their Repercussions on National Welfare*. Brisbane, 1946.

Bourdillon A.F.C. (ed.) *Voluntary Social Services: Their Place in the Modern State* London, 1945.

Bowers, Swithun. 'Social Work as a Helping and Healing Profession', *Social Work*, I,2, January 1957, pp. 57–63.

Brotherhood of St Laurence, *100,000 Depressed Pensioners*. Melbourne, 1958.

——. *'On Benefit' – A Study of Unemployment and Unemployment Benefits in Australia*. Melbourne, 1961.

Brown, Esther L. *Social Work as a Profession*. Russell Sage Foundation, 4th ed., New York, 1942.

Bruno, Frank J. *Trends in Social Work, 1874–1956: A History based on the Proceedings of the National Conference of Social Work*. New York, 1957.

Cannon, Ida M. *On the Social Frontier of Medicine*. Cambridge (Mass.), 1952.

——. *Social Work in Hospitals*. Russell Sage Foundation, New York, 1923.

Carr-Saunders, A.M., and P.A. Wilson. *The Professions*. Oxford, 1933.

Cawte, J.E. *Report on the Principles of Operation of Mental Health Services Overseas with Recommendations for South Australia*. South Australian Mental Health Association, 1961.

Child Welfare Advisory Council: The Delinquency Committee: *A Report on the Girls' Industrial School, Parramatta, N.S.W.: A Study in the Principles and Practices of Child Welfare Administration*. For the Australian Council for Educational Research, Melbourne, 1945.

——. *Report 1944, The Pre-School Child*. Sydney, 1944.

Citizens' Welfare Service, Red Cross Welfare Service, Catholic Social Service Bureau, Brotherhood of St Laurence: *Recommendations to the Commonwealth Government Concerning Rent Rebates and Their Financing,* Melbourne, October 1956.

Clark, C.M.H. *Select Documents in Australian History 1851–1900.* Sydney, 1955.

Close, Kathryn. 'Rallying Point for the World', *The Survey,* LXXXIV, 5, May 1948.

Cohen, Nathan E. *Social Work in the American Tradition.* New York, 1958.

Collings, J.W. *The Flying Doctor Service and its Influence on Outback Settlement.* A Pioneers' Memorial Trust Oration, 1943.

Connell, W.F., E.P. Francis, and Elizabeth E. Skilbeck. *Growing Up in an Australian City*, Melbourne, 1957.

Coyle, Grace L. *Social Science in the Professional Education of Social Workers.* New York, 1958.

Davey, Constance M. *Children and Their Law-Makers: a social-historical survey of the growth and development from 1836 to 1950 of South Australian laws relating to children.* Adelaide, 1956.

Dax, E. Cunningham. *Asylum to Community.* Melbourne, 1961.

Donnison. D.V. 'The Social Work Profession', *Case Conference* 3. No. 3, July 1956. pp. 63–7.

—. *The Development of Social Administration: An Inaugural Lecture.* London University, 1962.

Downing, R.I. *Raising Age Pensions.* Melbourne, 1957.

Elkin. A.P. (ed.). *Marriage and the Family in Australia.* Sydney, 1957.

*Encyclopaedia of the Social Sciences.* New York, 1930. Reprinted 1959.

Fitzpatrick, B.C. *The Australian People 1788–1945.* Melbourne. 1946.

—. *The British Empire in Australia: An Economic History. 1834–1939.* Melbourne, 1941.

Flexner, Abraham. 'Is Social Work a Profession?' *Proceedings of the 42nd National Conference on Charities and Correction*. Chicago, 1915.

Frankfurter, Felix. 'Social Work and Professional Training', *Proceedings of the 42nd National Conference on Charities and Correction*. Chicago, 1915.

French, David G. *An Approach to Measuring Results in Social Work*. New York, 1952.

Friedlander, Walter A. *Introduction to Social Welfare*. New York, 1955.

Garnett, A. Campbell. *Freedom and Planning in Australia*. Wisconsin, 1949.

Gollan, Robin. *Radical and Working Class Politics: A Study of Eastern Australia 1850–1910*. Melbourne, 1960.

Goode, William J. 'Community Within a Community: The Professions', American Sociological Review, 22, No. 2, April 1957, pp. 194–200.

Govan, Elizabeth S.L. 'A Community Program of Foster-Home Care, New South Wales, 1881', *Social Service Review*, XXV, 3, September 1951.

Greenwood, Gordon (ed.). *Australia: A Social and Political History*. Sydney, 1955.

Hamilton, Gordon. *Theory and Practice of Social Case Work*. New York, 1940.

Hancock, W.K. *Australia*. London, 1930.

Hasluck, Paul. *The Government and the People 1939–1941*. Canberra, 1952.

Hoffer, Joe R. 'Conferences of Social Work', *Social Work Year Book, 1954*. New York, 1954, pp. 128–35.

Hollis, Ernest V., and Alice L. Taylor. *Social Work Education in the United States: The Report of a Study Made for the National Council on Social Work Education*. New York, 1951.

Inglis, K.S. *Hospital and Community: A History of the Royal Melbourne Hospital*. Melbourne, 1958.

Kahn, Alfred J. (ed.). *Issues in American Social Work*. New York, 1959.

Kewley, T.H. 'Child Endowment in Australia', *Public Administration*, XVII, September 1958.

——. 'The Development of the Social Services', in C. Hartley Grattan (ed.), *Australia*. California, 1947.

——. 'General Survey of Social Services in Australia', *Economic Papers*, No. 7.

——. 'Social Services in Australia (1900–10): With Special Reference to Old Age and Invalid Pensions in New South Wales'. *Royal Australian Historical Society Journal and Proceedings*, XXXIV, 4, 1947.

——. 'Social Work and Training in Australia', *Social Welfare*, January 1952.

Kiddle, Margaret. *Caroline Chisholm*. Melbourne, 1950.

Klein, Philip. 'The Social Theory of Professional Social Work', In H.E. Barnes, H. and F.B. Becker (eds.), *Contemporary Social Theory*. New York, 1940.

Kuenstler, Peter (ed.). *Social Group Work in Great Britain*. London, 1955.

Lewis, Roy, and Angus Maude. *Professional People*. London, 1949.

Macadam, Elizabeth. *The Equipment of the Social Worker*. London, 1925.

——. *The Social Servant in the Making: A Review of the Provision of Training for the Social Services*. London, 1945.

Macintyre, Agnes. 'The Hospital Almoner', *Medical Journal of Australia*, 8 February 1930.

MacKenzie, Norman. *Women in Australia*. Melbourne, 1962.

Marsh, David C. *National Insurance and Assistance in Great Britain*. London, 1950.

Marshall, T.H. 'The Recent History of Professionalism in Relation to Social Structure and Social Policy' (1939) in *Citizenship and Social Class and other Essays*. Cambridge, 1950.

Massey, J.T. *The YMCA in Australia: A History*. Melbourne, 1950.

Medley, Sir John. 'Universities', *The Australian Encyclopaedia*, IX. Sydney, 1958.

Mendelsohn, Ronald. 'Social Services', in R.N. Spann (ed.), *Public Administration in Australia*. Sydney [1958?].

—. *Social Security in the British Commonwealth*. London, 1954.

Mess, Henry A. (ed.). *Voluntary Social Services Since 1918*. London, 1947.

Miller, J.D.B. *Australian Government and Politics: An Introductory Survey*. 2nd ed. London, 1959.

Morris, Cherry (ed.). *Social Casework in Great Britain*. London, 1950.

Morris, J. Newman. *Social Work in Hospitals: Some American Investigations*, Victorian Institute of Almoners, 1930.

Morris, Mary. *Voluntary Organisations and Social Progress*. London, 1950.

North, Cecil C. *The Community and Social Welfare: A Study in Community Organization*. New York, 1931.

Onians, Edith C. *Read All About It*. Melbourne, 1948.

Parsons, Talcott. 'The Professions and Social Structure', in *Essays in Sociological Theory Pure and Applied*. Glencoe (Ill.), 1949.

Peyser, Dora. 'A Study of the History of Welfare Work in Sydney from 1788 till about 1900', *Royal Australian Historical Society Journal and Proceedings*, XXV, Part II and Part III, 1939.

Portus, G.V. 'The University in Australia', in Edward Bradley (ed.), *The University Outside Europe*. Oxford, 1939.

Preventive Medicine Committee of the Australian College of General Practitioners (N.S.W. Faculty), *Social Work and Medical General Practice: A Pilot Study*. November 1961.

Price, A. Grenfell (ed.). *The Humanities in Australia: A Survey with special reference to the Universities*. Sydney, 1959.

*Proceedings of the First Australasian Conference on Charity, Melbourne 1890*. Melbourne, 1890.

*Proceedings of the Second Australasian Conference on Charity, Melbourne, 1891*. Melbourne, 1891.

Raynes, Harold E. *Social Security in Britain: A History*. London, 1957.

Red Cross Welfare Service – New South Wales Division. *Unemployment – 1960–61*. Sydney, October 1961.

Reiss, A.J., Jr. 'Occupational Mobility of Professional Workers', *American Sociological Review*. 20, No. 6, December 1955, pp. 693–700.

Reynolds, Bertha C., *Re-Thinking Social Case Work* (Social Service Digest). California, 1946.

Robinson, Virginia P. *A Changing Psychology in Social Case Work*. Chapel Hill, 1930.

Rowe, A.P. *If the Gown Fits*. Melbourne, 1960.

Royal Flying Doctor Service of Australia. *Royal Flying Doctor Service, Australia*. 5th rev. ed., 1957.

Saunders, Marion K. 'A Profession Chasing Its Tail', *Harper's Magazine*, New York, March 1957.

Sawkins, D.T. *The Living Wage in Australia*. Melbourne, 1933.

Sebire, Irene. *The Psychiatrist and the Social Worker*. Dorothy E. Poate Memorial Lecture, Sydney, 1943.

Simey, T.S. (Chairman of a Joint Committee of the British Federation of Social Workers and the National Council of Social Service). *Salaries and Conditions of Work of Social Workers*. London, September 1947.

Spence. C.H. *The Laws We Live Under*. Adelaide, 1880.

—. *State Children in Australia: A History of Boarding Out and its Development*. Adelaide, 1907.

Spencer, John. 'Historical Development', in *Social Group Work in Great Britain*. London, 1955.

Smith, Marjorie J. *Professional Education for Social Work in Britain*. London, 1952.

Stacey, E. Marilyn and S.M. Barker. *A Survey of the Employment Problems of Physically Handicapped Persons in New South Wales* (for the New South Wales Council of Social Service). Sydney, [1958?].

Stroup, Herbert H. *Community Welfare Organization*. New York, 1952.

Titmuss, Richard M. *Essays on 'The Welfare State'*. London, 1958.

Trethowan, W.H. *Report to the South Australian Association For Mental Health. South Australia Mental Health Association, 1961*.

Tufts. James H. *Education and Training for Social Work*. Russell Sage Foundation, New York, 1923.

*Universities Commission: What it is and What it does*. The Universities Commission, 1944.

Uren, Malcolm. 'A Brief Survey of the Development of Social Services in Western Australia', in *Jubilee Survey of Social Welfare in Western Australia 1901 to 1951, with Directory of Social Agencies* Perth, November 1951.

Waldron, F.E. 'The Association of Social Workers', *Case Conference*, 5, No. 7, January 1959, pp. 183–6.

Walker, SydnorH. 'Privately Supported Social Work', *Recent Social Trends in the United States*. Report of the President's Research Committee on Social Trends. New York, 1933.

*Who's Who in Australia*. 1933–34 (ed. E.G. Knox); 1938, 1944, 1959 (ed. J.A. Alexander).

Wickwar, Hardy, and Margaret Wickwar. *The Social Services: An Historical Survey*. London, 1949.

Wilensky, Harold L., and Charles N. Lebeaux. *Industrial Society and Social Welfare*. Russell Sage Foundation, New York, 1958.

Witmer, Helen L. *Social Work: An Analysis of an Institution*. New York, 1942.

Woodroofe, Kathleen. 'The Charity Organisation Society and the Origins of Social Casework', *Historical Studies, Australia and New Zealand*, 9, No. 33, November 1959.

Wright, R.C. 'A Profession of Reformers', *Case Conference*, 3, No. 7, January 1957, pp. 191–5.

Young, A.F., and E.T. Ashton. *British Social Work in the Nineteenth Century*. London, 1956.

Younghusband, Eileen L. *The Employment and Training of Social Workers*. Dunfermline, 1947.

—. *Social Work in Britain*. Dunfermline, 1951.

Zubrzycki, Jerzy. *Immigrants in Australia: A Demographic Survey Based Upon the 1954 Census*. Melbourne, 1960.

# IV. Other Published Material

## Directories:

Australian Capital Territory Social Workers' Group, *Directory of Social Agencies in the Australian Capital Territory*. March 1960.

Charity Organisation Society of Melbourne. *Charitable, Philanthropic and Welfare Work in Victoria: A Directory and Guide*. Melbourne, 1941.

Citizens' Welfare Service of Victoria. *Directory of Social Services, 1948*. Melbourne.

Fox, J. Carlile. *The Social Workers' Guide for Sydney and New South Wales*. Compiled for the Sydney Medical Mission. Sydney, 1911.

Jubilee Sub-Committee for Social Services. *Directory of Social Agencies in W.A.* Perth, November 1951.

New South Wales Board of Social Study and Training. *Directory of Social Agencies, Sydney*. Sydney, 1933.

New South Wales Council of Social Service. *Directory of Social Service Agencies*. Sydney. 1st ed. 1946; 2nd ed. 1952; 3rd ed. 1957.

Queensland University, Faculty of Education. *Directory of Social Services. Queensland*. Brisbane, 1958.

South Australian Council of Social Service. *Directory of Social Agencies, South Australia, 1956*. Adelaide.

Victorian Council of Social Service. *Directory of Social Services. 1953*. Melbourne.

# National:

Australian Association of Almoners (Australian Association of Hospital Almoners): Annual Reports 1939–57; and *Report of First Conference of Australian Association of Hospital Almoners*, Melbourne, January 1949.

Australian Association of Social Workers: Proceedings of Conferences: First, Sydney, September 1947; Third, Adelaide, August 1951; Fourth, Sydney, October 1953; Fifth, Melbourne, August 1955; Sixth, Adelaide, August 1957; Seventh, Sydney, August 1961.

——. *Papers presented at Casework Refresher Course, Melbourne 1949*; and *Selected Cases for Discussion*.

Australian Council of Social Service: *The First National Conference of Social Welfare, Melbourne, May 1960*; *Proceedings of the Second National Conference, Sydney, May/June 1962*.

Australian University Schools of Social Work, *Record of Meeting, Melbourne, August 1955*.

Boards of Social Studies of the Universities of Adelaide, Melbourne, and Sydney, *Report of the Conference held in Sydney, August 16th–17th, 1944*.

*Conference of the Australian Schools of Social Work, Sydney, 25th–27th May 1938, Summary of the Discussions.*

Post-War Reconstruction, Department of, *Training of Social Workers and Other Officers, Conference with Training Authorities, Melbourne, August 9th, 1945.*

*Proceedings of the Conference of Representatives of Departments of Social Studies in Sydney, Melbourne and Adelaide, July 4–6, 1941.*

## New South Wales:

Australian Association of Almoners (Australian Association of Hospital Almoners), New South Wales Branch: Annual Reports, 1939–58.

Australian Association of Social Workers, New South Wales Branch: Annual Reports, 1947–60.

Council of Social Service of New South Wales: Annual Reports, 1937–58; and other publications.

New South Wales Board of Social Study and Training: Prospectuses, 1929–39; Annual Reports, 1930–40.

New South Wales Institute of Hospital Almoners: Annual Reports. 1938–58.

Social Workers' Association of New South Wales: Annual Reports, 1941–46.

Sydney University Board of Studies in Social Work (Board of Social Studies): Annual Reports, 1941–57.

## Queensland:

Australian Association of Social Workers, Queensland Branch: Annual Reports, 1947–58.

Queensland Association of Social Workers: *Annual Report 1945–6.*

## South Australia:

Adelaide University Board of Studies in Social Science (Board of Social Science): Annual Reports, 1948, 1952–55.

Australian Association of Almoners (Australian Association of Hospital Almoners), South Australian Branch: Annual Reports, 1941–58.

Australian Association of Social Workers, South Australian Branch: Annual Reports, 1947–57.

South Australian Board of Social Study and Training: Annual Reports, 1936–41. (Department of Social Studies, Adelaide University.)

South Australian Council of Social Service: Annual Reports, 1954–58.

## Tasmania:

Australian Association of Social Workers, Tasmanian Branch: Annual Reports, 1947–50, 1954–58.

## Victoria:

Australian Association of Almoners (Australian Association of Hospital Almoners), Victorian Branch: Annual Reports, 1939–58.

Australian Association of Social Workers, Victorian Branch: Annual Reports. 1947–58.

Victorian Association of Social Workers: Annual Reports, 1937–46.

Victorian Council for Social Training: Annual Reports, 1935–42. (Department of Social Studies, Melbourne University.)

Victorian Council of Social Service: Annual Reports, 1947–58, and other publications.

Victorian Hospital Almoners' Association (Australian Association of Hospital Almoners): Annual Reports, 1932–38.

Victorian Institute of Almoners (Victorian Institute of Hospital Almoners): Annual Reports, 1930–48.

Victorian Institute of Hospital Almoners, Executive Committee. *The Origin and Development of Medical Social Work in Victoria.* Melbourne. July 1950.

## Western Australia:

Australian Association of Social Workers, Western Australian Branch: Annual Reports, 1946–58.

# V. Unpublished Material

## National:

Australian Association of Almoners (Australian Association of Hospital Almoners): records, including Central Council Minutes, 1940–57.

Australian Association of Social Workers: records, including Federal Council Minutes, 1946–58.

Commonwealth Office of Education. Training in Social Work in Australia. Sydney, May 1964.

Ogilvie. Katharine. Twenty Years A'Growing. MS.

Player, Alison. Report submitted to the Australian Association of Almoners following a visit to North America, May–August 1954.

Sumner, Dorothy. Report on Professional Social Work and Research Activities in the Commonwealth Department of Social Services to the Director-General of Social Services, March 1948.

## New South Wales:

Australian Association of Almoners (Australian Association of Hospital Almoners), New South Wales Branch: records, including Minutes, 1936–58.

Australian Association of Social Workers, New South Wales Branch: 1949 Conference Programme and Study Material; records, including Executive's Minutes, 1946–58, and Minutes of general meetings, 1952–58.

Lawrence, R.J. Statement on the Supply of Social Workers, prepared for a Seminar at the Department of Social Work, Sydney University, May 1962.

National Council of Women (New South Wales). Reports of the Standing Committee for Child Welfare.

New South Wales Board of Social Study and Training: small collection of records, Fisher Library Archives, Sydney University.

Ogilvie, Katharine. Points to be Considered in Favour of the Formation of an Institute. MS.

Pillinger, May. History of the Family Welfare Bureau.

Rees, Helen. Memorandum on the Establishment of a University School of Social Study. November 1939. MS.

Social Workers' Association of New South Wales: Executive's Minutes, 1932–46.

Sydney University Board of Studies in Social Work (Board of Social Studies): records, including Minutes, 1940–59.

Sydney University Department of Social Work. Survey of Professional Social Workers in New South Wales, 1956.

## South Australia:

Adelaide University Board of Studies in Social Science (Board of Social Science. Board of Studies in Social Science): Minutes. 1942–58.

Australian Association of Almoners (Australian Association of Hospital Almoners), South Australian Branch: records, including Minutes, 1941–58.

Australian Association of Social Workers, South Australian Branch: records, including Minutes, 1946–58.

Massey, J.T., and Stella Pines. 'Social Service as a Career', radio discussion, Adelaide, 17 February 1936. MS.

South Australian Board of Social Study and Training: records, 1936–41, including Minutes, 1936–40. (Department of Social Studies, Adelaide University.)

—. Reply to Questionnaire of the League of Nations Social Questions Committee. MS.

South Australian Social Workers' Association: records, including Minutes, 1942–46.

## Tasmania:

Australian Association of Social Workers, Tasmanian Branch: Minutes, 1947–52, 1954–58.

## Victoria:

Australian Association of Almoners (Australian Association of Hospital Almoners), Victorian Branch: records, including Minutes, 1938–59.

Australian Association of Social Workers, Victorian Branch: records, including Minutes, 1946–57.

Bethune, Dorothy. An Historical Survey of Almoner Work in Victoria. Prepared for the Committee of Management of the Royal Melbourne Hospital. MS.

Hamilton-Smith, E. The Scarcity of Social Workers. 1964.

Hartshorn, Alma. Medical Social Work in Victoria. MS.

Hyslop, Jocelyn. A Philosophy of Social Progress. Public Lecture, Melbourne University, November 1937. MS.

—. The Victorian Council for Social Training. Article sent to the *Hospital Magazine*, 27 July 1938.

Medley, J. Address. Annual Meeting, Victorian Council for Social Training, 10 May 1939. MS.

Melbourne University Board of Social Studies: Minutes, 1940–58.

Smith, S. Greig. Notes on Hospital Almoner System. Submitted to the Charity Organisation Society Executive Committee, February 1929. MS.

Victorian Association of Social Workers: records, including Minutes, 1935–46.

Victorian Hospital Almoners Association (Australian Association of Hospital Almoners): records, including Minutes, 1932–38.

Victorian Institute of Almoners (Victorian Institute of Hospital Almoners): records, including Minutes, 1929–36, 1944–50.

## Western Australia:

Australian Association of Social Workers, Western Australian Branch: Minutes, 1946–58.

# Theses:

Cairns, J.F. The Welfare State in Australia: A study in the development of public policy. PhD thesis, University of Melbourne, 1957.

Goodman, R.D. Teachers' Status in Australia. PhD thesis, The Australian National University, 1955.

Govan, Elizabeth S.L. Public and Private Responsibility in Child Welfare in New South Wales, 1788–1887. PhD dissertation, University of Chicago, 1951.

Kewley, T.H. Social Services: New South Wales and the Commonwealth of Australia. MA thesis, University of Sydney, 1947.

Lawrence, R.J. Australia-Wide Old-Age Pensions. BA (Hons.) thesis, University of Adelaide, 1953.

Ronaldson, M. The Development of Social Services in Victoria. MA thesis, University of Melbourne, 1948.

# Index

Note: Page numbers in italics indicate information contained within a table. A page number followed by 'n' (for example: 125n) indicates information contained in a note on that page.

www.ingramcontent.com/pod-product-compliance
Lightning Source LLC
Chambersburg PA
CBHW040152270326
41927CB00034B/3415